T0300414

TEAMS

Teams

Who

Needs

Them

and

Why?

RONALD J. RECARDO

DAVID WADE

CHARLES A. MENTION, III

JENNIFER A. JOLLY, PH.D.

Routledge
Taylor & Francis Group

LONDON AND NEW YORK

Teams

First published by Gulf Publishing
Subsequently published by Elsevier

This edition published 2011 by Routledge
2 Park Square, Milton Park, Abingdon, Oxon OX14 4RN
711 Third Avenue, New York, NY 10017, USA

Routledge is an imprint of the Taylor & Francis Group, an informa business

Library of Congress Cataloging-in-Publication Data

Teams : Who needs them and why? / Ronald J. Recardo . . . [et al.].
    p.   cm.
    Includes bibliographical references and index.
    ISBN 0-88415-852-7
    1. Work groups.   2. Self-directed work groups.   3. Organizational
effectiveness.   I. Recardo, Ronald J.
HD66.T438   1996
658.4'02–dc20   96-23261
                                                                 CIP

CONTENTS

Acknowledgments

The four of us would like to thank the hundreds of team members we have dealt with over the years. These team members provided the empirical data that made this book possible. Thanks to Les Vance, who help set the strategy for this book, oh, so many years ago. Thanks to M. L. LaFond, Kathy Molloy, Chris Meade, Debra Castelluccio, Denise Eltooney, Marsha Rohrs, and Anthony Hughey, who took the time to review all or parts of the draft. An all-embracing thanks to B.J. Lowe and Joyce Alff at Gulf Publishing—B. J. for seeing the uniqueness of this book in a crowded field, and Joyce for cracking the whip to keep the revisions moving to a final conclusion. Finally, thanks to the editors that made our draft a finished book worth reading. Special thanks to our significant others, Diane Pricone, Sandy Linfert, Clifford Jolly, and Kathy Mention.

PREFACE

There are over three dozen books on teams currently in print, all of them extolling the virtues of teams, few of them explaining what it takes to make teams successful. The failure rate for teams is very high, in many cases as high as 55 percent. The reason for failure is as simple as management's thinking that implementing teams will increase productivity 100 percent and thereby change the culture of the company overnight. Maybe. Teams are a specific solution to a specific business problem. They are not the universal solution to all business problems.

The content of most team books is based on anecdotal information, not empirical data collected over a long period of time. This book is based on performance measures collected from many sources over many years. We declared a team successful when it met four criteria:

1. *Did the team meet its specific objectives?* It is surprising that many teams do not have specific objectives. Odd but true. We have seen many cases where management has said unilaterally, "POOF! you are a team," and walked away letting the team fend for itself. Many other teams have productivity objectives, project objectives, customer satisfaction objectives, and financial objectives.

2. *Did the team meet its objectives on time?* This is a straightforward, easy-to-understand performance measure. Unfortunately, far too many teams are saddled with unrealistic time constraints imposed by managers with a "bias toward action" and limited knowledge about the time it takes for a team to settle in before it starts to perform optimally. These same bias-toward-action managers do not realize that teams need to spend a great deal of time planning. The more time they spend planning, the more likely they will be successful, sooner.

3. *Was the objective achieved within budget?* Teams require the same, if not more, resources that work groups do. Teams need someone to

hold their hands during their beginning stages, the equipment required to perform the job, the tools and techniques to help them solve business problems, and the training to help them understand how teams work. Without these resources and funding, teams are more likely to lengthen the time required to accomplish their objectives.

4. *Would team members participate on another team?* This is the most important performance measure of all. Team members who have had a bad experience on one team are less likely to want to work on another. In many cases, implementing teams is a management excuse to impose long hours and long weeks. For short-term teams such as simple problem-solving teams or cross-functional teams, being away from their departments is closely akin to disappearing from the work force: out of sight, out of mind with less recognition, fewer opportunities, smaller base pay increases, and smaller bonuses. In the age of high demand for knowledgeable workers, management should remember that they do not own what they think they own—corporate knowledge. Once corporate knowledge has been learned by an employee, that knowledge stays with the employee no matter where he goes, even across the street to the competition.

Other performance measures we used are too numerous to list, but there are some universals. We have found that the following list of performance measures are the leading indicators of success.

- Cooperation. A team member comes to you to ask for help, and you give it to him.
- Teamwork. You have slack time, ask another team member if he or she needs help, and you give it.
- The degree of backlog as a percentage of total work.
- The frequency and quality of management involvement.
- The degree and quality of planning.
- The ratio of planning to development or operations.
- The degree to which management understands and uses performance management techniques.
- The degree and quality of human resources support.
- How well team boundaries are managed.
- The degree to which the team was provided with the resources (material, equipment, time, money, etc.) they needed.

• The degree to which teams used tools and techniques to solve business problems, team problems, and measure team and managerial performance.

However, more research needs to be conducted to determine what makes teams successful. Many of the performance measures listed above are nonlinear. In simple terms, they act like economic diminishing return curves, (i.e., one more unit of management involvement that may actually impede team performance). This makes it difficult for both team members and management to understand the when and how of intervention. This book aims to bring us closer to that better understanding. It addresses when to use what kind of team, the obstacles management and team members face when they start to implement teams, how others have overcome these obstacles, and provides a section on tools and techniques to help teams become more successful.

INTRODUCTION

As the twenty-first century approaches, the turbulence that began to accelerate in organizations during the 1980s shows little sign of abating. Coping with this change, and striving to compete effectively in this environment, presents an immense challenge in a global economy. A constant theme sweeping through many organizations is cost cutting, which brings with it major changes in organizational structure. Vertical structures and functional silos are being replaced by horizontal and cross-functional structures. Layers are being removed, and white collar workers, especially middle managers, are losing their jobs or are having their roles changed extensively.

The traditional models of excellence many executives used to determine the best way to operate have frequently been discredited. Organizations that were once stable pillars of society can no longer be viewed as models to which others can aspire.

These changes raise critical questions. What is the best way to structure an organization to compete most effectively in the future? What kinds of organizations do we need? How should they be staffed? How can we ensure that employees have the skills that will be needed? What new technology will emerge, and how will it affect the way in which work is performed, and so on?

In an effort to work smarter, be more competitive, and meet customers' needs more effectively, organizations have moved toward team-based structures. Teams have been touted as one of the best ways to meet the challenges of the future. But how true is this for all organizations? Are teams appropriate for some organizations and not others?

As we review the past 50 years and consider some of the changes that have taken place in American businesses many theories of management and fads have emerged about how to run an organization. Employees have naturally developed a strong skepticism for the so-called flavor-of-the-month approach to management. With this in mind, many argue that the move toward teams is yet another fad that will pass with time and should therefore be ignored. Others argue that teams are the only way to compete effectively in the future and are here to stay.

Our position is that teams are not the panacea for all organizations. Team-based structures will be inappropriate for some organizations. Other organizations are clearly not ready for teams though management may be pushing for them. And, for some organizations teams can be extremely beneficial. The important thing to know is when to use teams and when not to use them and which teams are most appropriate to a particular situation.

Missing from most discussions about teams is a careful analysis of the right conditions for teams to be successful. Whereas many authors discuss the importance of teams, their characteristics, and what to do once teams are established, a systematic analysis of the factors that have to be considered to determine if teams should be implemented is missing. Many unanswered questions remain about the critical factors to consider to determine where and when teams are needed and the most appropriate types of teams and why.

In spite of the excitement about teams and the constant talk about how teams are one of the main answers to productivity problems, one thing we know for sure is that many teams fail. For instance, even when an organization talks about the need to put teams into place, dissension among departments within an organization is common. Under these circumstances, employees will do what they can to undermine teams.

In addition, many employees still operate in hierarchical organizations and organizations where autocratic management is practiced so that even though they are told to move to teams, the existing culture will not support team development. In yet other organizations, senior managers give lip service to teams, tell middle managers to make teams happen, and then walk away, leaving those in the middle frustrated and confused about what exactly they are supposed to do. Many employees are told to work as a team but are still rewarded for individual contribution and competition. These mixed messages result in a lack of effective team implementation. So the question remains, when do teams work and why?

Background and Purpose of this Book

We have worked with executives in organizations that are struggling to change. Some executives say that their organizations need more employee empowerment, some say that they are "going to teams," some say that they know that they have to change and to push decision making down to lower levels. Clearly, in an environment fraught with change, empowerment is not easy. It is very apparent to us that many organizations rush to put teams in place without really understanding what is involved and what critical factors must be assessed to determine whether teams are appropriate. Many executives and managers are confused about what it means to empower employees and how to ensure that teams work effectively.

In this book we address the strategic advantage of teams and look at the conditions that must be in place before teams can be implemented. We discuss how to implement different teams to meet the specific business needs of organizations. We show how those teams can optimally evolve and when they should be disbanded because they have outlived their usefulness.

This book is different from others of its kind in three main ways. First, it creates a bridge between the concept of teams and their application within organizations. Considerable academic work has focused on ways to implement teams and the ways they function in the workplace. Many assumptions have been made about when and where to implement teams, but little rigorous analysis has been done of all of the conditions that have to be looked at before the decision is made to use them. For this reason many attempts to put teams into organizations have failed. We contend that the decision to put in teams is often premature, and that teams might not be the right prescription for the problems the organization is facing. This is analogous to a patient going to a doctor with a headache, the doctor assuming the patient has a brain tumor, and then the patient having an operation without the doctor first doing a thorough exploratory examination, asking the right questions to establish the diagnosis and then ensuring that the appropriate treatment is administered.

Second, little has been written about the exact linkage of strategic direction of the organization and its culture to successful implementation of different types of teams. This book addresses this linkage. In doing so, the book examines the strategic and tactical aspects of teams.

Third, this book provides a link between the individual's approach and the organization's approach to teams. Little has been done to link, systematically, these two approaches—this book provides an integrated overview through organizational examples and case studies. Emphasis throughout is placed on customer satisfaction, acquisition, and retention; productivity and employee satisfaction; and performance management and learning.

Who Should Read this Book?

We see four main audiences for *Teams.* First, it is intended as a guide for middle- to senior-level executives who have either made a decision to move to teams as part of their organization's structure or who are debating whether to implement teams and are weighing the best strategies to use. It will provide them with practical and specific information about the issues that need to be addressed to successfully implement teams.

A second audience is internal or external consultants who are either trying to determine what teams should be implemented in an organization or who are trying to improve the performance of an existing team.

The third audience is employees who are already team leaders, team members, or team support staff and who are charged with maximizing team performance.

Finally, the book will provide useful information for students of organizations who are looking to the future to determine how organizations might be structured and what factors need to be considered when moving toward different structures.

Overview of the Contents

The book is divided into two parts. Part 1 consists of six chapters and provides a thorough conceptual overview of teams. In Chapter 1 we define what we mean by a team, look at the positive and negative implications of teams, discuss the major stages of team development, and examine the various types of teams. In Chapter 2 we provide specific guidelines about how to select the most appropriate types of teams for specific situations.

Chapters 3 through 5 discuss in detail simple problem-solving teams, task forces and cross-functional teams, and self-directed work teams. These chapters present the differences and similarities among the many types of teams, discuss design and implementation issues, identify the benefits of each type of team, and present case examples of successful and unsuccessful team applications.

Chapter 6 discusses the role of the manager in planning and successfully implementing teams.

Part 2 of the book is divided into three chapters and presents a wide array of tools and techniques. Chapter 7 discusses business problem-solving tools, Chapter 8 team assessment instruments, and Chapter 9 team effectiveness interventions.

PART 1

Conceptual Overview of Teams

CHAPTER 1

TRANSITIONING TO TEAMS

The Headlines

Every person in a medium- to large-size organization hears the word *team* or *team building* at least once every day. No less than 50 books praise the business worthiness of teams or team building in modern organizations. Americans have latched on to the concept "team" because the Japanese and the Europeans have used "teams" to improve productivity, customer satisfaction, and return on investment. Business, organizational, and psychological magazines and journals offer 20-point leads about the success of teams.

Teams are associated with a management model Ed Lawler calls high involvement, high participation (HIHP). HIHP emerged from sociotechnical theory, which originated in the coal mines of England during the early 1950s. This model suggests that increased productivity is achieved when workers are highly involved and participate in every aspect of the work they perform.

Though the self-directed teams approach, based on sociotechnical theory, faded in the 1970s, it re-emerged in many companies in the 1980s. Just-in-time (JIT) production greatly revolutionized the factory floor in the late 1960s in Japan and did the same thing in the United States in the late 1970s. The quality and productivity work of W. Edward Deming, Joseph M. Juran, and Philip Crosby have all pointed out the positive effects of involving employees in decision making, productivity improvement, and customer satisfaction. However, for the last 35 years HIHP has been largely a curiosity, not a mainstream style of management, in spite of impressive results like the following:

- Xerox plants using teams have 30 percent higher productivity than their traditionally structured plants.
- GE plans to eliminate layers of management through the use of teams.
- Proctor & Gamble gets 30 to 40 percent higher productivity in its team-based plants.
- Tektronix decreased product development time from 14 to 3 days using teams.
- GM reports a 30- to 40-percent increase in productivity in its self-directed, JIT plants.

The HIHP model has seven basic tenets:

1. Employees must be actively involved in designing processes and structures of the organization. This means that employees must be given all the information they need to be successful.
2. Employees manage the team, management manages the boundaries and the environment outside the team.
3. Employees are in charge of production and services; they have the authority to start, stop, or fix production.
4. Employees are cross trained to do several jobs and compensated for learning new skills.
5. High-quality products and high-quality work life are inseparable.
6. Continuous process improvement must be a way of life.
7. To a greater degree than in the past, employees hire, fire, and determine pay rates.

Costs involved with the HIHP model include training both managers and employees to work in such environments and supporting employees during the transition. Often dual systems are needed when employees migrate from an old system to a new one. Human resource personnel must be on-call to provide advice, support, and tools for managing change. Human resources also must learn to deal straightforwardly with managerial retrenchment—the single, most common threat to self-directed employees.

At about the same time sociotechnical theory was being developed in Europe, Douglas McGregor was beginning to wonder why traditional management systems, called the scientific management model (or command and control), didn't work anymore. The scientific management model focused on efficiency or time and movement in production. In the 1970s another management model appeared called the performance management model. This model stipulated that getting stakeholder buy-in was critical to increased productivity. The underlying theory in performance management is that employees need to know where they are going, how they are going to get there, and what their roles and responsibilities are. From this model we now have goals and objectives in our business plans.

But how does an organization get from a command-and-control model of organization to a high involvement, high participation organization? This is a very frequently asked question, *but it is the wrong question.* The right question is, "What strategies can this organization use to improve productivity, increase customer satisfaction, cash flow, and employee satisfaction?" If the answer to this question is teams, this book will show you how to get there, what problems you will face, and what tools and techniques you can use. Figure 1.1 shows three different models of performance management.

Everything Is Not Roses

While all the praise for teams is warranted when they succeed, they often fail. The whole concept of teams is countercultural to the modern American organization. Everything from organizational culture and multitiered hierarchical structures to structures that reward individual performance can impede the successful implementation of teams. Organizations that have the best track records implementing successful teams also have a long history of implementing them. They have learned from their successes and failures.

Part of their success is based on why they chose to implement teams. They have learned through the years that for all the measurement done concerning teams, only four measures are ultimately important:

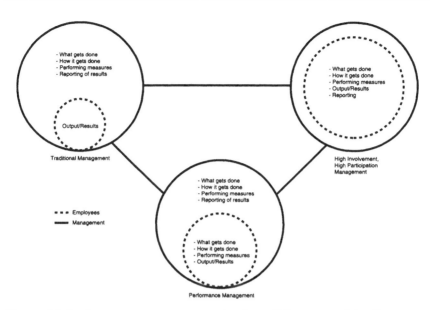

Figure 1.1. *Performance management in three different models of participation.*

1. Customer acquisition, satisfaction, and retention
2. Increased productivity
3. Employee satisfaction
4. Improved cash flow

It is no coincidence that these same four performance measures also happen to be the major drivers for most high-performing organizations. When investigating whether or not teams are right for an organization, these four important performance measures should be kept in mind. If teams cannot positively impact these four performance measures, chances are time and resources will be wasted implementing teams.

What Is a Team?

There is no common agreement about what constitutes a team. We, the authors of this book, work in organizations where our co-workers are called teammates and are collectively called a team. But they are neither teammates nor do they work on a team. Our co-workers work in intact work groups whose interdependence is very limited. In fact, they have more *interdependence* with people in other departments than they do with their department co-workers. Many of these people can carry out their responsibilities without the help of anyone in their department. In some cases, no one else in their department can do what they do.

So why do they call themselves a team? From what we can tell, the everyday use of the word *team* is a positive euphemism that implies that group members work together in harmony and in a spirit of cooperation. This means, by simple definition, that most of the groups called teams are not really performing as a team. In our definition, teams have specific characteristics. We define a team as:

A unified, interdependent, cohesive group of people working together to achieve common objectives. Whereas each person may have a specialized function, each person also needs the resources and support of others and must be willing to forego individual autonomy to the extent necessary to accomplish those objectives.

A successful team will have the following characteristics:

- *Definable membership.* This means defining the roles, responsibilities, and limits of decision-making authority of each member. Each team member must also be consciously aware of the deliverables for which they are responsible.
- *Membership stability.* Teams must have a core of individual members who will be with the team throughout the team's life. This core provides continuity.
- *Common goals.* Team members must understand the goals and objectives that they were brought together to achieve. Team sponsors and managers play a pivotal role in defining those goals and objectives and communicating them to team members. Of equal importance, the team members must think the goals are worthwhile so they will commit to achieving them.
- *Sense of belonging.* Team members must feel that they belong to the team and are full contributing members. This can be facilitated through ongoing discussions of team members' perceptions, ideas, and concerns.
- *Interdependence.* Teams are only teams if there is a large degree of interdependence. That is, one team member's performance is dependent upon the inputs and outputs of other team members.
- *Interaction.* Team members must interact with each other to be considered a team. Our experience suggests that the most successful

teams usually occupy the same physical space. Close proximity helps to solidify and bond team members together.

• *Common rewards.* Having common performance metrics and reward systems is essential to a team's long-term viability. Most organizations have compensation packages that reward individual, not team effort. This single factor is one of the most important underlying differences between members of intact work groups and teams. Intact work group members are in direct competition for rewards with one another, whereas team members work cooperatively together and should be compensated for what skills and knowledge they bring to the team, how well they work together as a team, and what the team accomplishes as a group.

Benefits of Teams

Some common benefits of teams are:

• *Better solutions.* A group of individuals brought together to solve a business problem is much more likely to come up with a better solution than is an individual working alone. The collective brain power of a team frequently out matches the single brain power of an individual. In a group of individuals there is more likelihood that an individual will be willing to say an idea is bad and needs to be reexamined.

• *Increased motivation of members.* Most managers are not trained, rewarded, or reinforced for making the workplace a sociologically and psychologically healthy experience and therefore misunderstand its importance in the forging of a good team. Employees who work in teams typically state they have received more support than they would have in a nonteam environment. In a well-run team the social interaction of team members is a positive and rejuvenating force. In most of the organizations we have worked in or have done scans on, members of successful teams often state that the experience was one of their best, most productive, and most creative.

• *Increased knowledge.* Teams provide all members with connections that can lead to new opportunities and new work experience that would be less likely to occur in a traditional work environment. People are exposed to other jobs and ideas that will make them more valuable in their own jobs.

- *Better use of resources.* In today's increasingly competitive environment, a key source of competitive advantage for many organizations is waste reduction. Teams are frequently a cost-effective way of reducing resource costs through sharing human as well as material and financial resources.
- *Increased productivity.* Teams go through a life cycle. During the early stages of that life cycle, team failures are very high and very frequent. It is not unusual for cross-functional teams and self-directed teams to have failure rates as high as 60 percent. But once through that life cycle, initial productivity gains of 40 to 100 percent are not uncommon, and sustained productivity increases of 15 to 30 percent are common. In organizations with a long history of implementing teams, their success rates are much higher, and consequently, productivity increases come more rapidly and with fewer failures.

Negative Implications and Risks Associated with Teams

Teams are not a panacea. When used appropriately, they can provide startling results. However, teams are not risk free. Some of the more common risks associated with implementing teams are as follows:

- *Loss of control.* Most Americans have grown up in this century without experience working in a communal or team environment. Furthermore, the compensation system in almost all corporations is based on rewarding the individual and *not* the team. Teams make many people feel as though they have lost some control or freedom over their work lives, whereas employees who have worked on factory floors or in the back office are much more likely to be at home in teams. Managers and supervisors tend to be threatened by teams because they have to surrender some of their traditional power to the team.
- *Imposed consensus.* With teams individuals may not always get what they want. All of us have identified and oftentimes offered what we think is the perfect solution to a problem; in teams, we may discover that we are the only one who thinks this is the perfect solution. In order for teams to work, a consensus among differing opinions must be forged and acted upon as a team.
- *Managing multiple relationships can be difficult.* In a team composed of ten members, the effort to manage relationships is complex. This is

especially true when the team is a task force or a cross-functional team because managers from other departments may have differing agendas.

• *Changing roles and responsibilities.* The roles and responsibilities of managers and employees change significantly when teams are implemented, and change is uncomfortable. Employees gain more power to influence work and are required to assume more responsibilities and be more proactive than in the past. Employees also tend to be held more accountable because they and not their bosses are responsible for key outputs. Managers become leaders instead of drill sergeants, coaches instead of control agents. To many employees and managers this shift in roles is disconcerting, particularly if they have not recieved enough training to take on the new responsibilities.

• *Cost.* Initially, teams are expensive to implement. Increased training costs and lost productivity can be expected. Sometimes redundant systems must be maintained during the transition period. Human resources systems may have to be redesigned, including compensation and the performance management system. For example, Coca Cola is moving some of its operations to self-directed work teams. They estimate that employees will require three months of classroom and on-the-job training time over an 18 to 24-month period before they are ready. In addition, they forecast a 16.6 percent loss in productivity during training periods and will have to build a new skill-based pay system to offset some of this productivity loss.

Kinds of Teams

Today, teams are configured in hundreds of different ways. All teams fall across a conceptual continuum from those that are reactive, tactically focused like simple problem-solving teams, to those that are more proactive and focus on being self-supportive, as in self-directed work teams. Based on our experience, we have identified four main types of teams. We do not mean to imply these are the only kinds of teams. These are only reference points. Definitions for these four major configurations are given in Figure 1.2. Each type of team is discussed in detail in the following three chapters.

Simple Problem-Solving Teams

On the left side of the continuum in Figure 1.2 are simple problem-solving teams. Simple problem-solving teams typically address intra-unit prob-

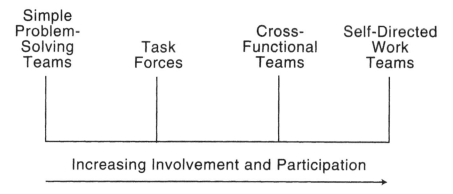

Figure 1.2. *The team continuum.*

lems over a fixed time frame (less than one year). Membership is typically mandated, and these teams tend to be reactive and tactical. They are typically easy to design and implement because they require little systems integration (such as adjustments in the compensation system).

Task Forces

Task forces are composed of team members with highly specialized skills, brought together from different functions across the organization for the purpose of solving complicated problems requiring a high degree of specialization. *Task forces conduct research and make recommendations but do not implement solutions.*

Cross-Functional Teams

Historically, cross-functional teams are composed of team members who are brought together from different functions across the organization to analyze, recommend alternatives, and solve complicated problems. Unlike a task force, a cross-functional team implements its findings and recommendations. Team members are often highly skilled or specialized, such as engineers, accountants, programmers and system analysts, designers, and representatives from management. More recently, as organizations adopt a higher involvement strategy to problem solving, cross-functional teams have been composed of members from every part and level of the organization. Some organizations have attempted to create permanent cross-functional teams, but the results so far are discouraging. The problems appear to be universal to all cross-functional teams. They include such things as lack of personnel resources, poorly detailed business plans, lack of clear roles and responsibilities, no clear chain of command, and lack of sponsor support. Fortunately, the reasons for this may be correctable over time (see Chapter 4).

Self-Directed Work Teams

Self-directed work teams (SDWTs) manage their own internal affairs. More than any other team, self-directed work teams evolve over time. They may come to control human resource decisions (hiring, firing, compensation, vacation scheduling, and so forth), often have budgetary and financial control, interact with customers, decide production schedules based on business goals, and generally have the authority to improve work methods.

Self-directed work teams are by far the most difficult type of team to implement because of the extensive systems integration required (they affect the information system, administrative control systems, human resource systems, and so on), they; correspondingly, have the lowest success rate.

Stages of Team Development

All teams, whether they are simple problem-solving, task force, cross-functional, or self-directed, go through a life cycle (see Figure 1.3), gradually progressing from one stage to another. The stages of team development

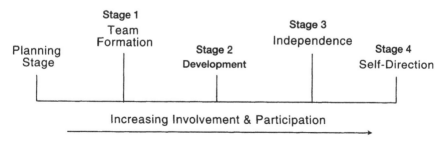

Figure 1.3. *Stages of team development from planning to self-direction.*

Figure 1-4.
Team Life Cycle.

	Preparation	Leadership	Team Activities	Training for Next Phase
Begin	Management lays fine groundwork for changing roles. Communicates the fundamentals of empowerment, coaching and teams through small interactive meetings.	Traditional/ Directive	N/A	Fundamentals of building effective teams
Stage 1 Team Formation	A group of individuals with diverse backgrounds, skills, and goals who have no methods for working effectively together. · excitment, pride, tentative attachment to the team, anxiety about the job ahead · decline in productivity	**Directive** · Organizes and directs the team's activities · Establishes and communicates performance expectations · Handles traditional supervisory tasks (hiring, terminating, appraisals, etc.)	· Establishes vision and unit mission · Clarifies roles and responsibilities · Identifies interdependencies · Develops operating rules · Learns about members' skills, expertise and gaps	· Technical skills · Team negotiations, problem solving, decision making · Effective communications · Conflict management · Effective meetings · Coaching facilitating
Stage 2 Development	Team members seeking to formulate common goals and establish operating methods to increase performance. *Characteristics:* · experiencing stages of team growth (storming, norming, performing) · productivity begins to increase	**Facilitative** · Establishes team boundaries · Coaches · Promotes team growth and independence · Encourages candor and flexibility of members · Handles traditional supervisory tasks (hiring, termination, appraisals, etc.)	· Works on business issues as a group · Self assesses how it is operating · Begins to manage how the work gets done	· Quality Improvement Process (ABPI) · Project/action planning · Technical skills · TBD based on team self-assessment

(continued on next page)

Figure 1-4 (continued).
Team Life Cycle.

	Preparation	Leadership	Team Activities	Training for Next Phase
Stage 3 Independence	Team members focused on common goals working interdependently to maximize performance through innovative methods. Characteristics: • high performance team • future focused • members business literate	**Shared** (Designated Leader) • Adjusts team boundaries • Fine tunes team processes • Ensures team's goals and accomplishments align with business objectives • Handles external issues that impact the team • Handles traditional supervisory tasks (hiring, terminations, etc.)	• Constantly examining its processes and practices towards improvement • Applying problem analysis/solving techniques to make high quality decisions • Self-assessing how team is operating and self-correcting	• Continually learning technical skills/business issues • Advance project management • TBD based on self-assessment • Team leader tasks (hiring, terminations, 360 appraisals, compensation, etc.)
Stage 4 Self-Direction	Team members plan the work and perform it, managing all (or most) of the responsibilities previously handled by team leaders/management. Fully interdependent with leadership shared among the members.	**Self Directed** • No designated leader • Team members have full responsibility and accountability	• Doing appraisals, hiring, firing, pay administration, rewarding, etc. • Constantly examining its processes and practices towards improvement • Applying problem solving techniques to make high quality decisions • Self-assessing how team is operating and self-correcting	• Continually learning technical skills/business issues • TBD based on self-assessment

are planning, team formation, development, independence, and self-direction. Each stage requires different kinds of preparation, leadership, team activities, and training. Figure 1.4 summaries each stage.

Planning Stage

In this stage the sponsor, team manager, and team leader draft the mission, critical success factors, objectives, deliverables, milestones, due dates, and activities the team will have to complete in order to be successful.

During this stage management determines the feasibility of using teams in the organization. It is essential that management understand the time and resources that are available to sustain the team's efforts. As important, management must lay down the groundwork for changing roles and responsibilities for managers and employees. Someone who has had some experience implementing teams should be brought in to help. Designing and implementing teams cannot be done solely from a book. It requires experience to understand the subtleties of what is often as much a psychological experience as a business experience. Our motto is *see one, do one, teach one.*

Implementing teams is a major change for an organization. Whereas there are many change management models, we recommend the *integrated business-planning model,* which states that a successful team must be part of the business plan and that managers and team members must be held accountable for their successful implementation. Building team implementation into the business plan, developing team implementation objectives, writing performance measures, and rewarding successful implementation will communicate to managers that teams are important to upper management and to the success of the business. To do otherwise decreases the likelihood that managers will pay serious attention to team success. Successful implementation also must be significantly rewarded to encourage future performance.

A communication plan must be designed and implemented to inform managers and employees about the need to take on new activities such as performance planning, coaching, and development. The best way to accomplish this is through organizational newspapers and small, informal meetings (less than 20 people). These meetings should be held in local plants or offices. They should be led by someone who has had a lot of experience working with teams, supported by a management representative.

This approach will provide management with information about the level of interest in teams and readiness for change. Quite simply, you will discover which managers in which departments are ready, or at least willing, to implement teams.

Leadership. Management during this preparation stage should be directive. That is, managers should do the following:

- Organize and direct team activities
- Establish expectations
- Handle traditional supervisory roles

Decide Who Will Sponsor the Team. Sponsors are the people who communicate the mission of the team, guide the team from a distance, and most important, go to bat for team members when they are in need. The sponsor is usually the person from whose budget the team is funded, for instance, a plant manager or a new product manager. While they do not have time to work hand-in-hand with the team, their frequent visits and intervention with other sponsors or parts of the organization are very important. Good sponsors let the team members know that their effort is important to the organization and that team members are important too.

Prepare a Business Plan. Three key factors will ruin a team: an ineffective sponsor, a weak manager, or the lack of a work or project plan. Most companies have a standard project or work plan. The plan is essential to success—it acts as a contract or covenant between management and the team. An example of a generic business plan that can be modified for all teams can be found at the end of this chapter (Figure 1.7). One for a cross-functional team can be found in Chapter 4. A simple motto to follow is *Plan the work, work the plan!*

Have Sponsors Select Team Managers, Team Leaders, and an Experienced Team Facilitator. (*This step does not apply to SDWT.*) Sponsors do not perform the day-in, day-out management of the team. Sponsors need someone who can operate between the team and the management hierarchy. It is the team manager's responsibility to guide the team on its own turf. But the team manager should be good at multi-tasking and boundary control because the ultimate advantage of teams is that one manager can manage several teams, one sponsor can manage several managers, thus reducing the size of middle management. A team facilitator can help all those involved in the team to avoid the many obstocles teams may encounter. A facilitator skilled in process consultation and conflict resolution can be especially helpful.

Training for the next stage. Ensure that sponsors, team managers, and team leaders receive training in integrated business planning, group dynamics, process consultation, and conflict management.

Stage 1: Team Formation

During this stage the sponsor and team members meet for the first time. During this meeting the sponsor presents the organizational mission to the team.

Preparing for the First Team Meeting. The sponsor is the person who provides the funding for the team and is often someone in charge of product development. The team manager will have overall performance responsibility for the team, including making sure they have all the resources they need to accomplish their mission. Like the sponsor, team managers may not have daily contact with the team but can be expected to support the team when needed. The team leader is the person who will be working with the team on a day-to-day basis.

We suggest that a two-day team meeting be held off-site. We like to avoid calling this meeting a "team building" meeting because it often has negative connotations. There are many purposes for meeting, only one of which is team building. We have used the term *team formation* successfully. It receives less resistance than does *team building*. The following activities occur in the two-day team formation meeting:

- Develop and document the organizational mission of the team.
- Identify and agree upon key deliverables and dates.
- Clarify roles, responsibilities, and spans of authority.
- Identify what and how many financial, human, and material resources are required.

Conduct the Team Formation Meeting. The team meeting should be led by the team leader. The team sponsor should be there to present the organizational mission for the team that sets the direction, expectations, and project targets as well as to provide background information about why the team is forming and to provide moral support. The meeting is mandatory for all team members and the team facilitator. The content and activities of the meeting are as follows:

- *Communicate the vision and mission of the team.* The sponsor is usually the person who communicates the vision and mission of the team. The vision tends to focus on a future end state and should be descriptive enough to create a picture in the mind of each team member. The vision is typically broader than the mission and is used to ensure team members are committed to the team. The mission identifies the team's direction and purpose. Two examples of organizational team missions follow:

"The Corporate-owned Variable Life Insurance (COLI) New Product Development Team will plan, design, develop, produce, and create a marketing plan for a variable COLI life insurance product that will have 5-percent market penetration by March 199x."
"In order to facilitate effective decision making within Rambunctious Life Insurance, we will provide immediate and direct access to accurate and relevant information, tools, and processes to analyze that information, consultation, and training."

- *Write the team mission.* The team should write their own mission. It should describe their purpose, deliverables, and how they plan to work together. This process will help establish ownership and begin to solidify the team.
- *Identify critical success factors, objectives, and other activities.* The team needs to come to agreement about what factors will help guarantee their success. These will serve as guiding principles for the team. For self-directed teams, the mission and critical success factors should be revisited bi-annually to ensure that the team is still headed in the right direction.
- *Outline strengths and weaknesses.* Strengths and weaknesses should be outlined and discussed. The strengths are what help the team get through the difficult times, and the weaknesses are what have to be guarded against all the time. Figure 1.5 lists strengths and weaknesses from a self-directed management-information team meeting.
- *Clarify roles and responsibilities of each member.* There is an amazing propensity among sponsors and managers to skip clarifying roles and responsibilities—this is a mistake. It has to be done, and it is better to do it in the beginning. Do not assume that everyone knows what the roles will be in the new team. Roles need to be clarified, and there are

Strengths	
Sponsor's support	Well-connected within the industry
We like what we do—self-motivated	Wide variety of skills
Confidence in each other	Bring out the best in each other
Meet regularly	Diverse group
Compatible personalities	Customer oriented
No hidden agendas	Recognize and willing to accept assistance
Commitment to team	Willing to spend the time
Individually well respected—	
collectively, we'll be better	We can be confrontational
Good chemistry	Conscientious
Enthusiasm and energy	Have reputation of doing good work already
Professionalism	Excellent business knowledge
Faith in team members by management	

Weaknesses	
Time commitment	Lack of acceptance outside of team
Insufficient access to management	Strong outside demands
Lack of cross training	Lack of balance between team and customer
Aggressive deadlines	Customers going over the top to management
Insufficient resources	Increased stress
Customer dissatisfaction	Speed of team transformation

Figure 1.5. *Strengths and weaknesses of a self-directed management-information team.*

many ways that this can be accomplished. Figure 1.6 is an example of a roles and responsibilities matrix from a cross-functional team.

Select or Define Team Processes. During the development stage, the team leader must be somewhat directive, nudging the team to begin to take more responsibility for making decisions, actions, and, ultimately, its survival. Remember, employees in most organizations have not been asked to help make decisions in the past, and they will be slow to take charge during this stage. But every team must decide for itself how it plans to work together, how meetings will be conducted, how conflict will be resolved,

Name	Activities	Products	Product Links
Arroyo	Product Champion		
Anderson	Create market strategy, industry perspective, competitors analysis, customer wants	Product profile	Illustrations
Armageden	Coordinate illustration software and send illustrations to the field	Illustrations and illustrations training	Tool
Biglow	Complete pricing of product, preparation of actuarial memo, setting assumptions, comparisons with other products	Final rates, actuarial memo, Non-forfeiture testing	Illustrations
Bleugreen	Represents policy holder and their attitudes	Tools	
DelFranco	Takes system specs and makes sure they support product, tests, and Q&A	Policy, document a record of policy on administration system	
Depaola	Takes rates and product specifications and loads onto system, verifies issue of document, develops illustration support	Proposals, illustrations, bales, policy documents	
Fourth	Represent customers, field agents and management	Advice and recommendations	
Goldstein	Represents communications and training and development	Prospectus and marketing materials	
Gottschal	Underwrites and issues, internal and external customer analysis	Policy	

Figure 1.6. *Roles and responsibilities matrix.*

how problems will be solved, and how decisions will be made. These are the first steps to more responsibility. Almost every company that has a management development program will have examples of problem-solving techniques, project plans, and other tools that the team will find useful in solving problems and making decisions. Don't try to reinvent the wheel—beg, borrow, and steal what you need!

Continue Detailing the Business Plan. We have used the terms *work plan* or *project plan* frequently. Whether the team is working on a project or will be a permanent self-directed team, a written plan is essential to success. At this point the team begins to provide more detail to the plan, including identifying milestones, due date, review points, performance measures, and individual, team, and project assessments.

Dealing with Complaints. There will be complaints about the team-building process from some team members; they will complain they could be getting some "real work" done back in the office or on the factory floor. Pay attention to those who feel this way and express their feelings so vocally. They could be telling you that they don't want to participate on a team. A judgment must be made as to whether the risk of disruption is less important than the potential loss of this person's participation on the team. Key managers and the team leader should counsel the team member and point out that participating on a team is becoming an everyday part of work life and that not participating may eventually have a negative impact on their salary and promotional opportunities.

The Team Facilitator. The team facilitator, who sits in the back of the room and watches the team work together, will be taking careful notes about the way the team interacts. At the end of the day, the facilitator will debrief the team about their patterns of interaction and discuss ways of overcoming negative patterns so that they can avoid problems in the future.

The Emotional Content of Stage 1. Excitement, pride, tentative attachment to the team, and anxiety about the job ahead are all part of the emotional content of the team during this stage. Again, having a team facilitator on hand who has worked with teams in the past, knows what the stages are, and can provide tools will be of great value to the team. If the team says they are "positively uncomfortable" at the end of this stage, you can consider it a success.

Stage 2: Development

Team Activities. During this stage the team's products are developed, and team members begin to grow into a solidified working unit. Team members will seek to formulate or refine their goals, objectives, and work processes. They will be trying out their new tool kits, finding out which tools work for them, and beginning to determine how they fit into the team. Teams begin to work on the business issues at hand, to self-assess how they are operating, and to take on more responsibility for the work to be done. Productivity can be expected to decrease for self-directed work teams as they take on more roles and responsibilities. Task forces and cross-functional teams will begin to develop a liaison relationship with their departments.

Leadership. In successful teams, team managers begin to be less directive and become more facilitative. Managers, with input from the team, should encourage increased candor, ask for feedback from the team about their performance, and begin to promote team independence.

Team independence is something the team manager must develop in the team. In many cases, team members have had little authority, limited control, and were never given problem-solving tools with which to work. Then suddenly, they are asked to assume responsibility for many operations and processes that are foreign to them. During this period, the team manager must patiently communicate, guide, and train all team members on how to take on more responsibility and make bigger decisions. Increasing the team's responsibilities without preparation or training will almost certainly cause the team to fail.

Training for the Next Stage. Simple problem-solving and self-directed work teams need training on the fundamentals of work effectiveness. All kinds of teams need training in project management, 360° feedback and assessment, coaching, and increased technical skills. Teams must be introduced to financial reporting, business planning, and budgetary decision making.

Stage 3: Independence

Team Activities. During this stage team members begin to gel as a working group and become less dependent on the team manager. The primary goals of this stage of team development are for the team to take on more responsibility for ensuring that the team aligns its performance with the business goals and objectives, increases customer contact, and continues to improve work processes. The team will also begin to go beyond the team boundaries, establishing contacts with other teams, sitting on task forces, joining cross-functional teams, and representing the department in plant or corporate meetings. Many teams begin to make financial decisions at this stage. Quite often teams take part in the yearly budget cycle and, in some cases, make financial decisions such as purchasing new equipment.

Leadership. Team members will refine their tool kits, find out which tools work for them, and begin to determine how they can run the team without supervision. The team manager will manage the team less and less and begin to manage team boundaries, both physical and political, as a primary responsibility. Team leaders will emerge to take over the role of the manager within the team. However, in a very short time, other team members will insist that the team be run by the team.

Training for the Next Stage. For simple problem-solving teams, task forces, and cross-functional teams, there is little additional training needed and, for that matter, would not be cost-beneficial. But self-directed work teams need much more training such as advanced project management and personnel policies and procedures including hiring, firing, performance reviews and feedback, compensation, and vacation scheduling.

Stage 4: Self-Direction

Team Activities. Team members receive business goals that have been developed at the location or maybe even corporate level, sometimes with team input. The team then develops its own business plan, writes its own objectives and action steps, assigns roles and responsibilities, performs all functions to accomplish the business plan, monitors and realigns its own performance with the plant or corporate business plan, and makes all personnel decisions.

Leadership. Team leadership is shared by all members of a team, sometimes on a rotating basis. The team manager manages the team's boundaries.

Team Training for the Next Stage. Training should continue to focus on business, organizational, and technical knowledge. Essentially, any training or conference you would consider for a line manager is potential training for self-directed work team members.

Summary

Spectacular results have been achieved by successful teams. Successful teams are driven by

- A desire to improve customer acquisition, satisfaction, and retention; productivity improvement; and employee satisfaction.

- Good managers who are rewarded for successfully implementing teams.

- A business plan that focuses on team involvement as a strategy.

• A commitment of time and resources by management.

• An understanding of the team life cycle.

There are four different kinds of teams from which to choose: Simple problem-solving teams, task forces, cross-functional teams, and self-directed work teams. Chapter 2 discusses how managers can select the right kinds of teams for their organization.

Figure 1.7
Detailed Team Development Business Plan

Section 1   Define the team's mission for the team
A. Mission
B. Critical success factors
C. Fundamental components
D. Resolve any conflict between the two missions

Section 2   Define roles and responsibilities (technical/behavioral)
A. Describe roles and responsibilities as they presently exist
1. Develop Roles and Responsibilities Matrix
B. Identify products and services associated with roles
C. Identify links with other products and services
D. Identify products and service links with other team members
E. Develop current organization map
Note: Roles and responsibilities and products and services establish the baseline from which all future operational decisions will be made. It describes who does what. From here, the team may wish to change, combine, rearrange, or eliminate responsibilities, or products and services. The organizational map will provide a horizontal view of the team functions, perhaps pinpointing disconnect points.

Section 3   Determine milestones and due dates
A. Determine what new tasks will be absorbed by the team, and when the team will take over responsibilities for them

B. Plan hours to complete work

C. Compare planned hours against actual hours

D. Ditto for hours per team component

Section 4   Develop performance measures (objectives, action steps, and indicators) for

A. Individual

B. Team

C. Organization

Note: Performance measures must be cross-checked with the new roles and responsibilities to make sure they are exacting fits and to ensure team members have control over them. Performance measures will be used to assess how well the team is doing as a team as well as individually.

Section 5   Determine training needs

A. Refer to the Team Life Cycle Chart as a baseline

B. Write training plan

1. Use current development plan as a model for writing training plan

C. Set training dates

Note: Accepting a new responsibility generally requires successful training, but always think about how any new training may be used in ways for which it was not originally intended. This may lead to accepting new responsibilities or increasing productivity.

Section 6   Develop communication plan

A. Identify audience

B. Define team charter (purpose, deliverables, etc.)

C. Define media

D. Define performance measures

E. Define milestones

F. Write communication

Note: The purpose of the communication plan is to ensure that the team's message gets desseminated accurately and broadly. The first communication should go out over the sponsor's signature. This will ensure that future communications will be taken seriously.

Note: Throughout the development of the work plan, please keep in mind the strengths you possess that will help you and the hindrances you must overcome to become a successful team.

CHAPTER 2

Selecting the Most Appropriate Type of Team

Teamwork, empowerment, and participation. These words are commonly spoken in the boardroom, hallways, and offices of most organizations. Although these concepts appear simple, few organizations have demonstrated a consistent ability to successfully implement teams. Throughout the world, organizations are using teams to solve problems, improve quality and customer service, and enhance productivity. But all teams are not the same. The first challenge for managers is to select the most appropriate team for the work that needs to be accomplished.

In Chapter 1 we discussed how teams can be viewed on a continuum. On the left side of this continuum, the teams tend to be reactive, to focus on intra-team issues, and to produce incremental results. As one progresses further right along the continuum the teams tend to be more proactively focused, to address broader (usually more strategic) issues, and to focus on creating employee self-sufficiency instead of simple problem solving. Four points along this continuum have been arbitrarily selected, and we have identified an example of a commonly used type of team at each key point (that is, problem-solving teams, task forces, cross-functional teams, and self-directed work teams (SDWT). This is not meant to convey that there are only four different types of teams that can be used in an organization. In reality there are many different types of teams. Our purpose is to select these four commonly used teams as markers to more readily enable the reader to apply the concepts to their own environment.

How to Select the Most Appropriate Team

Based on our experience, a review of the literature, and studying many successful and unsuccessful teams, we have developed a decision matrix for selecting the most appropriate type of team (see Figure 2.1). Our model consists of six decision dimensions:

1. What is the intended purpose of the team?
2. What are the existing cultural characteristics of the environment in which you wish to implement teams?
3. What resources will be required to design and implement teams?
4. How does the existing technology affect the usage of teams?
5. What are the prevalent workforce characteristics?
6. How much organizational alignment is required to institutionalize teams within the organization?

Before one can successfully utilize the matrix, an in-depth understanding of what should be measured under each dimension is required. Each is discussed in detail in the following sections.

What Is the Intended Purpose or Use of the Teams?

We have found that many organizations approach teams from the sole perspective of making employees "feel better" (to provide more input into decisions that affect them, to foster more autonomy, and so on). We believe the decision to use or not use teams should be based primarily on

Type of Team	Purpose	Culture	Resource Requirements	Technology	Workforce Characteristics	Organization Alignment
Simple Problem-Solving	Solve intra-team quality, productivity, and cost problems.	Participative, open communications.	6 mos. - 1 yr. commitment. Significant training required.	Technology allows employees to impact performance.	Willing to accept responsibility and take initiative in solving problems.	Modify performance management and reward systems.
Task Forces	Identify solutions to problems that impact multiple units. Don't implement solutions.	Participative, good cross-functional teamwork/cooperation, limited unresolved conflict.	Limited resource requirements. May require limited training.	Limited impact.	Flexible, able to commit large segments of time to project.	Limited impact.
Cross-Functional	Identify and solve problems that impact multiple units.	Participative, good cross functional teamwork/cooperation, limited unresolved conflict.	Membership may be permanent or temporary. Requires substantial HR support. 12-24 months for team to be fully functioning.	May require modification of information systems.	Members must have needed skill sets.	Modify recognition, reward, and performance management systems.
Self-Directed Work Teams	Create self sufficient work force. Increase employee and operational flexibility. Reduce overhead and improve productivity.	Highly participative, performance/customer focused, egalitarian, reward, risk taking/innovation.	3 - 5 year commitment requires significant training, process re-engineering, redesign of several business systems.	Technology allows employees to impact performance. Significant impact on information systems.	Willing to work under flexible work rules. Supervisors and managers must be comfortable with significant role change.	Significant impact, need to modify most HR, information, planning/goal setting systems.

Figure 2.1. *Decision dimension for selecting the most appropriate type of team.*

strategic advantage. Simply said, to what degree will teams support the business strategy and improve the strategic position of an organization? This presupposes that several elements are in place in the organization:

1. A business strategy is in place that is based on data that identifies strengths and weaknesses within the organization and opportunities and threats outside the organization.

2. The business strategy is tightly linked to the customers' requirements. This may appear obvious but all too often the business strategy is developed without appropriately considering customer requirements. Many organizations do not know the answers to the following questions: 1) who are the customers, and what are their desired product or service attributes (do they value price, packaging, professionalism of sales force, and so on)? 2) what is the relative weight or importance of these attributes? 3) do they vary according to each customer segment? 4) how satisfied are customers with the product or service delivery? 5) how well does the organization perform relative to its competitors?

3. The strategy has been clearly communicated and is supported by key stakeholders. Our experience in working with many executives suggests that even at this level there is typically little consensus on exactly what the business strategy is. If we ask five executives in the same company what the strategy is, we usually get five different versions. Since the business direction is not clear, executives from different functions sponsor initiatives that at times conflict with one another.

Figure 2.2 illustrates the link between the inputs and outputs of a well-designed strategic planning process. Although the more sophisticated organizations typically collect data on customers, competitors, markets, and socioeconomic trends, it is seldom integrated into the business planning process. However, the data may not be useful because it is collected in different time periods and by different functions. For example, the strategic and tactical plans may be developed in January, but customer data may not be collected until May. Therefore, business decisions (such as the development of a strategy, goals, and objectives) are made based on missing data. If this condition exists, the business planning process must be modified to eliminate these problems *before* assessing team readiness. If the target or strategy is not clear, it is exceedingly difficult to organize people to work together for a common purpose.

In many cases we have found that the business strategy is either nonexistent or inappropriate. When in doubt, study the strategic planning process shown in Figure 2.2. In many cases the strategic planning process is informal and is not based on data. The business strategy and goals and objectives are frequently not integrated into all of the organization's related systems (performance management, budgeting, reward, and so on). We once worked with an executive who described his company's strategic planning process as nothing more than the senior management team getting together once a year at a retreat and talking about their perceptions of the competition between holes three and four on the golf course.

If you are satisfied that your overall organizational and, if applicable, unit business strategy are sound, then you need to clearly identify the intended purpose and desired outcome for using a team. Each type of team has a specific purpose. Simple problem-solving teams are typically very focused. They are chartered to identify and solve tactical quality, productivity, and cost problems that affect a single department or work unit. Task forces, which usually report to an executive committee, are usually empowered to be fact-finding mechanisms. These teams are usually charged with recommending solutions to problems (such as, right-sizing, and merger integration) that cut across one or more functions or business units. The main difference between task forces and cross-functional teams is that the latter are responsible for both identifying and implementing approved solutions. Self-directed work teams are usually created to achieve the following outcomes: 1) to enhance productivity, quality, or customer service; 2) to reduce overhead and operating costs; 3) to increase employee and operational flexibility; and 4) to promote self-sufficiency in the workforce.

Also important is identifying all planned and ongoing initiatives. Since operational initiatives can impact one another it is imperative to evaluate the most appropriate type of team in light of these initiatives. A client we recently worked with tried to force fit self-directed work teams to support a merger-integration initiative. The cultural diversity between the German company that was autocratically run and its American counterpart that was very egalitarian and participatory made the success of this kind of team highly unlikely.

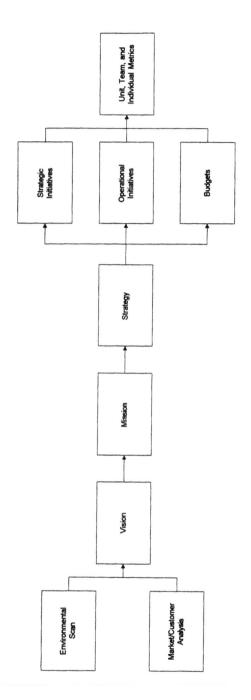

Figure 2.2. *An overview of the strategic planning process.*

What Are the Current Cultural Characteristics Within the Organization?

Culture is the prevalent set of attitudes, beliefs, and values held by the employees of an organization. As we discussed earlier, organizations may have an organizationwide culture and several subcultures. For teams to be successful in any organization the culture has to generally be participative, employees must be treated as valuable resources for the expertise they possess, communications should be open and unfiltered, and labor/management relations should be cooperative. For cross-functional teams and self-directed work teams, additional characteristics are required. Since cross-functional and self-directed work teams tend to address issues that transcend multiple functions we have found that they work best in environments that have the following characteristics:

- Little unresolved conflict and excellent cooperation among different functions or business units, labor and management, and among customers and employees.

- High customer focus. Customer focus is the essence of competitive advantage for most organizations. Cross-functional teams and self-directed work teams work best in an environment where the focus is on exceeding the needs of both internal and external customers.

- Culture that highly values results. Self-directed work teams and cross-functional teams tend to tackle complex problems. If the culture is highly political and managers are territorial, these teams are likely to encounter significant resistance and be much more difficult to implement.

- High employee flexibility. As organizations continue their right-sizing trends, employees must develop a broader competency mix. No longer will workers have the luxury of doing one thing very well. Employees must be willing to accept job rotation, cross training, and flexible work rules.

- Strong emphasis on new skill acquisition (such as problem solving and interpersonal skills) and employee development. The more complex teams require significant on-the-job and classroom training and coaching. The emphasis of this development should be on enhancing the competency levels of employees and creating an environment that challenges employees to do their best.

• Low mediocrity. Lou Peluso, a consultant with CSC Index, has coined a phrase that encapsulates the growing problem of mediocrity in organizations today. He believes that in too many organizations you have the "misinformed leading the uninformed." He believes that many executives in today's organizations are not the best and brightest but ascended to their preeminent position because they lasted the longest (they were the most politically astute). The best and brightest left long before to avail themselves of better opportunities in more progressive companies or as entrepreneurs. This acceptance of mediocrity is one of the largest problems in American organizations today. Self-directed work teams require a true pay-for-performance culture, not a culture that focuses inordinately on rewarding mediocrity.

What Resources Are Required?

We define resources as money and access to facilities, equipment, people, and information. Each of the four different types of teams has different resource requirements. Each requires different lengths of time for design, implementation, and institutionalization.

When evaluating resource requirements we recommend you consider the following:

1. Management commitment. How committed are all levels of management to the utilization of teams? Will senior management actively serve as role models? Are first-line supervisors threatened? What is the expected response of supervisors?

2. Adequacy of budget. Do you have an appropriate budget for the design, implementation, and maintenance of teams? Do you have sufficient resources (such as training capabilities or consulting assistance) to support teams?

3. Timing of introduction. Is it the right time to implement teams? Where are the organization, its products, and services in terms of their expected life cycles? How will teams affect any planned or ongoing operational initiatives?

Task forces are usually temporary teams (they dissolve after the problem is addressed) and tend to have a life expectancy of less than one year. In most cases employees who participate in task forces tend to take on team responsibilities in addition to their normal day-to-day jobs. Team members are usually selected either for their subject-matter expertise or because of their position in the organization. Our experience in working with task forces suggests that aside from some occasional training in such topics as problem solving, meeting management, or team skills, these teams require minimal resource support.

Cross-functional teams and simple problem-solving teams tend to require significantly more resource support. Since these teams are frequently ongoing, team members usually take on the responsibilities of the team in addition to their normal job responsibilities. Based on our experience, these teams require extensive senior management support, a budget for training, outside consulting expertise, and moderate organizational alignment.

Self-directed work teams are by far the most complex type of team. They require considerable process modification, changes to reporting relationships, and job redesign. Organizations that have been successful in transitioning to self-directed work teams tend to approach the process in an evolutionary rather than revolutionary style. This process commonly requires three to five years of continuous support until the teams are self-sufficient. In most cases organizations require significant outside consulting assistance to modify the culture and align the organization to support self-directed work teams.

What Are the Prevalent Workforce Characteristics?

Organizations are made up of people who have a diverse array of needs, wants, concerns, and competencies. Before selecting a specific type of team it is important to identify the prevalent workforce characteristics to assess fit. Different types of teams place different kinds of demands on employees. The following key questions should be answered when considering workplace characteristics:

1. What are the existing competencies (knowledge, skills, and experiences) of employees? Are new competencies required? Are there any competency shortfalls?

2. What are the needs of management and of employees? Does each group have high or low needs for

   • Achievement?

   • Security?

- Pay for performance?

- Job challenge?

- Willingness to accept responsibility?

- Willingness to take initiative?

- Recognition?

- Learning new skills?

- Flexibility in job assignments?

Self-directed work teams and cross-functional teams are the best fit when the workforce has high needs for achievement, job challenge, willingness to accept responsibility, initiative, and flexibility in job assignments.

What Technology Is in Place?

We define technology as the equipment (computers, telecommunications, production machines, and so forth) that actively supports the delivery of products and services. When assessing the impact of technology on teams, two key variables should be evaluated:

1. Is the current technology most appropriate for the products or services being delivered? Is it state-of-the-art?

2. How automated are the processes, and to what degree can employees affect (quality, cost, and so on) the final product or service?

In some manufacturing operations, employees turn on a switch to activate a piece of production equipment and then just load or unload the machine. Employees have little effect on the attributes of the final product being produced. For teams to be optimally utilized, employees must be able to impact performance. The role technology plays in selecting a team varies considerably. For example, when utilizing a task force, technological issues tend to play a minor role. But if you are assessing technology with respect to problem-solving or self-directed work teams, the impact of technology is significant. Typically there are critical issues relating to the adequacy or sufficiency of the information system and production equipment. This can obviously have considerable impacts on the resources needed to design and implement these teams.

How Much Organizational Alignment Is Required?

We believe all businesses are composed of an architecture that consists of the following three components:

- Technology: equipment, hardware, software, and data.

- Organization: This is the people element and consists of the organization's structure, job designs, unit boundaries, human resource systems, workforce competencies, culture, business systems (administrative policies, budgeting, planning), and physical layout of the work area.

- Process: The series of tasks that transform an input into an output (processes include order entry, new product development, and accounts receivable)

When transitioning to teams it is important to identify how the team you wish to implement will affect each of these components. In most instances one or more of the components may need to be modified to closely support the team you are implementing. For example, self-directed work teams typically require re-engineering work processes, modifying existing unit boundaries and physical layout, and altering reporting relationships. The performance management, reward/recognition, and succession plan may need to be modified to support the behaviors you are attempting to foster. The information system may need to be modified to provide new forms of information to support decentralized decision making. Employees may need to participate in a wide range of education from team building and communications to meeting management. And the culture may need to change to promote employee risk taking, empowerment, and a heavy emphasis on customer satisfaction.

How Do You Determine the Most Appropriate Type of Team?

We strongly recommend that an organization conduct a readiness assessment as a first step before utilizing any teams. A readiness assessment is a structured data collection and analysis process that is used to identify the following:

1. What type of team is most appropriate for a specific application or environment.

2. What issues need to be addressed to successfully utilize teams within an organization.

3. What resources are required to institutionalize teams within an organization.

The length of time and resources required to complete an assessment vary according to the scope of analysis. Most readiness assessments can be completed in less than two months. The following sections detail the five-step approach we suggest.

Step 1: Conduct an Archival Document Review. Identify and study relevant documents of the organization that can provide insight into any of the team decision variables. Depending on the size and sophistication of the organization, we typically review the following if available:

- Mission statement
- Vision statement
- Organization and unit business strategy and business plans
- Organization and unit goals and objectives
- Process flow diagrams
- Data from relevant previous employee/customer attitude surveys
- Employee handbooks and policy manuals

In most instances the document review will serve as a starting point and will allow you to identify missing pieces of the puzzle. For example, if the organization doesn't have a mission statement, vision statement, or business strategy, these may need to be developed before transitioning to a team-based work environment. In such cases, make sure that strategies are developed that will support team development.

Step 2: Interview Key Stakeholders. Once you understand the strategic direction of the organization it is usually very useful to interview, at a minimum, senior management and key customers. We have found that interviews with the senior management group can be extremely useful in determining how well the strategy is understood (is the strategy uniformly understood?) and the level of their commitment to execute the strategy.

Interviews with key customers can confirm their desired product or service attributes, the relative importance of these attributes, levels of satisfaction with the delivery of existing products or services, and feedback on how the organization performs relative to other competitors in the marketplace. Any unique issues that need additional clarification can then be added to the employee readiness survey that is administered in Step 3.

Step 3: Administer and Tabulate Employee Readiness Survey. Organizations have used surveys extensively since World War II. Surveys have become popular because they can identify 1) how an organization is performing relative to a number of dimensions, 2) employee perceptions and needs, and 3) perceptual difference across job or organizational groupings.

Although a lengthy discussion of survey feedback is beyond the scope of this book, we believe the following guidelines should be followed when using a survey:

1. Clarify the goal of the survey. Specifically what do you expect to learn as a result of the survey? How will this information be used?

2. Select a survey team. If you have internal expertise to tap, select team members who have enough formal authority within the organization to make change happen. Collectively these members should also have the full range of survey feedback skills (from survey administration to data analysis) to ensure the survey is successful.

3. Finalize survey design and logistics. Early in the process, the survey team must decide how respondents will be selected (either a census or sample), which business units to include, and what particular job groups are most appropriate to include. At this time survey administration issues (such as through in-house mail or by telephone) should be finalized. The survey team can then design and pilot test the survey instrument.

4. Administer and tabulate the data. Once the surveys have been completed, the data should be cleaned (nonsense responses eliminated), coded, and tabulated. Data tables may then be created to display the results.

5. Analyze the data. Data can be interpreted in a variety of ways. Generally, the focus is on identifying strengths and weaknesses, strategically prioritizing problems, and determining their root causes. This information can be incorporated into the overall design of teams.

Step 4: Conduct Focus Groups with Employees. Focus groups can be used in lieu of a formal survey or as a follow-up to a survey to elicit additional information. A focus group is a structured question-and-answer session with a group of people that affords several benefits. Focus groups are usually very cost effective, don't require much planning and analysis time, and can, therefore, yield considerable information and provide an opportunity for free-wheeling interactions (see Part 2: Tools and Techniques for an in-depth description of focus groups).

Step 5: Analyze Data and Determine the Most Appropriate Type of Team. The data from interviews, the team assessment survey, and focus groups should provide you with more than enough information to evaluate each dimension within the team decision matrix. Although there is no mathematical formula for selecting the most appropriate team, we have identified the characteristics needed for simple problem-solving teams, task forces, cross-functional teams, and self-directed work teams to be successful.

Figure 2.3 shows a simple method we have used to help several of our clients select the most appropriate type of team. In an effort to streamline the selection process we have developed a decision tree that utilizes the following seven decision dimensions:

Decision Dimension 1: Do teams support the strategy?

If teams do not support the business strategy, do not use them. They will consume resources that could have been applied to a more strategic initiative.

Decision Dimension 2: Does the existing technology allow employees to impact performance?

If the current environment is highly automated and does not allow employees the opportunity to significantly impact performance, we recommend not using teams unless there is an unusual and compelling reason that would justify qualitative benefits (improvements in morale, job satisfaction, etc.) in lieu of significant bottom-line results.

Decision Dimension 3: Will the existing culture support teams?

If the existing culture is not conducive to teams (employees are not interested in working as part of a team, not willing to accept additional

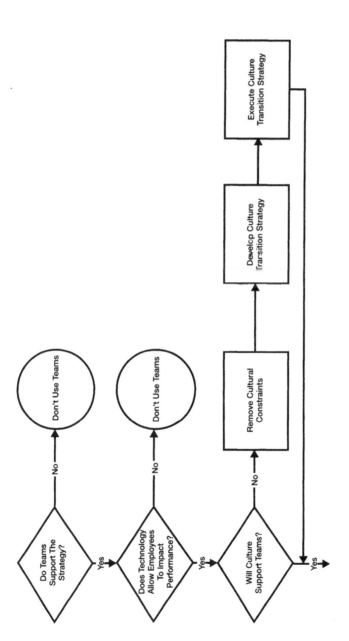

Figure 2.3. *A decision tree for selecting the most appropriate type of team.*

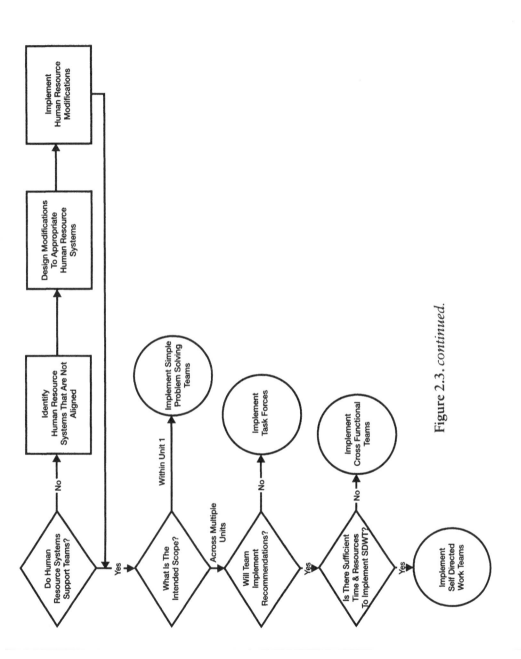

Figure 2.3. *continued.*

responsibility, not willing to learn new things, etc.) and teams are needed to support the business strategy, it is absolutely necessary to identify and remove any cultural barriers before attempting to implement teams.

Decision Dimension 4: Do the existing human resource systems support teams?

The performance management, employee selection, recognition, compensation, new employee orientation, training and development, and succession planning systems are the key human resource systems that are directly impacted by teams. Before teams can be successfully implemented, organizational alignment must take place. A key focal point of this alignment is the evaluation of key human resource systems to identify any gaps and the modification of one or more of these systems to more closely support the specific requirements of the team being implemented.

Decision Dimension 5: Is the intended focus of the team one unit or across multiple units?

If the purpose of the team is to solve tactical problems that occur within one unit, we suggest you implement a simple problem-solving team. Although this tends to be a reactive approach, it can provide considerable short-term benefits.

Decision Dimension 6: Will the team be involved in implementation?

If the team is not charged with implementation, use a task force. Task forces are teams that are chartered to collect information, perform root cause analysis, and recommend solutions to a problem that affects multiple work units. Because task forces are usually temporary, they work best when they deliver a single product. This keeps the group focused. We have found that task forces work well in most cultures that are participatory, with good teamwork/cooperation across organizational boundaries.

Decision Dimension 7: Is there significant time and resources available to implement self-directed work teams?

If the team is involved in implementation, we suggest you consider using a cross-functional team or SDWT. Cross-functional teams are much more complex task forces. Cross-functional teams tend to work well in environments where they deliver multiple products to many different customers. Since these teams are usually permanent in nature they require a significant amount of resources to align the organization to closely support them. Cross-functional teams frequently require consulting assistance in such areas as design, process consultation, modification of the MIS system, and the revision of many human resource systems.

If management has a time horizon of longer than two years and is not constrained too heavily for resources, then SDWT are recommended. Self-directed work teams require an extensive amount of resources and a three-to-five-year time commitment before full implementation occurs. Resources typically include external consulting assistance, considerable training, and an extensive organization alignment.

Summary

In this chapter we have compared and contrasted four different types of teams: simple problem-solving teams, task forces, cross-functional teams, and self-directed work teams. We have also presented a thought process and a decision free for selecting the most appropriate type of team. In the next three chapters we will discuss in detail simple problem-solving teams, task forces, cross-functional teams, and self-directed work teams.

CHAPTER 3

Simple Problem-Solving Teams

Introduction

Simple problem-solving teams evolved from quality circles. In the United States, organizations began to implement quality circles during the 1970s in response to worldwide competition in the manufacturing industry. At the height of their popularity in the early 1980s they had been widely adopted by most of the Fortune 500.

While quality circles lasted for many years in Japan, they were short lived in their original form in the United States. By the mid-1980s enthusiasm for them had decreased, and their widespread use began to disappear.

Many people have viewed quality circles as a passing fad and yet another unsuccessful management program. This rather dismissive view overlooks the fact that the difficulties associated with implementing quality circles provided valuable lessons in what to do and what not to do when implementing other employee involvement programs, especially simple problem-solving teams. In addition, many of the methods and tools that were introduced in quality circles are still successfully used by problem-solving teams.

We also believe that quality circles can be viewed as a demonstration of the danger of copying a process that worked well in Japan, without adequate consideration for the factors that are needed for success in another culture. In Japan, the emphasis on consensus management and long-term planning lends itself readily to the quality circle process, whereas the entrepreneurial culture and short-term focus found in the United States does not. Thus, both the national culture and the organizational culture should be considered in the implementation of such programs.

In this chapter we will present an overview of simple problem-solving teams. We will show their evolution by outlining the history of quality circles, discuss why quality circles failed, and what lessons have been learned from them. Following this, we will highlight the differences between quality circles and the simple problem-solving teams used by most organizations today to show what needs to be in place to ensure successful implementation of simple problem-solving teams.

The History of Quality Circles

The history of quality circles is important for several reasons. One reason is to demonstrate some of the profound influences the Japanese have had on American business. The second reason is that simple problem-solving teams were one of the main foundations for employee involvement programs that are so popular today. The third is to show how simple problem-solving teams evolved from them to fit the American culture.

W. Edwards Deming, a statistician for the U.S. Bureau of Census, is widely acclaimed as pioneering quality circles. In 1947, Deming went to Japan to work on a census with Japanese statisticians and convinced many of them that they could build their postwar economy using statistical techniques that he adopted from Bell Telephone Laboratories. Thus, the concept of statistical quality control, which came to be so important in Japanese organizations using quality circles, was actually developed in the United States. This approach became extremely important for the Japanese whose products at that time were generally regarded by the rest of the world as "junk." In less than five years the Japanese were able to change the perception of their products from poor to high quality. Deming's success in Japan has been attributed to two things:

- Production-level workers were taught statistical techniques for quality control. Then they were given the power to reorganize work so that product quality could be improved.
- Top management were convinced by Deming that it was necessary to have their direct involvement, understanding, and commitment to building quality products.

These are still key points in the successful implementation of employee involvement programs, but their importance was underestimated and they were often ignored in the United States when quality circles were first introduced. As we shall see later, appropriate training in problem-solving tools and a clear definition of the role of the manager are critical to the success of simple problem-solving teams.

In 1954, Joseph M. Juran, another American advisor to Japan, reinforced the importance of quality control, statistical methods, and management in Japanese industry. The Japanese went to extraordinary lengths to apply the steps recommended by Deming and Juran. Meanwhile, the Japanese Union of Scientists and Engineers (JUSE) began a campaign to teach their ideas to all production employees. Large numbers of supervisors learned the techniques of quality control, and the importance of quality was accepted throughout Japanese society.

All of this training in statistical process control techniques led Kaoru Ishikawa, a professor of engineering at Tokyo University, to develop a work system in 1961 called *quality control circles*. In 1962, 200 employees participated in the first 20 registered quality control circles. The term *circle* was used because employees sat around a table to discuss issues. Twenty-six years later, in 1988, there were approximately 10 million Japanese workers participating in more than a million quality control circles.

According to Ishikawa, the purpose of quality control circles was to:

- Develop oneself and others
- Increase quality awareness
- Encourage the creativity and brain power of the workforce
- Improve worker morale
- Develop managerial ability of circle leaders
- Implement and manage accepted ideas

The concepts being introduced fit well into Japanese society as a whole—a culture in which it is customary to obtain the ideas of everyone who will be affected by a decision and to obtain consensus on it. Theoretically, these would seem to have been laudable goals for the U. S. workforce and other countries too, so it is not surprising that the concept spread.

In 1974, quality circles began to emerge in the United States. This occurred mostly in companies with declining productivity and poor workmanship that were looking for ways to improve and survive against the competition. Having heard about the quality circle concept, a team of managers from Lockheed visited Japan and decided to copy the Japanese quality circles model and implement it within their own company.

The first formal use of quality circles at Lockheed was in the Lockheed Missile and Space plant in Sunnyvale, California. Initially the circles were a great success and resulted in significant cost savings for the company as well as reduced significantly the number of rejects ($30 million saved in three years). Interestingly, after one of the champions of the program left, the program languished and died. Today, Lockheed uses quality circles on a more ad hoc basis.

Other large organizations that implemented quality circles included General Motors, IBM, Westinghouse, Texas Instruments, and 3M. Each organization used its own specific names for the circles. For instance, at IBM it was "quality improvement teams," at Ford, "employee involvement circles," and at Xerox, "study action teams."

In the United States, only about 25 companies used quality circles in 1978. By 1980, many began to view them as a solution to all ills. Clearly they were not, however, and many of them failed. The process of statistical control, which was so favored by the Japanese, has met with varying results in the United States. So what went wrong?

What Went Wrong with Quality Circles and the Key Lessons that Emerged

It is probably accurate to say that the rise in popularity of quality circles can be attributed to managers assuming that if quality circles were successful in turning around Japanese businesses, they would most likely work in the United States and restore its competitive edge. Little thought was given to cultural differences that might influence the extent of their success, nor was sufficient attention paid to the critical factors that needed to be in place for their successful implementation.

Starting with a working definition of quality circles and then comparing them with simple problem-solving teams, we can begin to lay the framework for why quality circles lost popularity and understand the lessons learned from them and how they evolved into simple problem-solving teams.

A quality circle is a group of eight to ten people who meet voluntarily with a leader once a week to identify and resolve work problems. Typical problems addressed center around work flow, tools and equipment, safety and training, paperwork and communication, materials and supplies, quality improvement, and productivity improvement. In other words, anything to do with quality of work or quality of work life. Typically, projects chosen by circles were related to the four Ms: manpower, machines, methods, and materials. Areas that typically were *not* addressed included benefits, salaries, union contracts, grievances and personalities. Figure 3.1 outlines the main characteristics of quality circles.

Lessons Learned at Each Phase

Research indicates that problems with quality circles emerged at each of five phases. These were:

1. Start-up phase. Problems at this phase related to a lack of cultural readiness for teams, insufficient volunteers, inadequate training,

Purpose:	To improve communication between the line and management.
	To identify and recommend solutions to problems (some may be responsible for implementation).
Roles:	Team Leader
	Eight to ten employees from one work area.
	Coordinator.
	Facilitator.
Selection:	Membership is voluntary.
	Leadership may or may not be voluntary.
Type/Scope of Problems:	Circle selects its own problems, input can be obtained from management and non-circle employees; usually the problem is confined to one unit.
	In addition to quality, problems can also cover productivity, cost, safety, morale, and the environment.
Frequency:	Generally one hour per week.
Rewards:	Nonfinancial rewards are given.

Figure 3.1. *The main characteristics of quality circles.*

inability of volunteers to learn new skills, and lack of funding. All of these issues draw attention to the importance of conducting a readiness or feasibility study before implementing teams. This is a key lesson and the one that has been most consistently ignored by corporations.

2. Inital problem-solving phase. The team chose its own problems to solve. Conflict arose because of disagreement over which issues to tackle; sometimes there was inadequate knowledge to deal with an issue. Even when an issue was decided upon, it frequently did not have any significant impact on the organization as a whole.

   This draws attention to the importance of choosing strategic problems to focus on.

3. Presentation and approval phase. If a problem was identified and a solution was agreed upon, approval then had to be obtained from the next level of management. Because management was not heavily involved in the early stages of problem solving, they often resisted the ideas or they simply took no action. The lesson learned is that it is critical to include managers at all stages of team formation and implementation. This will significantly enhance the probability of a successful implementation.

4. Implementation phase. Quality circles were not typically responsible for the implementation phase. Therefore, even if approval was given to a proposal, the people who were expected to implement the ideas (often, the managers) didn't "own" the solution and would drag their heels during the implementation process. If the ideas were not converted to action, it is not hard to see that the motivation of the quality circle members was severely curtailed, and the program would often stop at this point. The lesson here is to involve all parties affected by an issue. In addition, it is important to give responsibility and accountability for problem solving and implementation to the same group.

5. Program expansion phase. If the earlier phases were completed successfully, the program could be expanded to other areas. Problems at this point arose when the program was not integrated into the culture of the main organization and an insider/outsider culture arose. Many members experienced a conflict between the day-to-day authoritarian decision-making culture and the quality circle's consensus decision-making culture. Some quality circles ran out of problems to solve; we have seen cases of members meeting for the sake of meeting and becoming frustrated because they could not think of any new issues

to address. Meanwhile, others who had to pick up their work while they were meeting became extremely resentful. Again, the lessons learned are the importance of assessing the readiness of the organization for teams and making sure that any problems to be addressed are strategic for the organization.

Additional Problems and Lessons Learned

In addition to the problems already discussed, the following problems also arose.

- Burn-out. After about 12 to 18 months working as a team, quality circle members often thought they had done enough or were tired of the process. At this point, an assessment should have been made about whether revitalization of the quality circle was required or whether it was time to stop and evolve to another type of team. When this did not happen, the quality circle was difficult to maintain. The lesson here is that teams will naturally evolve and mature with time (refer to the team continuum shown in Chapter 1, Figure 1.3) if management provides sufficient resources, such as training and materials.
- Design issues. The following team design factors contributed to the failure of quality circles:
  — Limited workforce involvement, which results in the "we-they" phenomenon and failure of the workforce to cooperate.
  — Dissatisfaction. Once the novelty wore off, the quality circle was seen as an *extra chore* by the participants.
  — People become tired of receiving nonmonetary rewards. In the original quality circles the people who developed the ideas were not rewarded financially resulting in a lot of resentment. We have seen cases where employees became tired of the same old tie pins, t-shirts, and plaques and wanted more share in the cost savings generated for the company. While they may be willing to take nonfinancial rewards in the beginning, resentment may set in over time if employees see the company realizing large savings as a result of their ideas, but they themselves receive no financial recognition. At this point motivation drops, and willingness to contribute dwindles

Simple Problem-Solving Teams

or stops. Over the years, companies have struggled with the best way to deal with giving financial rewards.

— The role of the manager, which often was overlooked in the original quality circles, is now seen as critical to the success of any team program.

Simple Problem-Solving Teams: How Are They Different From Quality Circles?

The major differences between quality circles and simple problem-solving teams are outlined in Figure 3.2 and discussed below:

- Membership. In simple problem-solving teams today, members are typically *selected* for their expertise to focus on a specific problem and to resolve it. In contrast, quality circles depended on *voluntary* membership. Originally, this voluntary participation was thought to be a strength, but later it was viewed as a weakness because an "elite" group was formed, the most appropriate people did not necessarily volunteer, and the members themselves began to feel "put upon."

Quality Circles	Simple Problem-Solving Teams
Voluntary membership	Select the best people to focus on the issue at hand
Continued indefinitely	Fixed time frame for project completion
Team members define problem to be worked upon	Project sponsored by organization
Fixed roles for members	Roles defined according to task to be accomplished
Management often left out	Management role clearly defined upfront
Rigid hierarchic structures	Flexible structures
Intra-unit	Can be inter-unit

Figure 3.2. *Major differences between quality circles and simple problem-solving teams.*

- Time frames. Simple problem-solving teams have a *fixed time frame* for project completion. Quality circles went on *indefinitely*, and, as we have noted, enthusiasm often waned.

- Task selection. Simple problem-solving teams are more likely to have their project sponsored directly by the organization. This means that the problems are *selected by management* and are more likely to be *strategic* in nature. As noted in Chapter 2, the task is very focused. Generally, the team is required to solve quality, productivity, and cost problems affecting a work department or work unit. In contrast, quality circle defined for themselves which problems they wanted to focus on. These problems were commonly not strategic in nature, which made the team's benefits difficult to quantify.

- Roles and Structure. Simple problem-solving teams have roles defined according to the task to be accomplished. As a result, *flexibility* and focus on the outcomes to be achieved are emphasized. Quality circles had multitiered structures and *fixed* roles for their members. Therefore, people could become locked into a role. This was potentially an obstacle rather than a facilitator to the accomplishment of task-related goals. Additionally, the multitiered structure added cost (overhead) to the employee involvement process and considerably lengthened the cycle times for implementation.

- Management sponsorship. Simple problem-solving teams emphasize the importance of *management sponsorship* on an ongoing basis. Quality circles involved management only during key milestones (such as solution selection and implementation).

- Project implementation. Simple problem-solving teams are responsible for *implementation* of the solutions. Quality circles made *recommendations on how to solve problems* but *were not responsible for implementing* the solutions. Thus, a greater sense of ownership of results and, consequently, higher levels of commitment and motivation exist among simple problem-solving teams.

- Rewards. Simple problem-solving teams usually receive some *financial reward* that is tied to problem resolution. In contrast, members of quality circles were not financially rewarded for their contributions even though they put in extra time and were able to save the company money. This became a major stumbling block.

The Philosophy Behind Simple Problem-Solving Teams

The main belief underlying simple problem-solving teams is that the people closest to the job are the ones best qualified to come up with solutions to work problems in their areas. By tapping the cumulative experience and expertise of employees, the organization benefits financially and gains a more committed workforce through personal development and individual motivation because of decision-making involvement. Other philosophical underpinnings include the following:

- Employees should be trusted. They will work toward the implementation of organizational goals if given the chance.
- There should be investment in training and treatment of employees as valued resources. Underlying this is the importance of building long-term commitment to the organization.
- Financial and nonfinancial recognition should be given for accomplishments. This is to show that the organization values the contributions of its employees.
- Decision making should be decentralized. This significantly shortens the time needed to identify and solve business problems.
- Work should be viewed as a cooperative effort. This implies *consensus decision making.*

Benefits of Simple Problem-Solving Teams

The overall benefits of simple problem-solving teams are an *increase in morale, increased productivity,* and an improvement in the *quality of work* without making big changes in policies, structure, or lines of authority. In addition, significant *cost savings* can be realized. Other benefits include but are not limited to:

- Improved interpersonal skills. Some people say that the methods they learn to solve problems help not only at work but also at home.
- Demonstration of new skills. People can develop and demonstrate skills that had not been apparent before. This can sometimes help in making promotional decisions and in individual development.
- Improved relationships. An increase in respect between the employee and supervisor can occur through a greater understanding of what

each one does. Sometimes conflicts can be worked through more readily by using the team techniques.

- Increased efficiency through learning new techniques. Employees often see discussion and problem solving as productive. The ability to use new tools, express their ideas, influence decisions, and gain recognition for their ideas is valued.
- Bottom-line results. When properly implemented, simple problem-solving teams generate results. For example, Honeywell saved about $1.5 million dollars in two years based on suggestions from teams; Hughes Aircraft improved the cleaning of parts and redesigned sample boards for assembly for a savings of $93,000 per year; and Northrop workers recommended a redesign of drill bits to reduce breakage and saved $28,000 per year.

Implementation Steps for Simple Problem-Solving Teams

Typically, eight steps are involved in the implementation of a simple problem-solving team. The key features of each step are expanded here:

1. Ensure organizational support
   a. Assess the level of top management support. There is general agreement that in order for problem-solving teams to succeed, there must be ongoing support from top management regardless of whether there will be an immediate financial payback. Some firms have encountered problems when top management will say that they want problem-solving teams without fully understanding what they require to be successful.
   b. Assess the support of middle manager. A major question to be asked is "Are middle line managers willing to have workers share in decision making?" Many supervisors are initially skeptical about problem-solving teams and see them as a threat to their own positions because they fear their power will be undermined. Any threat to the positions of middle managers should be eliminated. Train them about the benefits of teams and ask for their input at all stages of the program. We have seen extreme frustration and anger expressed by middle managers when their only involvement in teams was when solutions were being presented and they were being asked to rubber stamp them.

c. Assess the attitude and support of the union. In a unionized facili-
ty, it is critical to assess the union's receptivity to before deciding
on teams. Assurances should be made that any changes in work
methods will be approved through the usual channels. Because
simple problem-solving teams can increase positive employee/
management relationships, they are sometimes opposed by adver-
sarial unions. Therefore, union leaders should be included as soon
as possible in the planning phase, and officials should be asked to
participate at all stages. For the union to buy in, the program
should be seen as improving the organization's profitability and
workers' job security.

d. Assess the availability of personnel and funds. Most organizations
do not have the competencies (team design, human resource system design, change management, and so on) to design and implement teams without outside help. If an organization doesn't have
sufficient internal competency, funds may be needed to hire a consultant and to purchase appropriate training materials.

e. Assess the economic climate. Ideally, any widespread move to
implement teams should occur at times of economic stability and
when turnover of members is likely to be minimal.

2. Senior management identifies a strategic problem. The support of
senior management is usually advisable for any program to stand a
chance for success. Grassroots movements can sometimes succeed,
but their road is generally a tough one. It is important for the teams'
goals to be aligned with the strategic goals of the organization. Senior
management must provide strong and vocal leadership to each simple
problem-solving team and clearly identify which problems it wants
the teams to focus on.

3. Identify the objectives, deliverables, roles and responsibilities. We use
a simple formula to guide our efforts when designing simple problem-
solving teams: objectives + deliverables = roles + responsibilities. Simply translated, simple problem-solving teams should use a flexible
structure, and this structure should vary according to the desired
objectives and deliverables. This contrasts with the commonly used
roles found in most quality circles that include: a steering committee,
a coordinator, a facilitator, a team leader, and team members. Most
simple problem-solving teams utilize three roles: the steering committee, team leader, and team members.

a. Steering committee. The steering committee is generally a support, advisory, resource-allocation, and direction-setting group. The steering committee is also expected to establish overall policies and procedures for teams and to hear and respond to proposals from team members.

b. Team leader. Usually the leader of a simple problem-solving team is selected by management and is a supervisor or someone with subject matter expertise. This person also acts as a facilitator and may be drawn from the unit itself, from higher management levels, or from another work unit. The leader manages the meetings, makes sure that members participate, and makes sure that each step is executed properly. It is important that the leader is a self-starter who is willing to exert extra effort to ensure that the team operates effectively.

c. Team members. Team members participate in meetings, learn to use problem-solving and team-evaluation techniques, identify problems, collect data, recommend solutions to management, and implement approved solutions. They then track results after implementation.

4. Select team members. Care must be taken to choose members with appropriate expertise and whose skills can complement those of other team members.

5. Conduct training. Newly formed teams require training. This training should address a wide range of technical, team, and problem-solving topics. Managers, especially, have to learn a new way of operating, and it is important to provide them with the tools to do that.

6. Collect data on the root causes of problems. Simple problem-solving teams commonly follow a four-step process for problem solving (see Figure 3.3). Once a problem has been selected, data must be collected to answer the following questions:

- What is the extent of the problem?
- Who is causing the problem?
- Why is the problem occurring?
- When does the problem occur?
- Where is it happening?
- How does the problem occur?

Steps	Purpose	Possible Methods
Fact finding and Data collection	To determine the extent and cause of the problem, when and where the problem occurs, and how the problem occurs	Interviews Company records Check sheets
Problem Definition	To clearly define the problem; to find the main causes of the problem; to concentrate on the critical few causes	Pareto chart Histograms Problem stream analysis Presidential diagnosis
Problem Analysis and Identification of Solutions and Goal Setting	To identify root causes of the problem and to consider possible solutions.	Cause-and-effect diagrams Process analysis Verify results by checking with others GANTT, PERT, CPM charts
Recommended Solutions to Management Follow-up	To present solutions for approval To determine effectiveness of pilot program and whether to expand program	Formal presentation with supporting data Interviews Surveys Cost savings realized

Figure 3.3. *Four-step problem-solving process.*

Simple problem-solving teams use a variety of problem-solving techniques such as check sheets, work-flow analyses, (particularly useful in white-collar teams), interviews with experts or clients, archival document reviews, and cause-and-effect diagrams (sometimes called fishbone or Ishikawa, diagrams) to identify the root causes of a problem.

7. Teams identify solution(s). The data collection and analysis tools will allow a team to clearly identify causal relationships as well as to identify potential solutions. Depending on the complexity of the problem, a solution may or may not be obvious, or a cost-benefit analysis may need to be conducted to prioritize solutions. Again, depending on the limits of the team's decision-making authority, the team may then either implement their solution or may need to make a recommendation to the steering committee or senior management for approval to proceed further.

8. Implementation and follow-up. Quick results and success are important. Many companies we have worked with strongly believe that team projects should be small and uncomplicated to help create a record of successes. We concur with this philosophy. It is important to have a quick success. Polaroid calls this a "quick victory concept." It means that the initial problem should be solved and presented to management within eight to ten meetings. This provides quick feedback and positive reinforcement to the team to continue. This strategy is favored by many organizations today when they are going through change and trying to increase productivity.

Other Points to Consider in the Implementation of Simple Problem-Solving Teams

Remember, the nature of teams changes as organizations evolve. One of the mistakes that some companies have made is to use teams without thinking about the ways the teams may need to change and evolve as the needs of the company change. To keep the teams going, it is important to be aware of problems that might occur at each phase in their evolution in order to proactively deal with them.

When there has been a rigid adherence to certain teams even though they have not met the evolving needs of the company, failture of the team is guaranteed. When a long-term view is taken of simple problem-solving teams, they may be seen as having an effect that ranges from benefiting the individual to benefiting the organization through contributions to organizational change. In the latter case, the methods that they use may be adapted to fit any change in strategy. Consequently, the organization may start to change its focus to task forces, cross-functional teams and self-managing teams.

Basic organizational issues must be recognized. Problems can occur when companies go through the motions of forming teams without realizing the depth of some of the problems that their companies are facing.

Although for most teams the culture of the organization must be taken into account before introducing an employee participatory program, simple problem-solving teams may not be so sensitive to the type of culture if they are used purely on an adhoc basis to resolve a specific issue.

In summary, a simple problem-solving team can be used when a specific organizational issue needs to be resolved in a relatively brief period of time. For this kind of team, make sure to select appropriate experts, train them in problem-solving methods, and provide appropriate support and rewards.

Summary

This chapter has outlined the major characteristics of simple problem-solving teams and highlighted the issues that need to be addressed to ensure their success. In the next chapter we will review task forces and cross-functional teams to show how they differ from simple problem-solving teams and when they should be used within organizations.

CHAPTER 4

TASK FORCES AND CROSS-FUNCTIONAL TEAMS

Task forces and cross-functional teams are some of the hottest silver bullets in the business world. Task forces have been used since the development of modern corporations. Today we find task forces under such names as process mapping groups, productivity improvement committees, and workout sessions. Cross-functional teams are rapidly working their way into the heart of American business. Why? Because working across functional and organization lines has many advantages such as shortened time to market, increased productivity, and greater commitment from diverse groups on a single project. Further, task forces and cross-functional teams allow organizations to leverage fewer sponsors and managers over more projects, ultimately reducing costs and increasing productivity.

Brief History of Task Forces and Cross-Functional Teams

Task Forces

The concept of task forces came out of military organizations during World War I. The widespread use of the term revolved around the Allies' effort to locate and destroy the German battleship *Bismarck*. The term remained largely a military term until the 1960s when an increasing number of government and civic groups began using it. The problems these groups set out to study were large by anyone's scale, and it was the scale that helped to define the operating scope of a task force. Task forces perform the following functions:

1. Analyze issues and problems that have wideranging effects on a large number of people.
2. Identify as many possible solutions to these problems as they can.
3. Weigh the effects of each solution.
4. Select a solution or solutions.
5. Report their findings and recommendations.

Because of the size and cross-functional nature of their solutions relative to the size and nature of the task force, task forces can not be the group that implements the solutions.

Cross-Functional Teams

Cross-functional teams (CFT) were an obvious and logical extension of task forces. A group that represented all the "factions" of the task forces had to be given the authority and resources to implement the changes recommended by a task force. The term *cross-functional* was not in widespread use until the mid-1980s, when it became apparent that the more successful organizations were those that cooperated across functional lines. It became a necessary form of operation because of the speed and direction of change driven by customer demand and increasing downward pressure on costs. In short, the company that got to the market first had a distinct competitive advantage. This advantage could not last long because another cross-functional team in another company would build an equivalent product or service with better value. But the key is the cross-functional nature of the group: get everybody involved early on to be able to identify and solve any problems that might occur later. The best recent example of the overall efffectiveness of a cross-fucntional group is Dodge's Viper project. Historically, it took 36 to 48 months to get from design to the first car off the assembly line. The Viper was designed and rolling off the assembly line in 18 months.

Similarities and Differences Between Task Forces and Cross-Functional Teams

Task forces are composed of members from various departments or functions within the organization and are brought together to research, propose, and recommend solutions to one specific functional problem, such as increasing cross-functional selling of services in banks. Similarly, cross-functional teams are also composed of members from different functional areas and may be brought together to solve one specific functional problem, conduct research, or introduce a new product. Cross-functional teams, however, implement what they propose and recommend, task forces do not. Task forces disband after they have made their recommendations; some cross-functional teams are permanent.

Both task forces and cross-functional teams make use of highly specialized employees. For example, a task force could be brought together to reduce the time and effort required to put together an annual budget through process analysis, stakeholder interviews, and identifying barriers to reducing paperwork. To accomplish this formidable objective, accountants, business systems designers, programmers, various users, and human resources would be required to gather data and write a recommendation. Both task forces and cross-functional teams are subjected to multiple levels of review.

An example of a cross-functional team would be a group of experts and specialists brought together to work on a new product during the planning and design phases, much like what was accomplished during R&D for the Dodge Viper (a large project) or when Aetna Life and Casualty developed a new variable life insurance policy (a small project). Dodge reduced the amount of time from design to the showroom floor from the average of 36 months to 18 months, Aetna developed a 10-year term insurance in half the time originally planned, while getting rave reviews for its new product.

Benefits of Task Forces and Cross-Functional Teams

The following sections outline the key benefits of task forces and cross-functional teams.

Increased Functional Knowledge of Team Members. The least obvious and hardest to measure directly is the increased functional knowledge team members acquire while working with members from other departments. Once a team member has solved a specific problem, the time it takes to solve a similar problem will be reduced. This knowledge, leveraged throughout the organization, increases productivity and quality over time.

Increased Cooperation Across Functions. The cooperative nature of teams with their emphasis on solving business problems will, over time, help make the organization more productive by focusing on how to work toward cross-functional organizational benefits as opposed to individual competition.

Increased Productivity. Arthur Andersen & Company developed methodologies and training products for many years using subject matter experts (SMEs) from various functions (auditing, consulting, and tax), instructional design, graphic design, word processing, and secretarial. Typically, a project would begin when a partner had an idea that would either increase productivity, start a new business line, or bring additional revenues. The partner would contact a training manager and discuss the project. This was often done long distance and generally over a period of months. The partner and the training manager would meet to discuss the ideas and put together a business plan. The plan was then used to secure funding from an industry sponsor. Once the funding was secured, planning, design, development, and production could begin.

The partner or the sponsor would convene a meeting at the corporate training offices (SMEs) to discuss the idea. The SMEs would flesh out the idea and then convey this information to instructional designers, who in turn would organize the information. However, once this step had been completed, training materials took many months to develop and revise. Occasionally, the partner or a SME would check-in on the progress of the project. This almost always meant major, time-consuming revisions to the materials. The time to complete such a project was long usually, up to one year and expensive.

Fortunately, there were two things in Arthur Andersen & Company's favor: they had designed and implemented many just-in-time/group technology cell projects and the concepts were well known, even in the training community, and they had developed cost standards for new methodology and training products.

A study conducted by the Catalyst Consulting Group involved more than 40 cross-functional teams. Again, the results showed conclusively that if the critical success factors discussed below were followed, productivity and quality increased, cost and total product development time decreased. The data from the study were analyzed and the results provided the foundation for critical success factors discussed earlier in this chapter.

For example, one new product development project was estimated to cost $900,000 and take eight months to complete. Using cross-functional teams in group technology cell, and applying the critical success factors listed below, the total cost was $303,000 and took three months to complete. This is a clear example of how a cross-functional team can have a dramatic impact on cycle time and overall costs.

Increased cash flow. A bank in Connecticut used a task force composed of members from three different departments to increase previously untapped banking fees. The purpose of the task force was to develop procedures that would reduce some barriers that made it difficult to work cross-functionally and develop new operating procedures that would help identify and pass on business opportunities to other functional units, thereby increasing the overall profitability of the bank. The end result was an increase of over $1 million in fees for the fiscal year. Fees that would have been lost if not for the work of the task force.

Decreased Time to Market. Many new product development teams using the procedures outlined in this chapter have greatly decreased their time to market. In one amazing case involving the development of new consulting services, a cross-functional team developed a business plan based on customer requirements, established roles and responsibilities, established team processes and procedures, and substantial sponsor support. This allowed them to deliver the training for the new services for 75% less money and sooner, "scooping" several other consulting firms by several months.

Success Rates. The success rate for task forces and cross-functional team is often low. The data collected since 1990 by the Catalyst Consulting Group from several organizations indicate that less than 40 percent of cross-functional teams were successful, compared with approximately 75 percent of task forces. But what do we mean by "success"? Success means that the task force or the cross-functional team accomplished its objectives, on time, at or under budget, met or exceeded product or problem specifications, and members would elect to work on another task force or cross-functional team.

Why is there such a difference in the success ratios? Remember, task forces do not implement what they recommend, are not in control of the final outcomes, and, therefore, are usually not held responsible for them. Since a task force's responsibility stops at the recommendation stage, the likelihood of achieving its mission and objectives is much greater. Further, task forces are usually the favorite child of a powerful sponsor with resources to support the effort, whereas a cross-functional team is responsible for the planning, design, development, and implementation (or production) stages of its charged responsibility.

What Makes a Task Force or Cross-Functional Team Successful?

The following are some critical success factors that the authors have identified based on their research on task forces and cross-functional teams.

1. Ensure Sponsor Support. The single most important success factor for any task force or cross-functional team is sponsor support. The research done by one of the authors during his tenure with Arthur Andersen & Company clearly showed that task forces and cross-functional teams that had the support of a sponsor willing to work closely with the team during the planning and design phases of a project were more frequently successful than those teams with less or unsatisfactory sponsor support. Task forces tend to have more complete sponsor support than do cross-functional teams, greatly increasing their chances of succeeding.

Sponsor Involvement. This fact would be simplistic if involvement were not so misunderstood. But what kind of involvement are we talking about? In general, the more time a sponsor contributes to the team, the greater the chances are the team will deliver what the sponsor wants. For example, sponsors of task forces and cross-functional teams must take the time to communicate the vision and mission of the project if the team is to understand what it takes to be successful. Sponsors must be willing to come to the aid of the team when they need the sponsor's insights and suggestions.

Sponsors are critical to success at the end of a project also, when many loose ends may need to be wrapped up. However, as was discussed in the overview section of this book, nothing about teams is linear. That is, sponsor time adds value to the team up until the point of micro-management. It is at this point that the sponsor becomes a hindrance to the team, the cost of the project accelerates, the line of authority blurs, team interdependence drops, and productivity falls.

In short, sponsors should set direction and expectations at the beginning of a project, wrap up loose ends at the end, but stay out of the way (except when needed) during the middle.

Figure 4.1 provides a graphic representation of the sponsor-involvement problem. The figure is a diminishing-return curve. That is, at some level, increased sponsor involvement has a negative impact on the productivity of the task force or cross-functional team. The challenge for the sponsor and the team is to determine what the optimal level of involvement is before too much involvement becomes constraining.

2. Assign Flexible Managers. Based on our experience and research, we recommend that task forces and cross-functional teams have a dedicated team manager other than the sponsor. Task forces and cross-functional teams need upfront direction. However, the team manager must learn when to be authoritative and when to be empowering. In general, team managers must be more directive at the beginning of the team's life cycle and increasingly participative as the team becomes more mature.

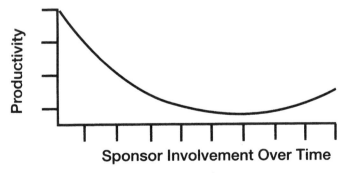

Figure 4.1. *Sponsor-involvement curve.*

Further, task forces and cross-functional teams must have managers that are proponents of performance management and thoroughly understand the complex nature of working in a team environment. In a short period of time, the manager and the team must work out roles and responsibilities, business plans, group processing, and establish the degree to which self-direction and empowerment will be enacted.

Leadership style is an important factor in team management and sponsorship. Our research has shown that cross-functional teams have succeeded with very traditional sponsors who took the time to communicate their vision and mission. But sponsors and team managers that took the time and effort to develop a comprehensive business plan, listened to team members' suggestions, and used good team processes were more successful. Further, our research clearly shows that "micromanagement" always drives the cost of a team project up in two ways. First, micromanagement tends to violate the JIT rules of review and revision, and, second, micromanagement prevents managers from working on more than one project at a time—both too costly in today's business environment.

3. Establish a Concept Design Group Before Forming the Team. Only new product development cross-functional teams need to establish a concept design group. The purpose of the concept design team is to conduct market research, calculate new product cost-benefit analysis, and make a "go, no go" decision about the new product. The concept design group is generally composed of subject-matter, market analysts, and any systems experts needed to determine the feasibility of the product or service being considered.

4. Develop a Business Plan. The business plan establishes the parameters under which the team must function. From our task force and cross-functional team debriefings we have discovered that one of the principle reasons for team failure is the lack of a business or project plan. For some reason, managers, imbued with thoughts of empowerment, often just throw projects over the wall to a team and expect them to be successful. For many reasons, this is suicide for the team because all task forces and cross-functional teams come from many parts of the organization, each with their own agenda. Therefore, to assure that the team has a unified focus, a business plan is essential. See Figure 4.2.

(text continued on page 69)

Figure 4.2.
A High-Level Business Plan for Cross-Functional Teams and Task Forces

1. Develop the organization and team mission
   A. Write the mission
   B. Determine critical success factors
   C. Determine objectives/metrics
   D. Identify needed resources (people, facilities, equipment, budget)
2. Determine and obtain resources
   A. Determine and secure capital resources
   B. Schedule and dedicate personnel
   C. Secure technological resources (machinery, hardware, software)
   D. Get sponsor commitment for long-term support
3. Determine training needs
   A. Refer to the Team Life Cycle Chart as a baseline
   B. Write training plan
   C. Set training dates
4. Determine team operating processes
   A. Establish a communication process within the team
   B. Establish how work will flow within the team
   C. Develop a team charter and operating principles
   D. Clarify roles, responsibilities, and limits of decision-making authority
5. Determine product specifications based on customer requirements
   A. Translate specifications into quantity, quality, capital, and cycle time metrics
   B. Identify links with other products and services
   C. Identify products and service links with other team members
   D. Develop current organization map
      Note: In the dozens of debriefings that we have conducted, one of the top three complaints we hear about is the lack of good, stable product specifications. Our advice is not to form a team until product specifications have been approved and signed-off on by management.
6. Develop performance measures (objectives, action steps, and indicators for) the:
   A. Individual
   B. Team
   C. Organization

Note: Roles and responsibilities and products and services establish the baseline from which all future operational decisions will be made. These describe who does what. From here, the team may wish to change, combine, rearrange, or eliminate responsibilities, or products and services. The organizational map will provide a horizontal view of the team functions, perhaps pinpointing disconnect points.

7. **Develop an implementation plan**
   A. Determine what new tasks will be absorbed by the team and when the team will take over responsibilities for them
   B. Determine milestones and due dates
   C. Plan hours to complete project
   D. Compare planned hours against actual hours

   Note: Performance measures must be cross-checked with the new roles and responsibilities to make sure there are exacting fits and to ensure team members have control over them. Performance measures will be used to assess how well the team did as well as how each team member did in the team.

8. **Develop communication plan**
   A. Identify audience
   B. Define problem
   C. Define purpose of the plan
   D. Define strategy
   E. Define media
   F. Define performance measures
   G. Define plan timelines
   H. Write communication
   I. Distribute communication

   Note: The purpose of the communication plan is to ensure that the team's message gets disseminated accurately and broadly. The first communication should go out with the sponsor's signature. This will ensure that future communications will be taken seriously.

9. **Support the team**

(text continued from page 67)

At a minimum, a team business plan must contain the following:
A. Defined customer requirements. Determining customer requirements, needs, and their quality requirements should be the first step that any cross-functional team takes. Customers should be

active participants in any cross-functional team. Their input will ensure that the final product or outcomes will be guided by their thinking, not just by assumptions. Customer wants lead directly to developing product or result specifications.

B. Written mission statement. Most sponsors of task forces and cross-functional teams have a specific problem they would like to solve or a product they would like to develop. In order for this to be accomplished successfully, the sponsor must take time to explain the mission of what it is he or she wants. In the many cases where task force and cross-functional teams have failed, one of the major reasons for failure is that the sponsor did not take the time to fully articulate the mission. In today's business environment, the "I will know it when I see it" approach is too costly in terms of time and resources to be an acceptable method of business operation.

C. Defined product or service specifications and quality requirements of deliverables. Specifications and quality requirements describe the features and characteristics of the deliverables and communicate to the team what the final product will look like, what it will do, and how it will do it, which in turn determine the scope of the project. Therefore, a task force or cross-functional team cannot go forward until specifications are completely understood. Further, these specifications will be used as the basis for performance measures when the team's work is assessed.

D. Established milestones and due dates. Milestones signify the completion of some subcomponent of the final product. Milestones and their due dates should be set for each subcomponent of the final product. Establishing milestones and due dates communicates another level of team performance expectations to team members. This approach works especially well when combined with JIT reviews.

E. Scheduled and dedicated team members. Scheduling and dedicating team members are difficult to achieve without the direct support of the sponsor. By dedicated we mean that a person is officially part of the team and will be working with the team throughout its duration. Scheduled personnel are those that are assigned to work with the team at specified times, such as during reviews. This does not mean that the employee must be with the team every minute the team meets; but it does mean the employee will be expected to meet with the team when requested and appropriate and deliver designated products to the team on schedule.

Unlike more permanent teams, the membership of task forces and cross-functional teams is largely predicated on the specialized skills each member brings to the team. The number of task force or team members is generally a straightforward proposition. Each functional department has to be represented. However, teams composed of ten or more members can become unwieldy and hard to manage.

If task forces or cross-functional teams are to be successful, there must be some continuity of the team members and managers. This continuity requires setting priorities and the added discipline of saying to management or other team managers, "No! You can't have Sandra—she is still working on the New Doodad task force," once Sandra has been committed to a team.

The addition or subtraction of team members causes the team to have to backtrack, introduce the new team member, bring them up to speed, and help them find a spot on the team. This is down time that costs the organization money. Unfortunately, most white-collar organizations do not consider labor a resource as important as capital. What often happens is that labor is squandered through lengthened time lines and unnecessary revisions due to lack of personnel dedication or bad scheduling. The following example illustrates the problem. A cross-functional team was formed to design and implement a new insurance information system within 11 months for sales agents information system in the field. After 13 months the project has 2 systems managers, 2 systems analysts, and 2 project directors. The project is 2 months overdue and management wondered why. The reason is simple. A vice president with theoretically greater needs than Sandra's vice president pulled Sandra off the team to work on another project. And this happened a number of times.

F. Defined roles and responsibilities. Our research shows that in almost 50 percent of the cases, cross-functional team members are never told what their role and responsibilities will be. Managers generally assume that they do not have to define roles and responsibilities for team members. Nothing could be further from the truth. Each member must know what functions they will perform and how and when they will perform them. Further, defining roles and responsibilities clarifies lines of authority.

One of the most amazing things to witness is when managers do two things: 1). "Alakazam! You are a team," and 2) walk away without defining roles and responsibilities, assuming everyone would know what to do. We have seen this happen so many times that it has become a standard joke. But the fact is this is a very expensive joke. Unfortunately, managers will probably continue to perform this magic trick until they are held accountable for such action in their business plan and are measured by the team through the use of 360° assessment and feedback (see 360° feedback in team assessment instrument section).

G. Estimated versus actual hours and costs. The business plan should include the estimated hours it will take to complete the project. In a worksheet, planned hours can be placed in one column, actual hours in the next column, and the variation between planned and actual in the next. See Figure 4.3 for an example.

Phase/Task	Planned Eastwood	Actual Eastwood	Variance Eastwood	Planned Hardwood	Actual Hardwood	Variance Hardwood
Pathfinding						
Research	2	2	0	4	2	−2
Review	2	3	+1	1	1	0
Design						
Developing items				5	2	−3
Reviewing items	2	4	+2	3	2	−1
Formatting items						
Revising items						
Totals	6	9	+3	13	7	−6

Figure 4.3. *Planned versus actual hours.*

The data can be further expanded by multiplying each team member's internal costs by the number of hours. We encourage management to consider this approach. It will provide them with an approximation of labor cost for developing new products and services. Amazingly, most organizations do not capture such data and therefore they do not know what it actually costs them to produce a new product or provide a service. Capturing such data will help to illustrate where capital is being spent and who is spending it and help management to make better economic and human resource decisions.

H. Estimated subcomponent costs. Similarly, we think that capturing the costs of each subcomponent will help management make better decisions about the cost-effectiveness of task forces, cross-functional teams, and new products and services. Costs to be captured should include such things as consultants fees, material costs, capital costs, internal operating costs (particularly if the organization is a "charge back" organization), and downtime. Every time a team has to stop working on his or her assigned task, the labor and the internal operating cost clocks are still running. In a team with eight highly trained professionals, this cost could be as much as $3,000 a day.

I. Decision-making authority. Team members need to know what they can and cannot do without managerial consent. This should be decided early in the team's development and in an open discussion with all team members present. It is an important topic that will, during some portion of the life cycle of the team, become a very important concern.

J. Performance measures. Almost all cross-functional teams are organized to solve a specific business problem. Most business problems are identified in the business plan as one of many objectives. The team as a whole should be held accountable for accomplishing this objective. But also, each team member should be held accountable for the quality of any deliverable produced. This includes the sponsor and the manager. Therefore, the team must develop some "team" performance measures that *every* member will be evaluated on by every other member (see Figure 4.4). To evaluate only the performance of team members and not the performance of the sponsor or manager violates the very essence of what a team is about.

5. Conduct JIT reviews. A business plan can be greatly facilitated if it is developed on a computer and the information is either projected onto a large screen with the use of an overhead or hooked up to a large-screen monitor. In either case, the purpose is to shorten the development time by making revisions then and there, eliminating the revision cycle. Review and revision cycles are very costly. Our studies using activity-based costing have shown that using on-line documentation is an exceptional productivity tool.

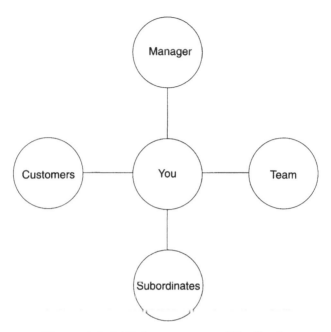

Figure 4.4. *360° Assessment and Feedback.*

JIT reviews have two distinct levels. *Level One* JIT review is one in which a SME and the SME's supervisor together review work that has been completed. For information-based products, the review should be done "while both are sitting at the computer." This means a copy to the work should be given to the supervisor before the review. Any suggestions or revisions of the work should be done when the supervisor finishes with the SME and makes any corrections on the computer. This completely eliminates the costly shuffling of paper revisions, greatly increases productivity, and reduces work cycle time and production costs. *Level Two* JIT reviews take place when the sponsor, or the sponsor's representative, signs-off on the subcomponent. Again, if the product is information-based, the review should be done with the SME sitting at the computer and inputting any corrections on the spot.

All of the authors of this book have been involved in JIT reviews with senior management in our respective companies. While JIT reviews are exasperating for most managers and sponsors in the beginning, our evidence clearly shows that *JIT reviews are one of the single most effective ways of drastically reducing review, revision, and work cycle time.* The first review reduces costs and the second review gets products to the market sooner.

JIT reviews become somewhat more complicated when the product is not information-based. However, the same principles can be used. For example, any changes to some physical component can be noted or changed in most CAD/CAM systems. The idea is to make changes or revisions as close to the product as possible.

6. The physical working environment. The design of the work environment can have a significant impact on cross-functional productivity for two basic reasons. First, boundary management is very important when a cross-functional team is put together to create a new product or service. All boundary crossings can have a negative impact on the productivity of the team.

Second, research conducted by the Catalyst Consulting Group suggests that close proximity of team members greatly increases communication of new ideas and decreases the time it takes to solve specific problems. Therefore, we have adapted the JIT group technology cell as the best model for the physical working environment for cross-functional teams. Figure 4.5 shows what the "cell" looks like.

   A. The cross-functional team should be located away from normal traffic patterns. Boundary crossings are disruptive and should be minimized as much as possible.

   B. Each team member should have all essential resources, his or her own computer, reference materials, etc., nearby.

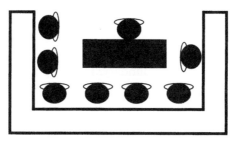

Figure 4.5. *Group technology cell configuration.*

C. Team members should face the wall of the cell. This is because working in a cell is very intense, and our research shows that people find facing each other over long periods of time makes them feel somewhat uneasy—there is no place to "hide" in a cell.

D. A conference table should be placed In the middle of the cell. This makes it possible for cross-functional team members to have JIT meetings whenever necessary.

E. The team leader should be located outside the cell's boundaries. The leader is a facilitator and coordinator, not a worker.

F. There is limited data on how well such a configuration would work for task forces because of their temporal nature and because members meet infrequently. But the concept of having all the necessary resources in one central place is difficult to discount. Furthermore, if productivity were to increase like it does in successful cross-functional teams using this configuration, the benefits would surely justify the costs.

Arthur Anderson & Company decided to place cross-functional teams in a group technology cell configuration. The reasoning was that close proximity of team members would decrease total work cycle time, increase product quality, and reduce total costs. In a preliminary study involving five teams, pre-, concurrent-, and post-conduct evaluations were made using individual interviews, questionnaires, and time and cost comparisons against standards. The results clearly demonstrated that cross-functional teams in group technology cells tend to realize dramatic improvements (45 percent reduction in costs and 60 percent reduction in task-related cycle times). It was from this study that preliminary cross-functional team performance variables were developed. These variables were used to conduct a more thorough and complex analysis of cross-functional teams.

7. Managing the boundaries. Boundary management is a fairly recent but important concept. What is a boundary? For our purposes, the boundary is the imagined or real physical boundaries surrounding a team. The concept emerged with the introduction of JIT, focused factories, and group technology cells. Focused factories and group technology cells have physical boundaries that designate what kind of operations take place, such as milling operations or upholstering car seats, and what kind of material exchanges take place across those boundaries. These concepts have been adapted to task force and cross-functional teams with great success.

The reasoning behind boundary management is straightforward: the fewer times team members or products cross the boundary, the greater the productivity. Further, the more vertically and horizontally specialized a team is, the more costly boundary crossings become. The team leader's job is to make sure that all of the resources that a team needs can be found within the team's boundary. No team member should have to leave the team to secure resources. Further, the team leader should limit the number of non-team members crossing team boundaries.

Managing relationships with constituents and stakeholders may be time consuming and tedious and may infuriate traditional managers. Managing a team means managing the relationships inside and outside the team, if the team is to be successful. Team leaders must become facilitators instead of movers, shakers, doers, or direction givers.

8. Team Support. Task forces and cross-functional teams need to be nurtured. Our experience has shown that a cross-functional team in a cell developing a new product can be exhausting. Working in a cell, while unquestionably increasing productivity, is very much like living in a fishbowl. Everything everyone does is visible. Peer pressure to conform to unwritten productivity standards is enormous. All of this, coupled with short time lines, makes this environment a difficult one to adjust to.

Sponsors and Managers of successful teams have been experts in performance management, particularly good at coaching, and exceptional in handing out pats on the back, "way to go," and 7:30 pizza parties. Equally important, good sponsors and managers have seen to it that the team received a much deserved "break" after a project was successfully completed.

Team members on successful teams have stated that they would work in such an environment again if they had the same sponsor or manager and because they felt like they were able to accomplish goals they thought would have been impossible to reach without the team. In contrast, sponsors and managers that did not nurture team members found that they were less likely to attract top performers when they asked for volunteers and had higher turnover rates after completion of projects.

Other Ways to Ensure Team Success

Team Formation Meetings. The team must spend time together developing a business plan that includes all of the points discussed earlier. We recommend that teams take at least two days off-site to put together the components of the business plan. Many managers are taken aback by this suggestion, but it must be remembered that a task force or cross-functional team that has to backtrack as a group is costly in terms of additional time in revision and lost opportunity costs. The time spent in developing a mission and a business plan will be more than made up during the development cycle of the project.

Training. Training is essential to the survival and success of any long-term task force or cross-functional team. Joining a team is a highly emotional experience, and team members need to understand how to manage the process. We recommend that managers and team members receive training in the fundamentals of integrated business planning, performance management, team design and development, and process consultation. Performance management will establish the ground work for developing performance objectives and measures, define how coaching works, and introduce review and assessment concepts. Process consultation is essential to understanding what is going on within a team at any given time and provides a nonthreatening way to discuss problems and solutions.

Rewards. Task forces and cross-functional teams have reward issues that do not exist in other kinds of teams. In self-directed work teams, team members are almost always from the same level and similar pay ranges. This is not the case for task forces and cross-functional teams. Some task forces have members from every function and level of the organization. The reward system has to be carefully thought through, especially if cross-functional teams become common in an organization. Why? Rewards, and how they are distributed, are one of the most divisive factors in modern organizations. Managers and sponsors who believe employees do not understand the reward distribution rates, how such decisions are made, and the large disparities between employees and management are misleading themselves. If the disparities between rewards for sponsors and employees are too great, or if the sponsor receives bonuses based on team performance and team members do not, it is very likely that the program to establish task forces or cross-functional teams will fail.

Debriefing the Task Force or Cross-Functional Team. We think that one of the most valuable efforts that an organization can do is to debrief task forces and teams at the end of a project. This should be conducted by a facilitator from outside the functions of the team members. The purpose of the debriefing is an honest and open evaluation of what went wrong and what went right. It should be structured in such a way that the same questions are asked of every team so that data can be compared over time. The information from the debriefing should be treated as "developmental" data as opposed to assessment or personnel decision data.

Customer-Value-Added Performance Measures

Almost all task forces and cross-functional teams are brought together to develop new products and services or solve complex problems. The following list of customer-value-added performance measures will help most task forces and cross-functional team develop better products and services in shorter time.

- Anticipation. Every team member has a responsibility to anticipate customer (or stakeholder and user) needs and requirements. This is not as difficult as it seems. A few hours spent conducting focus groups or telephone interviews, and reading between the lines of the data, almost always leads to a better fit with customer needs and requirements.
- Innovation. Innovative products and services based on good customer feedback analysis almost always turn out to be a money maker. Teams members should be encouraged to come up with innovative solutions to routine problems that get in their way and the customer's way.
- Expertise. Task forces and cross-functional teams can cost upwards to tens of thousands of dollars a day just in labor costs. What team members bring to the table is often vital to the success of the team. Therefore, all teams members should be evaluated on their expertise and business knowledge.
- Integration. Team members must think through how their portion of a project will integrate with all other parts, or how a new product or service integrates with existing products and services. Keeping the "big picture" in mind often reduces rework and redundancy. We feel that this should be a primary performance measure for all information technology teams because team members are often dazzled by tech-

nology without thinking about the consequences of its implementation, particularly for stakeholders and users.

- Alignment. Teams should keep a copy of the business mission and plan close at hand. Team leaders and members should frequently check to see if the project products and services are still aligned with the business mission and plan.
- Project management. If you can't manage a project, you can't manage a task force or a cross-functional team. Project management (i.e., milestones, due dates, quality, customer requirements, cost control, and intra-team functioning) should be a primary measure for all team managers and leaders.
- Translation. The new products and services that come out of task forces and cross-functional teams often have new language, processes, and procedures. It is the team's responsibility to make sure that customers, stakeholders, and users understand, in their own language, what these new products and services mean to them, and how they will changes their work.
- Application development. No new product or service should be introduced without first having in place the tools and techniques needed to sell, maintain, or service it.

Summary

The skills required for successfully implementing task forces or cross-functional teams do not require years of experience. In fact, we have seen new managers who were quite successful in implementing cross-functional teams. Success starts with a sponsor who is willing to share his or her vision and provide the team with the support they need. Next, a good business or project plan must be developed that outlines the team's mission, roles and responsibilities, milestones and due dates, and established team processes. Team, individual, and project performance measures must be written as well. All teams must be stable, and task forces or cross-functional teams are no exception. Therefore, team members should be dedicated or scheduled for the duration of the project. We also think it's important for the team to have a working knowledge of process consultation and conflict resolution.

Last, but not least, we think that there are ways to physically arrange task forces or cross-functional teams to have positive impacts on productivity and overall quality of products. Adopting some principles from JIT and group technology cell design may be one way to increase productivity. And bringing the team together during a team formation meeting to build the business plan and work out team operating procedures is a sure way to increase productivity.

In the next chapter we will discuss self-directed work teams. We will discuss their historical evolution, characteristics, components, and suggest a methodology for designing and implementing them. We will also examine several successful organizations that use self-directed work teams as a strategic advantage.

CHAPTER 5

Self-Directed Work Teams

What Are Self-Directed Work Teams?

We define a self-directed work team (SDWT) as a small group of employees (usually 5 to 20 people) who are responsible for carrying out a significant piece of work. This team is empowered to control their work environment and to strive for self-sufficiency. Although the exact roles and responsibilities of each team vary, SDWTs are usually responsible for most of the activities that relate to work planning, execution, and evaluation. Common roles and responsibilities of a SDWT include work scheduling, job assignments, material handling, preventive maintenance, housekeeping, personnel administration, record keeping, improving work methods, training, equipment set-up, assembly and fabrication, and safety.

Developing the capability to operationalize the concepts behind SDWTs is difficult for most managers and employees. The theory upon which they are based, sociotechnical systems theory, was developed by academics, and the vast majority of research and writing on the subject is conceptual rather than implementation focused. An accurate understanding of what SDWTs are is exacerbated by the many different variations of SDWTs that have evolved over the years. These variations are known as high-involvement work teams, super teams, autonomous work groups, and self-managing work teams. In the minds of most academics there are critical differences between each of these teams, but to those managers who are looking for a means to optimize their units' performance the differences are barely discernible.

SDWTs are not a new approach to job and organization design. They have been used in Europe and Asia for the last 40 years. Since the 1970s a number of companies in the United States, such as General Foods, PPG Industries, Inc., Proctor & Gamble, Sherwin Williams, TRW, General Motors, M&M Mars, Best Foods, and Cummins Engine, have implemented SDWTs in one or more of their facilities. Articles and books abound with stories of companies achieving dramatic results with SDWTs. The following are some examples.

- TRW's Oil Well Cable Division of Lawrence, Kansas, realized an 80 percent increase in work output over a six-year period while staffing levels only increased 12 percent. Turnover during this time was less than 1 percent and absenteeism was 2 percent.
- Donnelly Mirrors implemented SDWTs in the 1970s. At the end of the first year, the company realized cost reductions of $1.5 million, productivity increased 48 percent, and quality improved 8.5 percent.
- A team of clerks in the back office operation of a Federal Express office in Memphis improved quality by 13 percent and spotted and solved a billing problem that was costing the company $2.1 million a year.
- General Mills realizes 40-percent higher productivity in plants that use SDWTs as compared to their traditionally designed plants.
- Over a four-year period the Dana Corporation reduced its corporate staff from nearly 475 to less than 100. During this time the number of levels of management was reduced from 14 to 6 while sales increased four-fold.
- Westinghouse Canada at Airdrie, Alberta, reduced the cycle time for made-to-order motor control devices from 17 weeks to 1 week.
- Zilog's SDWT wafer fabrication plant in Nampa, Idaho, has had quality yields 15 to 25 percent better than the industry average ever since its start-up in 1978.
- Shenandoah Life Insurance Company reduced the cycle time of their policy application process from 27 work days (it required 32 clerks in three different departments) to less than 2 days. They are processing 50 percent more applications with 10 percent fewer employees.

Benefits

Although we've cited several success stories of well-designed SDWT initiatives, the exact types of benefits vary according to such variables as the objectives of the redesign effort and the specific application (white-collar staff function versus shop floor manufacturing setting) of SDWTs. Based on our experience with SDWTs we believe a well-designed program can provide benefits to both the organization and its employees.

From an organizational standpoint, we typically see significant improvements in operational and employee flexibility. Processes are usually redesigned to maximize the *overall* process and *not one link or unit* within the process. For example, the order entry process in most manufacturing companies includes a number of departments such as customer service, marketing, production planning, and shipping. Instead of redesigning the work flow in just the customer service function, SDWTs redesign the entire process and redraw, if appropriate, the reporting relationships and unit boundaries. Since jobs are redesigned to promote multi-skilling, this maximizes both operational and employee flexibility. Overhead and operating costs are invariably decreased because as work is leveraged down to the operating workforce, staffing levels of support and management are decreased markedly. Productivity is increased because output is significantly increased while input has been reduced. Functional silos are also minimized because work processes, information systems, and performance measures promote cross-functional cooperation thereby reducing the power of fiefdoms. Since the work itself is more challenging and motivating, absenteeism and tardiness tend to decrease. Interestingly, we also find in the short term that turnover increases. Because the work becomes more demanding we find that the "dead weight" most organizations carry on their payroll tends to self-deselect. Pressures from the team as well the redesigned work processes (that eliminate hiding places for this dead weight) immediately bring to light those who are unable or unwilling to carry their own weight.

Employees also tend to realize benefits as a result of SDWTs. Since SDWTs rely heavily on cross-functional training, on-the-job training, and classroom training, employees have greater opportunities for professional development. This, coupled with the fact that most SDWT initiatives use either a skill-based pay or gainsharing reward system, has enhanced employees' opportunities for career and salary progression. Since job redesign is an integral part of SDWTs, the redesigned jobs tend to provide greater opportunities for employees to participate in decision making and to take responsibility for their actions. We believe this increases employee perceptions of job and company satisfaction. Plants that adopt SDWTs provide more job security than those that are traditionally organized. Aside from those individuals who are displaced during the transition (who probably would have been displaced due to market conditions anyway), those who survive operate in a "leaner" organization that is better able to compete in the marketplace. According to our research, organizations that use SDWTs tend to have better quality and higher productivity, which allows them to compete more effectively. When an economic downturn occurs, these organizations are not hurt as badly as organizations that are traditionally organized.

History and Evolution of Sociotechnical Systems Theory

SDWTs are based on sociotechnical systems theory, which was originated by Eric Trist and his colleagues at the Tavistock Institute in London. During the early 1950s the National Coal Board asked The Tavistock Institute to conduct a study to isolate characteristics of high-producing and low-producing coal mines. The research team focused on the relationship between increased productivity and the application of state-of-the-art technology. Trist's initial studies centered around the difference between high-performing units with good group relations and successful diffusion of innovative work practices and those with low productivity, quality, high absenteeism and turnover, and poor labor-management relations. Trist concluded the following from this early study:

1. Productivity failed to increase in step with technological advances. High-performing units used autonomous groups of employees who had interchangeable roles (employees could perform multiple jobs from filling to cutting and loading). The high-performing units used minimal supervision and had high degrees of intergroup cooperation. The jobs were structured around "whole" tasks with definable products, ongoing feedback was provided to the employees, and the jobs fostered high task variability. Employees were empowered to make decisions that were previously made by management (such as, work scheduling and job assignments).

2. Low-performing units tended to be bureaucratic and utilized jobs that were repetitive and fragmented. Employees only knew their jobs and were not knowledgeable in upstream or downstream activities. Also, management tended to closely supervise these employees.
3. A production system is composed of a technology system and a social system. In order to optimize overall performance, each system had to be optimized to meet the demands of the external environment.

Trist reported his findings to the National Coal Board along with recommendations for reorganizing around work teams. Those mines that implemented his recommendations realized an average increase in output of 15 percent.

In the late 1950s the Tavistock Institute conducted additional research on work organization, this time studying a weaving shed at Ahmedabad, India. Two different studies were conducted on automatic and manual looms. Trist again concluded from these studies that there was a direct relationship between the technology employed and the way work was optimally organized. Productivity was low in areas where the technology 1) minimized worker interactions, 2) created jobs that were highly repetitive and allowed minimal opportunities for learning and development, and 3) fostered work processes that were highly fractured and convoluted. Trist also concluded that other systems within the organization (such as, the way workers were paid and, the amount of structure—policies, procedures, rules, regulations) also impacted worker motivation and productivity.

In the early 1960s the Tavistock Institute became involved in the Norwegian Industrial Democracy study, which focused on job design and further developed the sociotechnical theory by suggesting that work had to satisfy the social needs of the worker. Specifically, a well-designed job should provide conditions for learning, involvement in decision making, and opportunities for personal growth.

The importance of meeting the social needs of employees was never more evident than during strikes in 1972 between the UAW and General Motors at their highly automated Lordstown, Ohio, Vega plant. This was the first time that the key issue in a strike was the quality of the jobs themselves rather than pay.

In the late 1960s Saab-Scandia conducted additional research on SDWTs and established their first work group in 1969. Within four years approximately 130 production groups and 60 development groups were being used. Productivity increased considerably, downtime was reduced from 6 percent to 2 percent, and turnover on the chassis line was reduced from over 70 percent to under 20 percent. These successes led to the design and construction of Saab's Volvo plant at Kalmar, Sweden, in 1974. This highly innovative plant was one of the first to be specifically designed around work teams of 15 to 25 workers who were responsible for assembling complete subassemblies and sections of the car.

During the last two decades a number of highly progressive companies, primarily in the manufacturing industry, have been at the forefront of SDWT technology. Proctor & Gamble, Digital Equipment Corporation, and TRW have invested considerable resources to convert much of their manufacturing facilities to a SDWT approach. Executives from these companies believe that SDWTs have allowed them to reduce costs, improve productivity, improve labor-management relations, and enhance customer responsiveness.

Requirements for Success

Over the years a number of research studies have been conducted to determine what environmental factors are positively correlated with a successful transition to SDWTs. The studies and our personal experience suggests the following variables tend to support a SDWT transition:

- Egalitarian culture. SDWTs require a culture that deemphasizes status. Perquisites such as executive dining areas, separate lunch rooms and restrooms, and large offices should be avoided to eliminate barriers to communication and cooperation.
- Timely and targeted education. The redesign of jobs, unit boundaries, and reporting relationships typically creates critical competency gaps for such groups as first line supervisors, technical and administrative support functions, and employees whose jobs are redesigned. Education is needed to clarify new roles and responsibilities, to delineate decision-making authority, and to facilitate new skill (both technical and nontechnical) acquisition.
- Participatory management style. The transition to SDWTs requires a management team that is comfortable with empowerment and leveraged decision making. Supervisors and managers who are unable or unwilling to adopt this style of leadership should be identified, counseled, and, as a last resort, transferred or terminated. Employees must also want to accept new responsibilities (such as being process experts) that were previously handled by management or support personnel.

- Employment security. SDWTs are perceived very differently by each stakeholder group. Managers usually see them as a means of improving customer service, reducing overhead, and enhancing quality and productivity. Supervisors and employees may see them as a mechanism to reduce staffing levels. Fear of job loss is *real* because these groups of employees are frequently displaced when companies transition to SDWTs. It is, therefore, important for organizations to develop mechanisms to equitably address employee concerns. These can range from outplacement assistance and developing a skill bank to guaranteeing employment security and using seasonal or part-time workers as a means to address fluctuations in product and service demand.

- Stakeholder commitment. There are a variety of stakeholders who have "yes" and "no" votes regarding the ultimate success of SDWTs. It is important to solicit input and commitment from such stakeholders as unions, *all* levels of management, employees, suppliers, and customers. If you operate in a unionized environment, we suggest you involve the union at the earliest possible time (during the readiness assessment or early design stages). Since it commonly takes 24 to 60 months for an organization to fully institutionalize SDWTs, maintaining stakeholder commitment is critical to the overall success of this type of initiative.

- Rewards and recognition. No matter how you cut it, implementing SDWTs means more work. The focus is to get more output with less input. If carefully packaged, employees are typically willing to invest in the SDWT approach, but their investment must be rewarded appropriately. Management should have in place a base-salary system that rewards flexibility or a bonus-based system that rewards team output. We highly recommend managment consider a skill-based pay or gain-sharing compensation system.

- Task differentiation. SDWTs require work processes that allow the completion of a relatively whole task. If work is highly automated or existing processes do not lend themselves to task enrichment, then SDWTs are not a viable alternative.

- Boundary control. This relates to the extent employees can influence transactions (rates of inputs and outputs) within their work environment. In a SDWT environment employees are responsible for managing interactions and transactions within their own work area. The team leader is responsible for managing transactions and interactions between different teams or work units. This can include obtaining needed resources, facilitating inter-team communications, and troubleshooting operational problems that either are caused by or impact other areas.

• Task control. This relates to the degree to which employees can impact work output. This can include ability to choose work methods and scheduling work. If employees have minimal control over tasks, then SDWTs may not be a good fit.

Now that you have an understanding of the key success criteria for SDWTs, we would like to discuss issues that management should consider when designing and implementing this type of team.

The Design and Implementation of Self-Directed Work Teams

Sociotechnical systems theory is based on a view that an organization is composed of a series of processes where inputs are transformed to outputs that are valued by the customer. These processes occur within a social and technical system. Each system affects the other and is directly affected by demands in the external environment.

This view of organization or job design sharply contrasts with the way organizations are typically organized. Functionally, product, or geographically organized companies typically have problems with centralized decision making, are composed of narrowly defined jobs that promote specialization, utilize a structure that doesn't promote innovation and creativity, and have insufficient levels of intra- and inter-unit cooperation.

Table 5.1 compares the characteristics of traditional organizations and organizations that use a SDWT structure. Interestingly, organizations that utilize SDWTs tend to create an environment where employees are encouraged to be flexible, multiskilled, and work as part of a team to identify and redress variances. These types of organizations tend to foster open communications and reward employees for team performance or new skill acquisition.

When designing a SDWT we have used the following guidelines:

1. *Identify and strive to eliminate the causes of variance.* Variance is any unplanned event (such as poor quality of incoming materials or equipment failure) that critically affects an outcome. If a variance can't be eliminated, control it as close to its point of origin as possible. Incorporate inspection into jobs where possible. This shortens the time

Table 5.1
A Comparison of Traditional Organizations and SDWTs

Design Variables	Traditional Organization	SDWT-based Organization
Job design	Focus on specialization	Focus on multitasking
Leadership style	Leader directed	Employee directed
Reward system	Focus on individual initiative	Focus on team performance and employee flexibility
Information flows	Typically top down	Three way
Employee involvement	Commonly voluntary, focus on problem solving	Involuntary within intact work teams. Focus is on prevention.
Variance control	Controlled by management, technology, and support groups	Controlled at point of origin

needed to detect a variance, reduces rework, and decreases the need for interdepartmental communications.

2. *Avoid too much specification.* This refers to the amount and sophistication of documentation, rules, and policies. Only specify what is absolutely essential to maintain control of the process. Don't plan for contingencies you don't have to plan for. Too much specification impedes innovation, operational flexibility, and employee motivation.

3. *Design jobs that focus on the completion of a whole task.* Employees need to understand the overall process and how what they are doing relates to it; they must perceive their actions as adding value. Also, provide considerable skill and task variability (cross train, use job rotation, maintain flexible work rules), delegate decision-making authority to the lowest level, and provide ongoing performance feedback (from customers, the work itself, and peers).

4. *Ensure the information system provides timely and accurate information in a format that is usable.* It is critical to use technology as an enabler for performance improvements.

5. *Modify the role of the supervisor.* Most supervisors are responsible for planning, directing, and evaluating the work of others. In a SDWT environment, supervisors need to focus on being internal consultants, trainers, coaches, and boundary managers. Since these individuals are usually highly skilled, they should focus their attention on shortening the learning curve for other team members. For example, if a supervisor has 20 years of experience, he or she should strive to pass on their accumulated knowledge to other team members so that it doesn't take them 20 years to develop the same knowledge base.

6. *Unit boundaries should not separate employees who need to share information, work together, or learn from each other.* Focus on eliminating physical barriers that impede interactions.

7. *Modify the organization's impacted systems (human resource systems, planning systems, budgeting systems) to closely support SDWTs.* These systems should not send mixed signals—they should support the culture needed to institutionalize SDWTs throughout the organization.

Phases of Design and Implementation

SDWTs are not a panacea for all the maladies that afflict the modern organization. Rather, they should be used selectively when they closely support an organization's business strategy and thereby improve its competitive position. An organization that is interested in transitioning to SDWTs should conduct a readiness assessment as a preliminary step. A readiness assessment will answer three critical questions: 1) To what degree do SDWTs fit within the organization? 2) What are the best applications of SDWTs within the organization? (SDWT may be most appropriate for one or more departments, manufacturing cells, or SBUs), and 3) What are the requirements for a successful transition?

Over the years we have designed and successfully implemented several SDWT programs. The three-phase approach we use is based on the model illustrated in Figure 5.1.

Phase I: Organization Analysis

During Phase I the following five key activities occur:

1. A management advisory group (MAG) and a design team are established and trained.
2. A plan is created that outlines the scope, approach, and timelines for the project.
3. An analysis is undertaken of the demands and constraints that the external environment imposes on the organization.
4. The technical system is analyzed to identify inputs, transformation processes, and outputs for each operation; this will assist in the identification and control of variances.

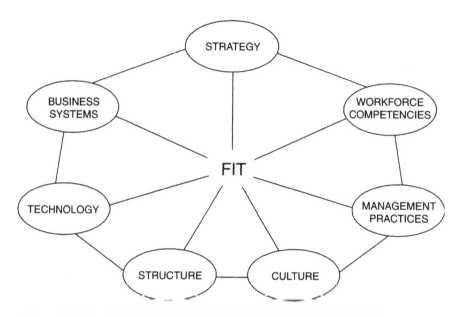

Figure 5.1. *Design variables for self-directed work teams.*

5. The social system is analyzed to identify ways to more closely align it with the technical system.

An initiative as complex as implementing SDWTs requires project management skills. This iniative starts with the creation of a project team. Depending on the scope of the project it is not uncommon to have a multi tiered project organization. Typically this consists of a MAG (usually 6 to 10 members) composed of senior management, union representatives (if applicable), and 2 to 3 members from the design team. The critical role the MAG takes on is the creation of a charter (see Figure 5.2). A charter typically outlines such things as the purpose of the redesign, the approach to use, timelines, expected outcomes, level of employee participation, and the design team's limits of decision-making authority.

MAG's Role. In addition to creating a charter, the MAG provides overall direction to the design team, ensures adequate resources, approves deliverables, members act as role models, acts as a liaison to corporate management, develops a vision statement.

Figure 5.2
The Team Charter Operating Procedures and Norms

Operating Procedures

The Membership of the Team
- There will be a cap of 14 teams members, roughly reflecting the organization's population.
- The quorum number for the team is 11, when it has achieved its 14 member cap.
  Otherwise, quorom is a super-majority (80 percent) of current team membership.
- Team members can be nominated by any team member; however, the initial team membership interview will be conducted by the supervisor, who will make a yes/no decision to present the candidate to the full team.
- The team will interview all candidates forwarded by supervisor.
- Membership to the team will be determined by first round team vote.
- Admission to the team requires a super-majority (9) of members voting in favor of the candidate admission.
- Team membership is not a right, but a privilege; therefore,
  missing five or more meetings could result in membership termination.
  missing three meetings in a row could result in team membership termination.
  dismissal from the team requires a quorum of members to recommend dismissal.
  dismissal from the team will be determined by first-round anonymous team vote.
  all subsequent votes will be by the showing of the hands.

Team Meetings
- Meetings will be held every other Monday, except for holidays; alternate dates may be assigned.
- There will be one meeting each in the months of July and August.
- The meeting will be limited to 2½ hours, with each agenda item allocated a specific time limit.
- At the beginning of a meeting
  the previous meet week's minutes will be reviewed.
  school updates will be given.
  old business will be discussed.
  new business discussed.
  the agenda discussed.

- Minutes will be kept for each meeting.

  Minutes will be kept in bullet point fashion.

  The scribe will summarize accomplishments and next steps on agenda before close of meeting.

  The scribe will be responsible for following week's agenda.

  Each team member may call three working days prior to meeting with new items.

  The keeping of minutes will rotate weekly.

  No one should keep minutes twice before any team member has done two.

- Team members have the right to invoke the team conflict management decision-making process by calling for a second and a simple majority vote.

The Role of the Moderator

- The supervisor will be the primary moderator but will elect others to fill post to help leverage knowledge. This monitor will

    recognize new business from floor.

    recognize people to speak.

    monitor/reduce side bars.

    call time outs during heated debates.

    limit speakers to not more than five minutes per issues.

    invoke the team conflict management decision-making process by calling for a second and a simple majority vote.

Further, everyone will do one stint as moderator before any team member has done two.

The Team Norms

We will show respect for other team members by
    not using put downs.
    being open minded.
    listening carefully.
    eliminating cliques.
    keeping focus on issues, not personalities.

We will communicate effectively by
   calling, if not coming.
   keeping disagreements within the team.
   thinking before speaking and being concise.

We will build and implement a business plan by
   developing realistic short/long term goals.
   building and implementing an accountability matrix.
   using a formal decision-making process.
   developing an "outside the team" communication plan.

We will show active involvement by
   regular attendance.
   sharing equal responsibility for implementing ideas.

Beliefs
   We can make a difference.
   A positive attitude will help build a better organization.

Design Team's Role. The design team is typically responsible for: learning about SDWTs; conducting an environmental, technical, and social systems analysis; educating employees regarding SDWT concepts; recommending the overall design to the MAG; acting as a role model; facilitating vertical and horizontal communications; and leading the implementation process.

The design team should work closely with the MAG and is typically composed of 6 to 12 employees from each function within the scope of the project. The team is usually empowered to collect data, educate themselves and other employees, keep employees informed about the project, and implement approved recommendations. Two key activities the design team should complete early in the project are the creation of a commitment plan and a communication strategy. The commitment plan should identify 1) the stakeholders impacted by SDWTs, 2) winners and losers—(some groups of stakeholders will be positively impacted by SDWTs by gaining more input into decision making and, having jobs that provide more growth, whereas others will be losers—(they will lose power, status, and so on), 3) people whose support is essential for success, and 4) any outstanding concerns from any stakeholder group. The communication strategy should identify the communication vehicles (meetings, videotapes, and so on) that will be used to convey each message, specify the frequency of communications, identify methods to counteract rumors, and develop mechanisms to solicit employee input and to address their concerns.

Once the design team has completed its preliminary tasks it can focus its attention on conducting an environmental analysis. The objective of this analysis is to identify the organization's interdependencies with external stakeholders. It also should identify the present and anticipated demands the environment places on the organization as well those factors that influence organizational performance. Key questions to ask in an environmental analysis include:

1. Who are the organization's stakeholders?
2. What demands does each stakeholder *currently* place on the organization?
3. What demands is each stakeholder expected to place on the organization in the *future?*
4. Can the organization influence these current and future demands?
5. What effect will changes in demand have on the organization?
6. How well is the organization meeting these demands?
7. What constraints or opportunities do these stakeholders create?

In most instances these questions will generate a large amount of data. The data must then be synthesized, and a desired future state, or vision, must evolve from this synthesis.

Technical Systems Analysis. The technical system includes work flows and processes, procedures, instructions and information, techniques, tools, equipment, machines, and physical space that are used in transforming the organization's inputs to outputs. The focus of the technical systems analysis is to reduce the probability of key variance from occurring.

The technical systems analysis usually begins with an indepth work analysis. This frequently employs one of the many process mapping technologies. Additionally, data should be collected on the physical work setting (amount of light, temperature, noise levels, orderliness, and so on) and spatio-temporal layout (anything that can affect the amount and quality of interpersonal interactions). Key aspects of the technical systems analysis include:

1. Identifying the mission or purpose for each process.
2. Creating a process map for each process. This includes identifying the inputs, outputs, transformation processes, information flows, and existing unit boundaries. These maps should note bottlenecks, points of inspection, cycle times, activity costs, and productivity and quality problems.
3. Identifying the sources and causes of variance.
4. Understanding how key variances are controlled, the information needed to control variances, where the information comes from, how the information is used, and how employees are kept informed about the effectiveness of their efforts to control variances.
5. Examining how the social system actually controls or copes with variances in the technical system.
6. Strategically prioritizing key variances.

Social Systems Analysis. The social system consists of the people who work in an organization, their attitudes and perceptions toward the organization, their expectations and needs relative to their jobs, supervisory-subordinate relations, worker interrelations, the way jobs are grouped into units, and the tasks that are completed. The primary emphasis of the social systems analysis is to identify what employees want in their jobs and the extent to which the job is fulfilling their needs, and to understand and improve the effectiveness of focal roles (individuals who can most readily impact key variances).

The data for a social systems analysis is usually collected through any of the following methods: focus groups, interviews, archival document reviews (review of quality of work life indicators, such as trends in employee surveys, absenteeism rates, grievances, and turnover rates), observation, and surveys of employees.

Typically, the analysis focuses on four key activities that occur in all organizations: goal setting, adaptation, integration and coordination, and long-term employee development. Analysis of the goal-setting process addresses how well the basic business mission, strategy, and goals have been communicated and accepted by the workforce. It should also address levels of involvement in the process and stakeholder's understanding and commitment the strategy and goals. It includes the strategic and business planning activities and budgeting processes. Adaptation refers to how well the organization is able to identify and react to changes in its environment.

It relates to the appropriateness of current policies and practices that impact risk taking, environmental sensing, innovation, and feedback from customers, suppliers, and competitors. Integration and coordination concerns the effectiveness of the activities of individuals to get interrelated units and people to work together. It includes policies and practices regarding conflict management, organizational communications, and cooperation. Long-term employee development concerns the effectiveness of policies, procedures, and systems that are designed to develop the knowledge, skills, and abilities of the workforce. This can include the training and development, performance management, reward and recognition, and selection and advancement systems.

In addition to analyzing the effectiveness of these systems, it is also important to identify employees needs, perceptions, and attitudes relating to 1) the most important and least important attributes of a job; 2) the extent to which these attributes are present in their current job; 3) issues, systems, and processes that are preventing them from doing a better job; 4) the nature and effectiveness of communications (that is, who interacts with whom? when? and how?), and 5) how can goal setting, adaptation, integration, and long-term employee development be improved?

Phase II: Detailed Design

During this phase, the design team analyzes the data from the environmental, technical, and social systems analyses. Utilizing the vision statement, charter, design objectives, and the list of critical variances, the team identifies as many redesign alternatives as possible. At this point it is important not to put any unnecessary boundaries on idea generation that will curtail creativity. Once a large list of redesign alternatives is developed, a cost-benefit analysis should be undertaken to prioritize the alternatives.

When the design team feels confident their alternative design will appreciably improve the organization, they should select their preferred modifications and create a detailed action plan with budget and present it to the MAG for their review. A well-developed action plan will identify proposed modifications to inputs, transformation processes, outputs, unit boundaries, technology, job design, staffing levels, and organization systems and processes. At this time the MAG will usually do one of three things: approve the plan, request a pilot test of the design on a smaller scale, or identify issues and concerns they have that must be addressed before final approval. If the design team has done its homework it is extremely unlikely the MAG will veto the plan outright.

Phase III: Implementation and Evaluation

During this phase, a number of implementation teams are usually created to assist the design team in carrying out a myriad of activities. These teams are usually composed of representatives from the units that are impacted by the redesign and are responsible for addressing the nuts-and-bolts issues (such as, modifying work processes, and revising performance standards).

One of the critical activities that implementation teams and the actual SDWTs must complete is a code of conduct that dictates the ground rules for interactions between team members. Unless this is addressed early in the process, we tend to find significant dysfunctional behavior occurring in the team. See Figure 5.3 for an example of a code of conduct that was used by a Fortune 200 manufacturer of mailing systems.

- Members will become skilled in all team and team leader roles; members will assist each other in developing skills.
- All relationships and actions should lead to increased trust and confidence.
- Communication will be open and honest, without fear of negative consequences.
- Team values will reflect individual member values.
- All interactions, problem solving, and decision-making activities are done in a supportive atmosphere.
- Solutions to conflicts will be sought assertively and cooperatively.
- Suggestions, comments, ideas, information, and criticisms are offered and received with a helpful attitude.
- Team members will help each other reach their fullest potential in technical knowledge and share their knowledge and skills with each other.
- Efforts will be made to keep stress, anxiety, fears, and unnecessary pressure at the lowest possible level.
- Goals set by the team will be attainable; members will give mutual help in attaining goals.
- Each team member has 100 percent responsibility for team success.

Figure 5.3. *Sample code of conduct.*

During the implementation process, a number of employee groups, including the implementation teams, should participate in a wide range of educational opportunities. Listed below are the common topics addressed during a SDWT transition:

- An overview of SDWTs
- An overview of the redesign plan (to set expectations). Minimally, this should include modifications to the mission, vision, physical layout, unit boundaries, job design, and changes to the organization's systems and processes.
- Project management
- Change management
- Job and organization redesign principles
- Team facilitation
- Team skills
- New role of the supervisors
- Relevant job content training

Summary

In this chapter we discussed the conceptual underpinnings of SDWTs and key design and implementation issues. In Chapter 6 we will discuss the important role management plays in leading the transformation to teams.

CHAPTER 6

THE ROLE OF THE MANAGER IN TEAMS

When new CEOs are brought in, or those already in place are charged with bringing about change, they generally surround themselves with a team of executives who already have the same values and beliefs as they do. In fact, these executives may be part of a cross-functional team, whose role is to help execute their strategy by putting into practice the values and beliefs that are needed to support it. Generally speaking, if someone fails to buy into the values and beliefs and refuses to support the strategy, they either remove themselves voluntarily because they cannot or will not adjust, or they are eventually told, as Lee Iaccoca would say, "to get out of the way."

The extent to which success in implementing teams occurs at lower levels depends on having managers in place further down in the organization who also:

- buy into the strategy
- adopt the values and beliefs required to implement the strategy successfully

101

- currently operate in a fashion conducive to a team; or,
- are able to change their behavior to operate in a fashion conducive to teams

It is at these middle levels that the role of the manager becomes extremely difficult. This is especially true if these managers have been accustomed to operating in a hierarchical organization, have previously been rewarded for autocratic styles of management, and are then told to implement teams. Even when the CEO sets an environment for teams, the transition to teams may still be difficult. This change becomes even more difficult when managers are told, as often happens, to implement teams but the level above continues to operate in a hierarchical fashion.

Therefore, there are two major challenges facing managers:

1. Lack of Support. Often senior management tells middle managers to "put in teams," and then walk away expecting teams to happen. In doing this, they often provide little, if any, support and guidance. They are often surprised when nothing changes or teams fail. When this takes place, and in our experience it is a fairly common occurrence, middle managers are often blamed for failing to execute senior management's directives, even though these may not be clear, and there are mixed messages and conflicting goals.
2. Role ambiguity. This is closely linked to the first point and occurs when managers are caught in a conflict of operating with a hierarchy above and a team below or when managers say to employees, "Now you are empowered" without themselves knowing what this really implies. Under these circumstances, employees become anxious and consequently resistant to change as ambiguity surrounding expectations increases. Stress is frequently felt. One manager that we worked with said that she thought that she had empowered her team because she let them get on with things by themselves. She hadn't realized that she was supposed to work with them to help set mutual goals and let her expectations for team members be known. When she went through a 360 degree feedback process, all of her direct reports complained that they had no idea what she expected them to do or what they were supposed to do to achieve the goals of the organization.

Because we believe that the role of the manager is of critical importance to the success of teams, in this chapter we examine the changing role of managers as new organizational structures, and especially those involving teams, emerge. The resultant role may be so different that a new title such as coordinator may be needed.

In this chapter we will:

- Summarize some of the underlying forces that have an impact on the manager's role and why it is so important to pay attention to the role of the middle manager.
- Compare the skills of managers in "traditional" organizations with those expected in "high performance/high participation" organizations.
- Examine the role of the manager in the specific types of teams we have identified.

Forces Affecting the Manager's Role

As we have indicated in previous chapters, the nature of management in many organizations is being altered as a result of several forces. At a macro level, the most important of these are:

- Intensified competition both globally and domestically
- Widespread corporate renewal and restructuring
- Plant and product obsolescence and excess capacity
- Rapid changes and improvements in technology

These forces have had a significant impact on the structure of organizations. Organizations have become flatter, reduced corporate staff, made use of part-time workforces, moved production offshore, and broken large systems into smaller ones. And, as we have noted in other chapters, teams have become very much a part of this new organizational model. In some organizations, the traditional functions of the middle manager have disappeared. All of this has had an impact on the manager's power, status, security, and work load.

Listed below are some of the other major trends that are taking place that have an impact on the manager's role:

Information Overload

Managers will have to become more accustomed to allowing more involvement among employees in the decision-making process. With all of the changing forces that are taking place, it is becoming increasingly difficult for one person to possess the required knowledge and experience to make fully informed decisions, and these individual decisions are more prone to errors and oversights. Therefore, the manager's role will become more of a coordinator who ensures that the right people with the right backgrounds and skills are available when important decisions have to be made.

Even Greater Emphasis on People Management

Managers will have to spend more time managing change than managing the status quo. This means an enormous change in mind-set, together with the acquisition and application of new skills and a much greater emphasis on managing people as well as the workflow will be required.

Continued Chaos

Managers will have to deal with uncertainty resulting from changes inside and outside the organization. They will have to act as integrators and help others to make sense out of chaos. They will have to be big-picture thinkers and also detail oriented. A major challenge will be to remain big-picture thinkers in the context of the current trend to break work processes into small parts. To do this, well-managed cross-functional teams will be essential.

Increased Complexity in Technology

Some estimate that scientific knowledge has been doubling every 6–10 years since the 1960s. As rapid changes and improvement in technology occur, there will also be increases in the complexity of technology, and it is likely that additional technical skills as well as business skills will be needed. Implications of this for the manager can be enormous. Questions that will have to be addressed are: a) will managers have to keep up-to-date, b) will they have to rely on people reporting to them, c) will they have to participate in special training on a regular basis, and d) will they stay in the manager's role for a much shorter period of time than before.

Increased Diversity in the Workforce

Organizations will become more multicultural, which will provide numerous challenges for the manager who has never had to consider the needs of employees from different cultural backgrounds in getting teams of people to work together.

Other Issues in the Workplace

Managers will have to spend more time on legal issues such as sexual harassment, workers with disabilities, and so on.

Managing these issues presents some major challenges that may be exacerbated at the top as well as the middle levels where, as we have already noted, those people who rose in the organization were rewarded for the very behaviors that are now no longer espoused. In fact, some of the "mavericks" who conducted themselves in ways that are now valued were most likely the ones who left because they were unable to operate in the old culture.

All of this is further complicated by the fact that in the past (and even today), management was the career path many employees chose for moving up in the organization and receiving greater financial rewards. This has often resulted in a variety of problems that are counterproductive to the kinds of organizations and the management behaviors that are needed today. They include:

- Poor job matches. Many good technicians were rewarded for their performance by being promoted into management where they were like fish out of water and failed.
- Politicking. Many people who were hungry for power rose in the organization by treading on others or by using their political power to advance. Unfortunately, many didn't have the interpersonal skills or adaptability required to manage effectively at higher levels, especially in the new organizational structures.
- Lack of technical expertise. In the past, many people believed the philosophy that a manager is a manager is a manager. For this reason, people were promoted into management positions and put in charge of functions where they had little and, in some cases, no technical expertise. Many of these managers have ultimately failed because they had no credibility, were unable to help in effective problem solving and frequently made poor decisions because of a lack of understanding of the most important factors which needed to be taken into account in order to make a good decision.

In spite of their drawbacks, many of these practices are still adhered to and the people who advanced in this way may still be in place. Therefore, although many organizations have bought into the concept of employee involvement in decision making through the use of teams, old management practices still exist and the role of the manager in this transition process has generally been paid less attention. A key issue in moving to new organizational forms is that training and preparation for new demands has not occurred at middle and upper management levels.

So, it seems that managers can be faced with unrealistic expectations, lack of adequate support, and lack of clarity about how to move from traditional systems to the new team-based, customer-focused, organization designs.

Why Is It So Important to Pay Attention to the Manager's Role?

Fewer management layers and the need for greater flexibility in processing work has probably had a greater impact on managers than almost any other employee group. By the year 2000, many believe that of all employees, executives and managers will have undergone the most radical re-thinking of their roles. In moving to the new model, all levels of management are forced to relax their tight control over employees as the spans of responsibility increase, and lower levels are required to manage themselves.

As supervisors and managers increase their spans of control, they often experience a loss of power and may have less energy for close supervision. The teams they manage are unlikely ever to be static due to constant shifts in customer expectations, technology, products, and services, and often require a continuous retraining. Management control over employees shifts to a role of gaining commitment on new ways to work. Therefore, managers may find themselves having to deal with self-managing teams and empowerment, business processes rather than functional silos, and constant change in information technology that requires that information be distributed rapidly to any part of the organization.

Major challenges for managers are:

- To steer their organizations through transitions
- To find new and effective ways of managing in organizations that have been transformed, especially when the transformation includes employee involvement and teamwork.

As we have already indicated, a major impact on the effectiveness and productivity of the organization can occur if the role of the middle and upper level manager is overlooked. These managers play a key role in helping teams to work effectively and in acting as a link to other parts of the organization. If insufficient attention is paid to them, they can act as barriers to effectiveness in the following ways:

- Resistance to new behaviors

  Traditional bureaucracies were designed for making repetitive decisions on products/services with long-life cycles in a comparatively stable environment. This was appropriate at one time and was not in conflict with customer requirements. However, the new breed of manager must be able to operate in a variety of situations and organizations that are increasingly complex and be able to deal with different values of the emerging workforce. A major shift in behaviors may, therefore, be required. This shift is extremely difficult, if not impossible, for some managers, and they will do whatever they can to be disruptive and fight it. This shift will be particularly hard in the many cases where managers have been selected and rewarded in the past for behaviors that are no longer acceptable. For example, the "new" manager may be expected to change from being an authoritarian boss who told people what to do, to a "participative" coach who is expected to solicit ideas from other people and operate through consensus decision making. The difficult question facing him or her is, "What on earth does this mean and how on earth am I going to do it without totally losing sense of who I am?"

- Resistance to change from perceived threat to security

  When downsizing or delayering occurs, the middle manager is the one who is generally the most hard hit. The AMA reported that while middle managers were only about 5 percent of the workforce at the 836 companies it surveyed in 1992, they accounted for 22 percent of the layoffs (*Fortune,* Vol. 127, No. 4, February 22, 1993, pp. 80–86). Consequently, apart from resistance to learning new behaviors, at these levels there is frequently some resistance from middle managers whose jobs may become threatened when teams are implemented, and it is at the middle levels of management that the team is most likely to fail.

- Resistance due to perceived loss of status

  Not only is there a threat to managers in terms of loss of jobs, there is also the threat of having to manage and lead work groups through transitions. They then have to figure out how to manage (if they are kept in place), in the new company that emerges when they have no idea what this really means for them and the immediate impact appears to be loss of power and status.

• Role ambiguity affects performance

When senior managers decide to bring about change in the organization, they may know that they have to involve people at the bottom but they may have no idea what it means for the people in the middle. Given that the current mindset of senior managers is that change necessarily means cutting the middle layer, they frequently shy away from dealing with those people in it. This means that there can be a repetition of the situation found in quality circles when middle management became the "frozen layer" that was not necessarily eliminated but was not included in the change. Therefore, when asked for their support at a later date, they refused to provide it. By not providing guidelines for middle managers and helping them define and carry out their new roles, a critical piece needed in the shift to teams can be lost and their failure predicted in advance. In addition, if the critical role of the middle manager is overlooked altogether, time, money, and self-esteem are all lost.

How to Ensure Management's Success

There are four major factors that should be in place to avoid resistance to change from managers and ensure their success when teams are introduced. These are:

• Involvement from the beginning
• Commitment from the top
• Training and development
• Appropriate rewards

Why are these factors so important? Let's look at each one in turn.

Involvement from the beginning. Many employee-involvement efforts will backfire unless the critical role of the manager in the transition is recognized and the managers are involved in the process of change from the old to the new right from the start. Unless this happens, managers feel a lack of trust.

G.E. Aircraft found that when supervisors were needed to support change, such as redesign of the work, their involvement was needed as soon as possible in design planning and decision making. This could cover inclusion in design teams to designing segments of a new work system.

After managers understand the new work system, they should take part in the design of their new roles. Once more, a lesson can be learned from quality circles where those managers who were left out often resisted and sabotaged efforts to make changes and implement projects.

Commitment from the top. Based on our experience, the leadership at the top of the organization should be committed to teams or failure is likely. The process of consensus decision making, which is critical for teams, may take longer than senior management thinks it should. Meanwhile the managers in the middle are held accountable for getting the results within a set period of time.

When managers don't get the support from above, they occasionally work outside the system, go underground, form a plan, form a team. and get out new work. Some of them gain credibility by bringing in large sums of money for their organizations by using the plan and implementing new methods of processing work or meeting customer needs. However, this way of proving a point is not easy.

Training and Development. Once managers have a better understanding of those skills required to perform their new roles, support and training through coaching and counseling either by their own boss or by an outside consultant can help the manager through difficult transitions. Formal training also needs to accompany this. Specifically this would include training managers in understanding their new role, how to coach and counsel subordinates, managing multi-disciplinary teams, and learning how to tolerate reasonable mistakes from subordinates.

The use of feedback to the manager from his or her subordinates, peers, and boss through instruments measuring perceptions of how the manager performs when measured against multiple criteria along a number of dimensions is increasing. This 360-degree feedback process aims to help develop the persons being assessed so that they can continuously improve their skills. This system views the customer as everyone with whom the manager works. In the future, it is likely that it will become even more important to give individual managers more frequent feedback on their work.

Appropriate rewards. Support can also be provided through new reward systems and helping managers to deal with plateauing, which frequently occurs in a flatter system. If the manager's position is not eliminated but the opportunities for advancement disappear, this should be discussed. If the position is eliminated, help in finding another position should be offered while the manager is still on the payroll. If the manager stays, new pay incentives may be needed so that pay is tied more closely to performance of the team, and less to the annual merit increase.

Comparison of the Manager's Role in Traditional and High Involvement/High Participation (HI/HP) Organizations

In this section, we will talk about managing performance at three different levels of participation. We will examine the differences between the most traditional type of organization and the most participative one. This will provide a jumping off point for demonstrating the different types of behavior required of managers, the challenges faced in moving from one type of organization to the other, and how there can be a variety of different mixtures between the two.

The traditional model of management developed out of the work of Frederick Taylor, the founder of American industrial engineering, and Lillian and Frank Gilbreth. Often called scientific management or command and control management, this approach sought to reduce work to its simplest pieces. The emphasis was on output and getting the most done in the least amount of time. It was an approach readily adopted by entrepreneurs, such as Henry Ford, who at the time found the approach invaluable for assembly line work.

Employees had little say in how the work got done and had no contact with customers. Customer input was, for the most part, ignored.

In examining these models, it is important to realize that we are not necessarily advocating one management model for an entire company. Several companies use the traditional model, the high performance/high participation model and models in between (which we have generally lumped under the heading of performance management models typical of Management By Objective—MBO systems), simultaneously.

Figure 6.1 contrasts the main roles of the manager in traditional and HI/HP organizations. The role of the manager in performance management models falls somewhere in between these two models. Figure 6.2 demonstrates this shift in employee/management roles for the three levels of participation, namely traditional, performance management, and high performance, high participation. Figure 6.3 highlights the main differences

(text continued on page 114)

Traditional	Participative
Managers expect order, control and subservience to rank and authority.	Managers expect commitment and participation.
Managers lead by telling others what to do.	Managers lead by example. Organization of work is decided by the employees.
Territory is defended against other groups.	Manager of boundaries, encourages cooperation and resolves conflicts within and between teams.
Communication is generally vertical. Selective filtering occurs, information is hoarded.	Horizontal and vertical communication with more emphasis on the former. Negotiation at different levels.
Decision making is done mostly by the manager regardless of expertise. Implication is that the manager has the answer to everything, and in fact, is expected to know all the answers.	Decision making is by consensus. Others are invited to join in. Implication is that "the whole is greater than the sum of the parts." Manager facilitates process.
Manager has the last word on performance appraisals. Feedback is rarely given and then people only hear when something is wrong.	Employee input and discussion is encouraged and valued. Information is shared. Feedback is given with recognition for good work. Guidance provided when problems occur.
Initiative is discouarged. No risk taking and no questioning of the status quo.	Initiative and reasonable risk taking is encouraged. Development of trust is critical.
Blame others for mistakes.	Mistakes seen as a learning experience.
Focus is internal.	External focus, customer driven.
Manager called supervisor or boss.	Manager called sponsor, leader, internal consultant, coordinator.
Follows chain of command.	Deals with anyone necessary to get the job done.
Tries to master one discipline.	Tries to master a broad array of managerial disciplines.
Tends to be activity driven.	Tends to be results driven.
Encourages internal competition.	Encourages sharing and teamwork.

Figure 6.1. *Manager's role in traditional and high involvement/high participative (HI/HP) organizations.*

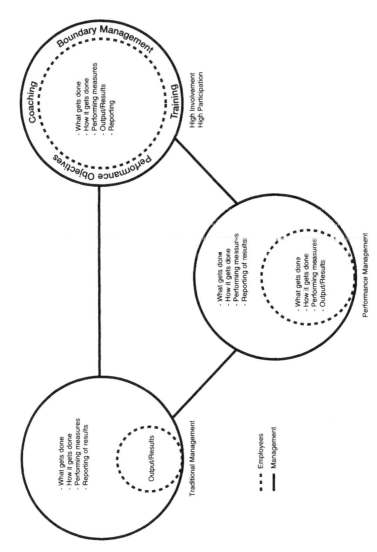

Figure 6.2. *Managing performance in three different levels of participation.*

	Traditional	Performance Management	High Involvement/ High Participation
Role of Subordinate	Highly specialized called "subordinate." Little contact with customers and upper management.	Stakeholder in achieving objectives. Some control over shaping direction of work.	Cross trained to do several jobs. Highly involved participant in business. Called "team member or Associate."
Supervision	Emphasis on control. Give directions, no input from subordinate.	Control still under manager sets goals for subordinates.	Management of teams - boundaries and environment.
Performance Planning	Little planning of work. Focus on output. Work broken into small units.	Set business goals for each team or individual. Employee has some input into how performance is measured.	Plans developed by employee and manager to meet corporate objectives. Performance measures jointly agreed upon.
Assessment	Command and controls.	Appraised and evaluation.	Employees decide on measures to be used.
Coaching	Virtually none.	Informal discussions between manager and employee.	Teams are responsible for coaching.
Development	Viewed as the individual's responsibility. An unwarranted cost to company.	Informal discussions between manager and employee.	Teams are responsible for coaching.
Rewards	Straight wages.	Variety of rewards — straight wages, perks, bonuses, non-cash recognition.	Compensation for learning new skills. and/or based on team performance.

Figure 6.3. *Management/employee rules for the three models of managment.*

(text continued from page 110)

among the three types of organization from the perspective of employee/ management interaction.

In the next section, we will look at the ways in which managers have to operate in a participative organization and will then look at the specific implications for the different teams that we have identified.

The Role of the Manager in Moving to Teams

In many traditional organizations, there is an emphasis on daily fire fighting, and competition among work groups is encouraged. Management methods are often in conflict with quality and customer service. In an organization that emphasizes quality, the focus of the employee shifts from top management to the customer as the controller of the employees' actions and generally the focus is on teamwork with continuous improvement, doing the right thing right the first time, and taking ownership at all organizational levels.

When managers become team leaders, there are two major roles that they have to perform. One is their role as a member of the team. The other is their role as the manager of the boundaries of the team in its relationships with other members of the organization, and its relationships with clients, other stakeholders, and competitors outside the organization.

In the next section, we will discuss these two main roles of the manager, what actions need to be taken, and what skills have to be acquired to transition into these new roles effectively.

Role Within the Team

If we start to think about the characteristics and behaviors needed for success among managers in a participative work environment, it is important to remember those characteristics that are needed for teams to be effective. This is because the manager's role is to move the team towards this desired state and to help maintain it.

Managers have to ensure that their teams have the following characteristics:

- They operate in a *supportive* environment.
- They have *clear, worthwhile goals* that all members agree upon.
- All members are *committed to the goals.*
- The team *members are competent.*
- Members obtain the *help and input* of one another to succeed.
- *Standards of excellence* are established and *prompt feedback* is provided.
- There are *rewards for the team* and not just for individuals.
- Have a clear charter and operating principles that focus efforts and clarify *roles and responsibilities.*
- They *collaborate* with one another and share information openly.

With this in mind, the major activities of the manager are to:

a. Create a Supportive Environment. The major role of the manager in relation to the team is to create an environment which *supports effective decision making.* The manager has to act as a facilitator in the decision-making process and has to help the team reach effective decisions. This is critical to the team's ultimate success. The environment should allow people to take *educated risks.* Blame has to be eliminated and *learning stressed.*

When a supportive environment is created in which team members can trust the manager and one another, it is more likely that change can occur.

b. Develop Trust. The greatest challenge to the manager is to develop trust among team members. Team members have to be given responsibility and allowed some autonomy to carry out decisions. For trust to be achieved managers have to demonstrate:

- Integrity. This means that they tell the truth, don't try to hide things, accept responsibility when they make a mistake, and don't try to put the blame on others when an error is made. They make sure that team goals take precedence over their own individual goals.
- Open Communication. This means that they demonstrate receptivity to new ideas and are willing to be persuaded to the viewpoints of others. It also means that they share ideas and realize that different viewpoints can result in new and creative ways to solve problems. They should encourage communication and demonstrate that ideas have been listened to by acting on them or discussing them even if they disagree. They provide feedback to group members and encourage members to give feedback to one another.

• Fairness. This means that they treat people with respect and courtesy. They avoid politicking to further their own ends and avoid showing favoritism among employees. Management must present challenges, encourage educated risk taking, reward and recognize superior performance, and support the team in its decisions. Therefore, an effective team leader will give all team members the self-confidence to act and the responsibility to make changes.

Consistency in these behaviors is critical.

c. Create and Communicate a Clear Vision. Managers need to be able to look at the organization and be able to determine where it needs to go to be able to compete and survive in the future. This means that they have to have a vision of where they want to take their team.

To formulate this vision, they have to be able to *read the environment* well. This requires that they *understand the needs of their customers and other stakeholders;* have a good comprehension of political, social, economic, and technological trends that are taking place, have developed specific ??? performance expectation with their suppliers; and have a good grasp on how their *competitors* do business.

Generally it is the chief executive of an organization who writes case studies that set a vision for the future state of the organization; however, passing this responsibility along to lower levels can be equally important. To do this means creating a sense of shared purpose and getting team members to feel excitement when the goal for which the team is striving is perceived to be worthwhile.

The organization's vision has to be translated into *clear goals* that have to be communicated and agreed upon. The members have to understand their roles within the context of these goals. Managers should help set clear goals and should establish a few clear priorities. The managers should know when to give direction and when to let the team decide on issues. In conjunction with this, they should make sure that team members communicate openly with one another and work through their own disagreements. They must be able to help the group to think through activities and establish plans. They should set high standards and give guidance on how to achieve them as well as give prompt feedback. The best team leaders constantly look for ways to improve doing things and will bring the team along in this endeavor.

Once the team has been selected, it has to sit down to figure out how to achieve its goals. This means planning an attack, working out strategies, being clear about the role of each team member, and defining objectives and action steps.

The leader can create trust by being honest, open in sharing ideas and listening to ideas, consistent in behavior, and by treating team members with respect. This should help to augment the skills of team members rather than just compensating for the lack of skills.

Note that the people who were good managers in the old system should have no difficulty shifting to the new system.

d. Act as a Role Model. Just about the worst thing that the manager of a team can do is to become caught up in his or her own self importance. If the manager's self interest starts to take precedence over that of the team, it is more than likely that the team will not be effective. Thus the team manager must have the welfare of the team in mind and act accordingly. This means acting with integrity and behaving in a way that sets the tone.

Team managers should provide a model of expected behaviors. They should have values and principles that they consistently live by and should hold others accountable for standing by these values and principles. Key among these values are integrity and treating others with respect and dignity. Their values and principles should be clear to others, and they should hold others accountable for living by these values and principles. They should demonstrate commitment to goals by working at them as hard as the team members and should deal directly with performance issues.

e. Select Effective Team Members. It is most important that team managers understand what is needed to reach the goals that have been set (hopefully by themselves) and that the right players are in place to accomplish them. They should select good people with appropriate skills. One of the main drawbacks to managers who become caught up in furthering their own self interest is that they may surround themselves with people who are not perceived as a threat to them and, in doing so, may surround themselves with an ineffective team. If the right team members are selected and an appropriate atmosphere of trust is created, members are willing to compensate for one another's weakness.

All of the above requirements mean that the manager has to have good skills in facilitation, the ability to sort through a great deal of data, and be able to identify the most relevant pieces. They should possess the ability to learn quickly, to communicate effectively, and to act consistently and with integrity. Needless to say, identifying managers with all of these skills is a major challenge to many organizations.

Role as a Manager of Boundaries

One of the most difficult tasks a manager faces in leading a team is managing the boundaries between the team and other parts of the organization. As we noted earlier, middle managers often find themselves caught between the demands of senior management to whom they report and those of the team for which they are responsible. One company that we work with is typical of this. Managers find themselves running a team below them and dealing with a rigid organizational hierarchy above. The result is role ambiguity, stress, and burnout. Only about one in four managers succeed in this environment. The key features of these managers are:

1. They are very smart.
2. They are very adaptable and are able to change roles from being directive to collaborative.
3. They demonstrate the ability to live with high levels of ambiguity without being too stressed by it.
4. Generally, they have support from the level above.
5. They are skilled in negotiation and the ability to influence others.

The ability to manage boundaries can become critical when two organizations merge and teams are formed of members from two different cultures. The ways in which the boundaries are managed can vary from one organization to another. GE Broment, for example, uses standing committees, ad hoc committees, and task forces to do this.

The role of the manager in managing boundaries is detailed in Figure 6.4 .

Figure 6.4. The Role of the Manager in Managing Boundaries

> • Ensure effective communication vertically and horizontally. This means communication to and from upper management and from the team and to any other person involved. This requires outstanding negotiation skills.
> • Link different work teams. This is particularly important for teams that may depend on one another to reach a mutual goal.

(continued on next page)

- Train inexperienced employees. In most organizations, management is more experienced than those employees who report directly to them. An effective manager should therefore leverage his/her expertise to each team member, greatly reducing their learning curve.
- Make sure necessary equipment and supplies are available. A big part of boundary management entails providing the team with the needed resources (facilities, equipment, access to people, budget) to achieve their objectives.
- Facilitate the workflow. An effective team manager is like a baseball coach. He can't hit, run, or catch the baseball for his players, but can and should work with each team member to put each in a role that optimizes his/her talents. Once this has been accomplished, attention should be focused on developing a process for allowing the player to work most effectively.
- Resolve conflicts with other groups or with senior management. One of the most difficult things to work out is where the responsibilities at different levels in the organization end. This is especially difficult when there are teams at all different levels.
- Integrate relevant information from other sources to present to the team in order to meet business goals.
- Ensure that the team meets the needs of customers both within and outside of the organization.
- Communicate a vision for the company. The vision should be steady and consistent. This vision should be supported by strategic and tactical plans.
- Translate the vision into guiding principles and practices that become an organization's belief system, showing how the company will go about its business.
- Demonstrate the constancy of purpose in his/her behavior and communications to members of the organization.
- Identify the external customers for the products and services of the organization.
- Make sure that the customers' needs are reflected in the attributes and characteristics of the products and services
- Make sure that the resources of the organization are directed to meeting the needs of the customer and to continuous improvement of the product and the service to the customer.

Once the team has been selected, it has to decide how to achieve its goal. This means planning an attack, working out strategies, and being clear about the role of each team member.

The skills required of managers may vary somewhat in accordance with the emphasis the organization places upon these skills and the way in which these skills are translated at different levels. Figure 6.5 provides an

Figure 6.5. Management Behaviors Matrix

Top	Middle	Supervisory
Vision: Establishes vision Communicates it Models it Translates it to next level	Communicates top level vision Develops for our business unit Models vision/value Describes expected behaviors	Communicates company vision Translates to unit Develops/communicates local level vision/mission Models values and creates mission described by vision
Market/Customer Focus Identifies right niche Manages existing relationships	Translates marketing strategy into plans and systems for finding and keeping customers	Conducts customer surveys Studies indicators of customer's satisfaction Maintains data on best practices and applies them
Financial Excellence Monitors financial results Takes corrective action Manages "public" reaction to stock price Maintains confidence in future of company Develops/communicates realistic financial strategies	Translates operational results/strategies/issues into bottom line Implements process for monitoring value added	Sets realistic budgets Holds those accountable for cost effectiveness Communicates role of team/unit business unit financials
Operation Excellence Understands overall business operations and systems critical to results Understands output desired in business unit Sets overall operative standards	Understands workflow, information flow Maintains data on current resource use Defines desired business processes against customer specifications	Understands quality requirements of customers Puts processes in place to ensure efficient cycle time, waste, quality and delivery Monitors against cycle time, waste, quality and delivery

Figure 6.5. Continued

Top	Middle	Supervisory
States what is expected/ desired	Communicates gaps and standards for operation Coaches for success desired state Ensures strategy connected to customer	Removes obstacles to achieve
Strategic-Collaborative Resource Use		
Ensures resources are in place to:	Ensures efficiency of resource use	Ensures people, technology have capacity/competencies needed
—meet market strategy	Bench strength	to produce quality products and
—achieve excellence across lines of business	Technology	services
—develop candidates for own succession		Ensures bench strengths Applies technology to reduce
—ensure procession place to ensure resources support business needs		costs, enable best use of people Uses resources/teams across functions
—reward others for meeting business standard		
—analyze decision factors		
Responsive decision making		
Includes key players as needed in decisions	Develops and implements strategy for filling gaps	Uses resources/teams across functions
Weighs long-term vs. short-term issues	Process in place for information technology	Develops information sources
Makes thoughtful decisions in time to make a difference	Applies variety of decision-making methods Trains others in responsive decision making	
Empowerment		
Removes bureaucractic barriers to decision making	Removes bureaucratic barriers to decisions	Removes bureaucratic barriers to decisions
Frees up resources and information for access to all levels	Frees up resources Holds employees accountable for results	Frees up resources Holds employees accountable for results
Holds employees accountable for results	Rewards employees for positive results	Rewards employees for positive results
Coaches, trains others Rewards employees for positive results		

example of how a Fortune 100 financial services company decided on the core activities for their top, middle, and supervisory managers and how these activities were translated into expected behaviors for the three levels.

The Manager's Role in the Four Types of Teams

In this section, we will look at the four types of teams and the manager's major role within them.

Simple Problem-Solving Teams

The general role of the manager is to provide resources, model correct behaviors, act as a facilitator and coordinator, act as a decision maker, communicate to higher levels, and help align the goals of the team with the organization's goals.

The Task Force

A task force can operate in almost any kind of culture, regardless of the leader of the organization. This is because the members usually meet for a relatively short (3–6 months) period of time to resolve a specific problem and make recommendations for its implementation.

The members will most likely be drawn from various parts of the organization and are often selected for their different perspectives as well as to provide them with a developmental experience. Usually the task force will have a chair or chairpersons responsible for "managing" the process. The main management skills required are group facilitation skills, the ability to delegate and coordinate activities, and the ability to plan and organize to make sure that the task is completed on time.

The manager or chair of the team has to be able to influence others, but this skill may not be too demanding because the team project is generally sponsored by a higher level manager who has position power over all members of the task force itself. In addition, members are generally viewed as good performers and have the reputation for having specific expertise and getting things done.

Cross-Functional Teams

The most difficult issue is managing the boundaries across functions. Also, managing the egos and different personality types involved in the team and getting them to work effectively together can be difficult. Generally these teams have a sponsor who has daily contact with the team, brings tasks to the team members, and helps keep team members away from organizational conflict. The manager has to clarify roles and responsibilities and makes sure systems are in place to support teams. Teams are usually formed for strategic business reasons and can trace back the activities required of them to the overall business plan.

Self-Directed Work Teams

In contrast to the role of the traditional manager whose major functions centered around planning, organizing, leading and controlling, and using authoritarian methods, self-directed work teams view the role of the manager as a facilitator and a coach. Managing boundaries and alignment of the team's goals with the goals of the organization are key. The manager's role changes as the team evolves to become more and more independent.

When the team is first put into place, the main activities of the manager will be to create and maintain trust, create a learning environment, develop the team's ability to solve problems, and provide focus and vision.

At the next stage, the focus will be on decision-making skills, acting as a teacher of group skills, and identifying what people need to learn and mentoring.

Later on, as the team begins to manage itself, the manager becomes a coach, a facilitator and helper, a consultant for advice, a manager of boundaries, and a mediator.

All of these required changes place a spotlight on the importance of identifying the right managers for the future and training them in the appropriate skills. Different recruiting strategies may have to be adopted in organizations trying to bring about the changes needed to compete in the year 2000. Different training strategies will probably be required. In fact, there has already been a qualitative shift in what companies expect from executive education to meet the needs of emerging structures. This often involves getting managers together to discuss the organization's new vision and strategy and placing less emphasis on case studies.

Summary

This chapter concludes Section One of this book. In Section Two we will present a number of tools and techniques for improving the performance of any team.

PART 2

Team Tools and Techniques

Part 2 of the book provides managers, team members, and team facilitators with a wide array of tools and techniques we have found to be particularly valuable. These tools are applicable no matter where your team is or what industry it's in. Many individuals often confront us with an old, tried, *but not true,* ploy about how they need something specific for their industry because it is so different from every other industry. To be blunt, this is just "hog wash!" The following selection of tools has been used in almost every industry listed by the Department of Commerce. All teams face the same issues no matter the industry. These issues include business problems that must be solved in order to be successful, ways in which the team can be more effective internally, and ways to measure performance of the team. To this end, we have provided a set of tools, divided into three logical sections: business problem-solving tools, team assessment instruments, and team intervention tools.

Section One, Business Problem-Solving Tools, has several old familiars including Pareto analysis, focus groups, flowcharting, brainstorming, and force field analysis. We have also included some less familiar techniques such as Komatsu diagramming, spider diagramming, storyboarding, and cost-benefit analysis. This selection of tools will help you break any business problem into its functional components, examine its structure, guide you to some alternative solutions, and help you determine the best way to solve most business problems.

Section Two, Team Assessment Instruments, introduces the concept of 360° review and how to use it in a team setting. Team leaders also need feedback and we provide you with a team leader evaluation questionnaire. We also provide teams with tools to evaluate their meetings, and their internal or external consultants.

Finally, in Section Three, Team Effectiveness Interventions, we provide you with a selection of team effectiveness interventions, a consultant's way of saying "ten ways to help yourself become a better team." In this section, we demonstrate how and why each team needs to develop norms and set up operating procedures even before they get started on "the more serious stuff." We have tools and techniques to help you identify and solve team issues, set up effective meetings, identify and solve performance problems, learn how to handle conflict and improve coaching techniques, and learn who is communicating with whom and what that means.

We think that you will find these selections of tools valuable. After you have tried a tool or technique once or twice, don't be afraid to make changes to it so that it better fits your business needs. In short, don't be a slave to tool and technique convention. We have, for example, used focus groups for everything from conducting structured task analysis, to determining customer needs, to developing performance measures. Communication maps and spider diagrams both have their foundations in sociograms used in sociology, and both techniques can be used to track wayward operations. Don't forget that one of the reasons you are in a team is to give you and your team members an opportunity to try new and different things. So once you have the hang of how to use a tool, try modifying it for other situations. You will soon find that you can increase the size of your tool kit by simply giving one of these tools a little tweak.

CHAPTER 7

BUSINESS PROBLEM-SOLVING TOOLS

Overview of Problem-Solving Tools

Business Problem-Solving Tools	Purpose
1 Pareto Analysis	A technique used to graph problems of a system, process, machine. Generally, 80 percent of all problems are generated by 20 percent of all causes—this technique helps to identify that 20 percent.
2 Focus Groups	Used to collect face-to-face data, generate ideas, or solve problems in a structured way; focus groups are structured Brainstorming sessions.
3 Executive Diagnosis	Executive Diagnosis
4 Matrix Design and Analysis	Identifies relationships
5 Storyboarding	A visual planning, organizing, and communicating tool modeled after the storyboards used in the motion picture industry where every scene is sketched out and planned in detail.

Business Problem-Solving Tools		Purpose
6	Flowcharting	Flowcharting uses standardized symbols to "map" the way work "flows" through a job, process, machine, or program.
7	Problem Stream Analysis	Identifies root causes and set procedures for correction
8	Data Flow Analysis	Similar to Flowcharting, but the "mapping" is only concerned with the flow of information through a system
9	Komatsu Diagram	A variation of a Tree Diagram, using charts and graphs instead of text.
10	Spider or Target Diagram	A two-dimensional plot of concentric circles that helps to identify specific issues or problems.
11	Brainstorming	Designed to generate ideas in volume. Brainstorming groups are generally composed of individuals who would not ordinarily get to offer their suggestions under "normal" circumstances.
12	Force Field Analysis	Identifies the factors ("forces") to drive a condition to, or constrain it from, a certain position.
13	Cost-Benefit Analysis	A structured approach to determine the benefit of any costs incurred for a project, product, or service.
14	Morphs	Combinations of other tools.
15	Comment Analysis	A set of procedures used to sort, categorize, analyze, and interpret written comments.

Pareto Analysis

What Is It?

Pareto Analysis is a tool that separates important concerns, causes, and results from less important ones. It is based on principles developed by Vilfredo Pareto, an Italian sociologist and economist who lived from 1848 to 1923. The Pareto principle states that 80 percent of the "effects" of any system are due to 20 percent of its "causes." Though the "80/20 rule" is not always literal, Pareto's premise generally holds true, that is, the overwhelming majority of effects arise from a critical few causes.

Why Do It?

Human and capital resources are becoming more critical and less abundant for most organizations today. In addition, competition is getting stiffer. Therefore, organizations must make wise decisions about where to commit resources. Pareto Analysis will focus resource commitment in the areas that are most important.

How to Do It

1. Collect the data
   a. Use data from Brainstorming, Process Monitoring, or another data-collection technique. Record the frequency of each cause by category.
   b. Ensure that categories are delineated and descriptive enough to communicate exactly what causes are involved. Avoid redundancy and generalization.
   c. Combine rare or poorly defined causes in an "other" category. No specific causes should be included in this category.
   d. Total all occurrences.
2. Sort the data from highest to lowest frequency. Enter on a worksheet such as the one shown in Figure 7.1. Always list "other" last.

XYC Company Pareto Analysis Worksheet
Machinery Downtime Causes, 1996

	Cause	Frequency (Hours)	Cumulative Percentage
1	Change orders	257,188	64.0
2	Machinery breakdowns	64,297	79.6
3	Unscheduled stops	40,186	82.2
4	Material not available	20,093	94.6
5	Parts not available	10,046	97.1
6	Waiting on lab tests	5,023	98.3
7	Order errors	2,512	98.9
8	Operator error	1,256	99.2
9	Labor not available	628	99.4
10	Power interruption	63	99.4
Other	Other	2,364	100.0

Figure 7.1.

3. Calculate and record the cumulative percentage represented at each cause. For example, if the total of the occurrences is 100 and the frequencies of the first two causes are 40 and 20, then the cumulative percentages would be 40 percent and 60 percent, respectively.
4. Graph the data (Figure 7.2).
   a. Draw a vertical bar chart with two y-axes.
   b. Label the left y-axis "frequency," the right y-axis "cumulative percentage," and the x-axis "cause".
   c. Scale the left y-axis based on the total from step 1.d. Scale the right y-axis from 0 percent to 100 percent. Make sure that the 100-percent line corresponds with the total of the left y-axis.
   d. Plot the frequency data as vertical bars. Plot the highest frequency cause against the left y-axis and proceed to the right, plotting each cause in decreasing frequency. Remember to plot "other" last.
   e. Plot a dot for the cumulative percentage at each cause.
   f. Connect the dots to make a line.
5. Interpret the data.
   a. Draw a straight line at 80 percent (on the right-hand y-axis) across the entire chart (Figure 7.2).

XYZ Company Pareto Analysis Worksheet
Machinery Downtime Causes, 1996

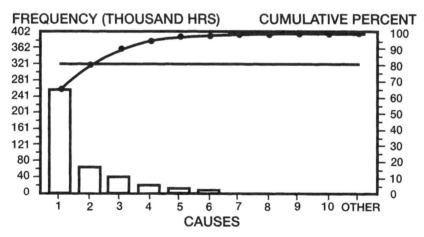

Figure 7.2.

b. The point at which this line crosses the cumulative percentage line (from step 4.f) is the "Pareto" or "critical" point (Figure 7.2).

c. Take corrective actions for those causes to the right of the critical point that are easy, low in cost, and quick to implement. Do not take any time in action planning for the noncritical causes.

d. Conduct action planning for the critical causes.

  i. It may be necessary to conduct a second-level Pareto Analysis on the critical causes.

  ii. If so, display the data in a horizontal bar chart:

    (1) Collect the data.

    (2) Sort the data.

    (3) Graph the data (Figure 7.3).

      (a) Draw a horizontal bar chart. Label the *y*-axis "frequency" and the *x*-axis "cause."

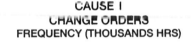

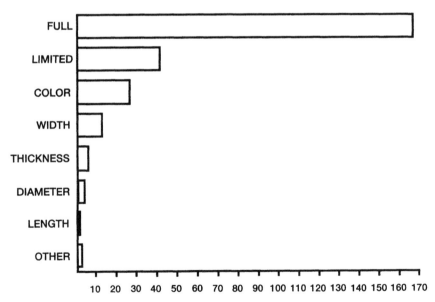

Figure 7.3.

(b) Scale the *y*-axis to about 10 percent or so above the highest frequency.

(c) Plot the causes as horizontal bars in decreasing order from top to bottom on the chart. Label each bar top with the frequency of the bar. Remember, again, to plot "Other" last (Figure 7.3).

(4) Interpret the data.

Case Example

A major manufacturer has made a capital investment of $2.5 million to improve its technology. It has bought five copies of one machine and installed them in five locations in two states. A technology transfer agreement has been signed with the machinery manufacturer that controls the start of the warranty period. The buying company must make sure that the machinery maker constantly knows how each machine is running.

It does this by maintaining a set of Pareto charts that it sends to the machinery maker weekly. There are two charts for each installation. The first shows the major faults on each machine in the most recent week. The second shows the major faults on each machine since the beginning of the installation. By comparing the two charts, both the buying company and the machinery maker can quickly determine if problems are being solved.

A final set of two charts shows the same data for all five machines combined. By comparing the latest week and whole installation charts on this basis, the two companies can make agreements about what machine components should be redesigned because they produce common faults at all locations.

Additional Information

Brassard, Michael. *The Memory Jogger Plus+*, Methner, MA: Goal/QPC 1989.

Lynch, Robert F., Werner, Thomas J., and Lynch, Livia C. *Continuous Improvement: Teams & Tools*, Atlanta, GA: QualTeam, Inc. 1992.

Focus Groups

What Are They?

Focus groups can be used for collecting data, generating ideas, and solving problems. Focus Groups offer a number of advantages over many other data-collection tools because they are simple and cost effective to run, provide multiple views on a specific subject area, and provide a vehicle for freewheeling interactions.

Based on our experience in running Focus Groups, we have developed the following guidelines to aid in planning and facilitating a session:

- Keep participation limited to a manageable size—8 to 13 participants is optimal; this allows for a free exchange of ideas and allows the facilitator to keep control of the session.
- Do not include superiors and their direct reports in the same session. Also avoid including "blockers" (people who will adversely affect group interactions—secretary to the president, union president, and so on.)
- When selecting participants, only select people who are interested in participating and have appropriate knowledge of the subject under discussion. Pay careful attention to the demographics (age, sex, and so on) of the participants and functional composition of participants.
- Do not schedule sessions for longer than 2½ hours. As fatigue sets in, the usefulness of the data will decrease markedly.
- Select a setting that ensures privacy and is conducive to obtaining the objectives of the session.

How to Do It

Utilizing a Focus Group involves three steps.

1. Plan the meeting. Select a facilitator who is skilled in group dynamics, conflict management, group problem solving, and meeting management. We have found that the most effective facilitators are sensitive to what is said, good listeners, able to express themselves clearly and are keenly intuitive; they are able to communicate the objectives of the Focus Group session and the categories of information to collect and to develop questions for each category. We strongly suggest the questions progress from broad and easy-to-answer questions to specific questions. Always ask questions about sensitive or volatile issues last. Do not use close-ended (yes/no) or leading questions. In some instances it may be

necessary to develop and administer a questionnaire prior to the Focus Group. Once the Focus Group protocol has been completed, a list of stakeholders should be identified to invite to the Focus Group. Each should receive an announcement that specifies the purpose of the focus group, its location, scheduled time and length, and expected outcome. Select a neutral location for the meeting. Arrange the chairs in the room in a circle and provide for either a secretary, flip chart, or tape recorder to accurately record data that is generated in the meeting.

2. Conduct the meeting. At the outset of the meeting, the facilitator should introduce him or herself; confirm the purpose of the meeting, review the agenda, and time allotted for each topic or issue; identify the roles of the facilitator and participants; and discuss why each participant was selected, expected outcomes of the session, and how data will be used. The facilitator must quickly establish the norms (only one person will talk at a time, raise hand before speaking) for the meeting and stress confidentiality. Although the data will be reported, individual confidentiality should not be compromised. Before starting the discussion ask participants to introduce themselves. When the session has been completed thank each participant for their involvement, reconfirm next steps and how data will be used, answer any questions they might have, and close on time.

   During the meeting the facilitator should focus on:
   • Collecting data on the various issues discussed in the session.
   • Ensuring good group process (equal participation, eliciting opposing views).
   • Clarifying points.
   • Keeping the participants focused on the topic.
   • Managing conflict.
   • Summarizing key points and agreements.

3. Analyze the data. If a facilitator is taking his or her own notes, we strongly suggest writing up notes, immediately after the completion of each session. Detailed analysis of the data usually occurs at a later date. During this analysis the facilitator must digest and synthesize the data. Irrelevant comments are coded and themes may be sorted by topic. Trends are studied and interpreted, and tentative conclusions are developed. Supporting documentation (quotes to support perceptions) and recommended next steps should be noted for inclusion into an executive summary. If an executive report is developed, it should detail the size and make-up of the group, and include themes, verbatim comments, and detailed recommendations.

Case Examples

The Focus Group Protocol on the next page was used to evaluate how well an internal consulting department of a Fortune 50 company satisfied the needs of its customers.

Quality Analysis Focus Group Protocol

1. Build rapport (10 minutes). Good afternoon and welcome to our session. Thank you for taking the time to participate in this Focus Group. My name is _____ and I work for _____. The objective of this session is to identify how well the XYZ Consulting Department is meeting your needs and identify opportunities to improve their value-added to you. Since you are all customers of the XYZ Department you have been invited to share your perceptions and ideas on this topic. Please feel free to share your point of view even if it differs from other's opinions.

   Before we begin let me suggest the following ground rules. In order for us to understand one another, I request only one person speak at a time. We will be taping the session because we don't want to miss any of your comments. We will be on a first-name basis, but in our report to management there will not be any names attached to comments—I guarantee the confidentiality of each of your comments. We are just as interested in negative comments as positive comments, and at times the negative comments are the most helpful.

   Our session will last approximately two hours. Before we begin, please introduce yourself to the rest of the group.

2. Understanding the strategic direction of the company (20 minutes).
   • What is your core business strategy? What are your differentiating product attributes; pricing, product functions and features, quality, and so on?
   • What are your key success factors?
   • What initiatives is your unit currently involved in?

3. Perceptions of client organization's products and services (30 minutes).
   • What role, if any, has the client organization played in helping you to improve your organization's competitive position? How?
   • What other roles have they played?
   • What roles should they play?
   • What specific services or programs have you found to be most useful? Why?

- Which services or products have you found to be least useful? Why?
- Looking ahead, what additional services or products would you like them to offer?
- If there were one thing the XYZ Consulting Department could do to increase its usefulness to your efforts here, what would it be?

4. Identify next steps; thank interviewees for their assistance (5 minutes).

Additional Information

Anderson, Al. "A Step-by-Step Way to Conduct Focus Groups." *Training,* Dec. 1978.

Axelrod, M. "10 Essentials for Good Productive Research." *Marketing News,* Mar. 1975.

Bogdan, R. and S. Taylor. *Introduction to Qualitative Research Methods.* New York: John Wiley & Sons, 1975.

Ensman, Richard. "Focus Groups: How and When to Use Them." *Successful Meetings,* Vol. 41, No. 8, July 1992.

Greenbaum, Thomas. "Don't Lose Focus: Tips for Effective Focus Groups." *Bank Marketing,* Vol. 25, No. 2, Feb. 1993.

Hitchcock, Darcy, and Willard, Marsha. "Measuring Team Progress." *Journal for Quality and Participation,* Vol. 15, No. 5, Sept. 1992.

Love, Barbara. "Focus Groups, Fast and Cheap." *Folio: The Magazine for Management,* Vol. 22, No. 11, June 1993,

Executive Diagnosis

What Is It?

Imagine you're planning to take a long, unfamiliar trip. Before you could even buy a road map to help you plan your course, you would need two pieces of information: where you are or will start from and where you are going. For organizations, Executive Diagnosis is a tool that is used to answer the first question "where are you?" More specifically, Executive Diagnosis identifies the strengths and weaknesses of an organization. But, before we can proceed with a discussion of Executive Diagnosis, we must discuss the Organizational Performance Model, on which Executive Diagnosis is based.

The Organizational Performance Model. The Organizational Performance Model is a representation of the factors that predict the ability of an organization to promote and survive paradigm shifts and to sustain satisfactory performance. Organizational Performance Model identifies two interacting sets of features that characterize any organization. These are the defining features and the sustaining features.

The defining features (or "definers") identify the characteristics that make each organization unique. They predict the ability of an organization to promote and survive paradigm shifts. There are three such features: structure, culture, and externals. Structure includes the hierarchy of an organization or its tiers of management and nonmanagement, the nature of its decision making, the nature of its relationship between management and labor, the design of its jobs, its reporting relationships, its unit boundaries, and, in public organizations, the role of its directing boards. Culture addresses the management style, politics, norms, beliefs, values, and policies of the organization, especially regarding employee involvement, participative management, and general quality-of-work-life issues. Externals are those things outside of the organization that influence it. This includes customer regulatory and legal requirements, policies, and demands; labor union requirements; technological changes; shifts in socioeconomic and monetary trends; and competition. The definers can be viewed as equal slices in a pie (Figure 7.4). Some definers will play a larger role than others in some organizations, but for this discussion, let's say they are all equal.

Figure 7.4. *The defining features of an organization.*

The other set of features of an organization, the sustaining features (or sustainers), determine the degree to which an organization can sustain successful performance inside the framework of the definers. The sustaining features are commitment, systems, and resources. Commitment addresses the willingness, primarily of top management, to devote resources to organizational improvement. No organization can sustain meaningful improvement if there is no commitment. Systems deal with the existence of adequate processes to guarantee improvement. This includes such systems as information management, human resources, strategic and operational planning, administration, budgeting, and productivity and quality improvement. Resources weighs the existence of human, financial, and other assets dedicated to achieving improvement. Even when commitment and systems are in place, improvement is unlikely with inadequate resources.

The sustainers can be viewed as three interlocking circles. The circles interlock such that when each is as large as it can be—representing maximum performance—a small space remains that prevents all three from intersecting (Figure 7.5).

The size of this space represents the potential for unsatisfactory performance (Figure 7.5). When the circles are as large as they can be, the risk of

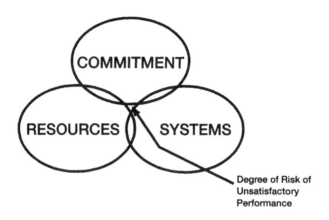

Figure 7.5. *Sustaining features of an organization.*

unsatisfactory performance is very, very low. As the circles decrease in size, the risk of unsatisfactory performance increases.

The interaction of the definers and sustainers is shown in Figure 7.6. In addition to limiting unsatisfactory performance, high "sustainer performance" also limits the influence of definers. This serves to "buy the time" that an organization will need to change paradigms. This paradigm shift must take place before any organization can reshape its definers and prepare for the future.

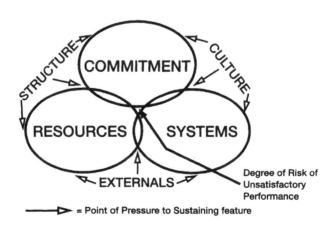

Figure 7.6. *Organizational performance model bringing it all together.*

Why Do It?

When used with Organizational Performance Model, Executive Diagnosis gives organizations a tool that can be used to 1) estimate sustainer performance, 2) identify specific action plans to improve it, and 3) position themselves for significant, positive change.

Executive Diagnosis will help an organization to keep focused. When it is used properly there will be more "successes" and fewer "failures". It will also deter the "program-of-the-month" mentality.

How to Do It

Eight steps are involved in implementing Executive Diagnosis:

1. Identify health/strength indicators to be used.
2. Identify qualifiers for each health/strength indicator.
3. Assign owners for each health/strength indicator.
4. Rate sustainers for each qualifier.
5. Identify determinants.
6. Produce summaries and graphs.
7. Identify causes for determinant performance.
8. Develop action plans for determinants.

Step 1: Identify Health/Strength Indicators to Be Used. Executive Diagnosis is much like a physical examination—a doctor looks at each major system (respiratory, cardiovascular, and so on) of the human body and evaluates the health or strength of each. Likewise, Executive Diagnosis starts by conceptually dividing the organization into distinctive areas of performance. These areas are called health/strength indicators.

Step 2: Identify Qualifiers for Each Health/Strength Indicator. Each indicator has a set of criteria that "indicates" whether an organization can achieve and sustain success. These criteria are called "qualifiers." Typical health/strength indicators and qualifiers are shown in Table 7.1. The indicators and qualifiers will vary from organization to organization.

Step 3: Assign Owners for Each Health/Strength Indicator. An owner should be assigned for each health/strength indicator, and a list of owner responsibilities should be developed and agreed upon. Impressive results can be achieved when ownership is assigned "cross-functionally." For

Table 7.1
Basic Health/Strength Indicators and Qualifiers

Health/Strength Indicator	Qualifier
Sales	Evidence of a goal-oriented sales plan. Evidence that competitive analysis is an everyday facet of business. Evidence of a comprehensive plan to out-perform competition. Evidence of partnerships with customers. Evidence that value-adding customer services are being developed, pursued, and implemented. Evidence that sales performance is improving from year to year.
Profitability	Evidence of a goal-oriented profit plan. Evidence that profitability is improving from year to year.
Quality	Evidence that customer satisfaction is improving from year-to-year. Evidence that customer satisfaction is superior to competition. Evidence that a structured quality improvement process is in place. Evidence that quality improvement activities are under way at all levels of the organization. Evidence that Quality Function Deployment activities are taking place. Evidence that measurable quality levels are improving from year to year. Evidence that quality improvement is a specifically stated objective in every job description.
Cost Reduction	Evidence that a structured cost-reduction process is in place. Evidence that cost reduction activities are under way at all levels of the organization (including value analysis, short cycle manufacturing, flexible manufacturing, and/or JIT manufacturing). Evidence that Qualty Function Deployment activities are taking place. Evidence that measurable cost levels (variable and fixed) are improving from year to year. Evidence that cost reduction is a specifically stated objective in every job description. Evidence that concurrent engineering is taking place. Evidence that idle inventory and idle depreciation costs are declining.

example, this could involve assigning a manufacturing manager the "sales" indicator, and so on.

Step 4: Rate Sustainers for Each Qualifier. Look at each qualifier and rate it in relation to the sustainers (commitment, systems, and resources). This

Table 7.1 (continued)
Basic Health/Strength Indicators and Qualifiers

Health/Strength Indicator	Qualifier
Productivity	Evidence that equipment capability has been analyzed and understood. Evidence that equipment capacity utilization is improving from year to year. Evidence that process reliability has been analyzed and understood. Evidence that process reliability is improving from year to year.
Delivery	Evidence that delivery commitments are being met. Evidence that cycle times are being reduced from year to year. Evidence that order expediting is being eliminated.
Safety	Evidence that safety awareness programs are in place and active at all levels of the organization. Evidence that frequencies in all categories of unsafe incidents are decreasing. Evidence of compliance with all governmental safety regulations.
Morale	Evidence of an active suggestion and participation program. Evidence that participative management is in place and active. Evidence that self-directed work teams are in place and active. Evidence that an effective recognition system is in place and active. Evidence that an effective reward system is in place and active. Evidence that decision making follows input from all levels of the organization whenever possible.
Environment	Evidence that environmental awareness programs are in place and active at all levels of the organization. Evidence that frequencies in all categories of environmental incidents are decreasing. Evidence of compliance with all governmental environmental regulations.
New Product Development & Innovation	Evidence that Quality Function Deployment activities are taking place. Evidence that new products represent a significant portion of total sales each year. Evidence that innovation is encouraged, recognized, and rewarded.
Service & Responsiveness	Evidence that customer contact is consistently practiced. Evidence that customers are consistently invited for site visits. Evidence that customer concerns are satisfactorily addressed.

rating should be based on a 1 to 5 scale with 5 being the best. Definitions should be given to each point on the scale to increase the chances that different people will mean the same thing when they rate a qualifier.

Step 5: Identify Determinants. There will be three ratings for each qualifier (one for each sustainer). The lowest sustainer rating for each qualifier should be highlighted. This rating is called a "determinant." A determinant is the sustainer that has the most influence in making a qualifier's score as low as it is (Table 7.2).

These determinants, the underlined figures in Table 7.2, are very important evidence of organizational performance. Remember, as the "health" or "strength" of sustainers deteriorates, there is more room for the definers to influence performance and higher risk for unsatisfactory results. Con-

Table 7.2
Sample Qualifier Ratings for Cost Reduction Health/Strength Indicator with Determinants

Cost Reduction	Commitment	Systems	Resources	Total
1. Evidence that a structured cost-reduction process is in place.	2.20	2.40	2.60	2.40
2. Evidence that cost-reduction activities are under way at all levels of the organization.	1.80	2.20	2.20	2.07
3. Evidence that Quality Function Deployment activities are taking place.	1.75	1.75	1.75	1.75
4. Evidence that measurable cost levels (variable and fixed) are improving from year to year.	2.20	2.20	2.80	2.40
5. Evidence that cost reduction is a specifically stated objective in every job description.	1.60	1.20	1.60	1.47
6. Evidence that concurrent engineering is taking place.	1.20	1.60	2.60	1.80
7. Evidence that idle inventory and idle depreciation costs are declining.	2.80	2.80	2.40	2.67
Total	1.94	2.02	2.28	2.08

versely, when an organization is at "5" ratings, it will be better able to over-come deficiencies in structure, culture, and external pressures, and it will be better able to survive the paradigm shifts necessary to alter its definer characteristics.

This exercise is repeated for each health/strength indicator. An overall score for each health/strength indictor is developed showing each indicator's "qualifier determinant" (the qualifier for each indicator that has the lowest total rating) as well as its "feature determinant" (the sustainer with the lowest total rating).

Step 6: Produce Summaries and Graphs. A summary should be produced that shows the total score and identifies 1) the feature determinant for each health/strength indicator, 2) the organization's overall feature deter-minant, and 3) the "indicator determinant"–the health/strength indicator with the lowest total rating (Table 7.3).

Finally, the overall scores should be put in graphical format. A good way to show this is as a 3-D bar chart (Figure 7.7). This format quickly points out where the strengths and weaknesses of the organization are.

Step 7: Identify Causes for Determinant Performance. Before any improvement can take place, it is very important to know the root causes

Table 7.3
Executive Diagnosis Summary Showing Indicator
and Feature Determinants

Summary	Commitment	Systems	Resources	Total
1. Sales	4.50	3.00	4.50	4.00
2. Profitability	4.50	2.60	2.80	3.30
3. Quality	2.77	2.90	2.82	2.83
4. Cost Reduction	1.94	2.02	2.28	2.08
5. Productivity	1.60	1.20	1.60	1.47
6. Delivery	2.50	2.50	3.60	2.87
7. Safety	4.90	4.80	4.25	4.65
8. Morale	3.34	3.19	3.65	3.39
9. Environment	3.00	2.67	2.67	2.78
10. New Product Development & Innovation	2.95	2.25	2.50	2.57
11. Service & Responsiveness	3.35	3.50	2.95	3.27
Total	3.21	2.78	3.06	3.02

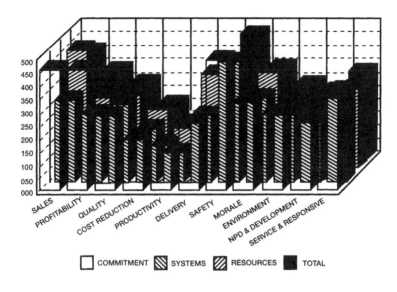

Figure 7.7. *Sample executive diagnosis summary chart.*

for "determinant performance." For example, under the health/strength indicator of quality, one of the qualifiers may be: Evidence indicates that customer satisfaction is continually improving and significantly superior to competition." In this case, suppose that resources was identified as the determinant. Root-cause analysis would then be conducted to determine what practices, policies, or processes are involved with this determinant performance—for example: "Not enough resources allocated for non-crisis customer contact; also none allocated solely for the purpose of fact finding in relation to competitors."

Step 8: Develop Action Plans for Determinants. After all determinants have been identified and analyzed, action plans for each determinant must be developed. The plans should be devised to directly produce determined performance improvement. In the above example the plan might be: "Establish the following measurement parameters for engineers: number of days spent face-to-face with customers and suppliers, number of hours spent on competitive analysis per period."

The Timing of Executive Diagnosis

Except for steps 4 through 6, all activity should take place in controlled discussion sessions. More success is realized when these sessions take place away from the normal work environment. This cuts down on such distractions as phone calls, visitors, and other interruptions. More importantly, being away from the work environment makes it easier for people to get into a different mindset, leave their territorial armor behind, and be open to evaluating different ideas.

The discussion sessions are divided into two parts. The first is a three-day session that covers steps 1 through 3.

- Day 1 is used for health/strength indicator identification. Identification of qualifiers should also begin. Qualifiers should be chosen because of their primary support of customer-satisfaction-related performance. If any qualifier doesn't primarily support customer satisfaction, then some justification for using it must be given. This should be done to ensure that the organization doesn't spend time and resources trying to improve on things that don't really matter.

  Besides primary customer-satisfaction-related performance, other justifications could be legal or regulatory compliance or conformance to company policy. In relation to conformance to company policy, the justification of the policy itself should be brought into question. Depending on the level in the organization that the Executive Diagnosis team holds, this may not be practical.

  Having a good mix of process and results-oriented qualifiers is important. "Process-oriented" means that emphasis is placed on *how* things are done. "Results-oriented" means that emphasis is placed on the outcome. In the example we used earlier involving the health/strength of the "quality indicator," both actions that were planned (spending time with customer and in competitive analysis) are process-oriented.

- On day 2 identification of qualifiers should be completed. A prioritization of qualifiers and indicators should take place. This should help the Executive Diagnosis team understand which qualifiers and indicators are most critical to organizational success. Prioritization Matrix Analysis is a useful tool to use for this. Prioritization Matrix Analysis allows for the identification of the factors that have the most bearing in a given situation.

- On Day 3 the health/strength indicator owner responsibilities list should be developed and communicated. This list may turn out to be only primary and may be adjusted later after the root-cause snalysis and action planning sessions are complete.

  After this session there should be a two-week time period to allow the individual ratings to be done. The results should be tabulated and provided to everybody far enough ahead of time so that the owners for each health/strength indicator can predict what information will be needed for root-cause analysis. They should begin to collect facts and data to present during the second focused session. This period represents steps 4 through 6 of Executive Diagnosis. By doing the actual ratings before the next session, the focused meeting time can be used to perform analysis on determinant scores to find root causes and to develop plans and contingencies for improvement.

After this two-week period, the second session, this time five days, should begin.

- On day 1 the facts and data about determinant performance are presented. This information should increase the chance that everyone on the team will start from the same base of knowledge, then the analysis and planning that is done will be more thorough and everybody will be able to bring their own expertise to bear on determinant "opportunities." Care should be taken to make sure that facts and data are presented in terms and formats that are familiar to the organization and its members to avoid wasting valuable time.
- On days 2 and 3 root-cause analysis should take place to determine specific reasons for determinant performance. This relates Step 7 of Executive Diagnosis. When in this stage, and when in the process of developing plans to improve determinant scores (step 8), Brainstorming should be used to help with idea generation. Flowcharting, Y-diagrams, and Process Mapping can also be used to find root causes. Force-Field Analysis, Interrelationship Diagraphs, and Affinity Diagrams can be used to show interrelationships of varying causes and effects. Structured Tree and Value-Time Analysis can be used to gauge the overall effect of the determinant performance outside the bounds of the immediate functional area being looked at.

This session is critical to the effectiveness of step 8, which takes place on days 4 and 5.

- On day 4, action and contingency planning takes place. Matrix Analysis can be used to define ownership, and Process Decision Program Charting can be used to develop contingency plans. Prioritizing the action plans may be difficult, but it is critical. Since there will be one determinant score for each qualifier, if the organization attempts to act on all determinants at the same time there is a danger that 1) there may be no or limited success because the resources of the organization are being spread too thin, or 2) so many things will be done at one time that there will be no way for the organization to gauge success. In the latter case, some things that are being done may have negative effects while other things may have positive effects. Whereas the net effect may look like no change at all, some things are actually working and some things aren't. This may cause the organization to move away from some things it should be doing and allow it to keep doing some things it really shouldn't be doing.

Though the temptation is great to conduct root-cause analysis and action and contingency planning in parallel, these two activities should not be done together. More success will be gained if root-cause analysis is done on all determinants and then action planning is done in a different session. There is a tendency, when mixing root-cause analysis with planning, to start making plans much too soon and never to get to the root cause of the problem; the causes identified first are often acted on, but many times these are only symptoms. Any plans made to address symptoms will not deal with the real issues and may require work later to solve the same problem again. Furthermore, there may be a high degree of failure and frustration leading to no success at all. In any case, it may be harder to get involvement in later efforts due to lack of momentum.

- Day 5 is used for implementation planning. In this session the details for timing and follow-up of the plans from day 4 are worked out. While doing this, the Organizational Performance Model must be used as a guideline, especially in relation to sustainers. The Executive Diagnosis Team must ensure that the commitment, systems, and resources are all in place to implement the plan. Many well-intentioned plans have failed because they didn't mesh well with the capabilities of the organization trying to carry them out.

The definers cannot be forgotten either. Does the organization have the structure, culture, and externals to carry out the plan? Will any external partners have to be informed or consulted? Will there be any potential breaches to compliance or conformance issues? Another role of implementation planning is the determination of what measures must be used to gauge success. Benchmark dates for performance review should be set. There should be predetermined thresholds of performance that dictate planned actions.

This way, a lot of time and energy won't be wasted during the implementation deciding what alternate routes to take. This will serve to reduce in-fighting and territorial disputes that may arise. It will also promote joint ownership of the plan by the Executive Diagnosis team.

Any measurements that are used should be ones that primarily support customer-service-oriented performance. The same criteria that applies to qualifier justification should be utilized here.

A summary of the timing of Executive Diagnosis:

Session 1   Day 1: Indicator and qualifier identification (steps 1 and 2).
Day 2: Qualifier identification, prioritization of indicators and qualifiers (step 2).
Day 3: Development of indicator owner responsibilities (step 3).
Rating Period (2 weeks) (steps 4–6).
Session 2   Day 1: Presentation of determinant facts and data.
Day 2: Root-cause analysis (step 7).
Day 3 : Root-cause analysis (step 7).
Day 4: Action and contingency planning (step 8).
Day 5: Implementation planning (step 8).

Additional Information

Kano, Noriaki. "A Perspective on Quality Activities in American Firms." *California Management Review,* Vol. 35, No. 3, Spring 1993, pp. 12–31.

Townley, Preston, "Decentralizing for Competitive Advantage," *Across the Board IIC Supplement,* Jan. 1994, pp. 24–29.

Vogl, A. J. "It Could Happen to Us," *Across the Board,* Vol. 30, No. 8, Oct. 1993, pp. 27–32.

Matrix Design and Analysis

What Is It?

Matrix Design and Analysis is a tool that makes the communication of relationships, influences, and interdependencies easier by representing them graphically. Using Matrix Design and Analysis, any volume of non-quantitative data can be logically displayed, evaluated, and even quantified. This characteristic, in particular, makes Matrix Design and Analysis a valuable decision-making tool because it facilitates the evaluation of the strength of key relationships.

Why Do It?

Many times successful project implementation depends on effective communication of responsibilities and objectives. Most people respond more to visual explanation than to written or oral directives. Any time a large amount of information has to be organized, compared, evaluated, and communicated, Matrix Design and Analysis is the tool of choice.

How to Do It

1. Clearly identify the objective or desired outcome of the analysis. This objective must address what specific information will be conveyed by the completed matrix and who it will be conveyed to. This will guard against overlooking information critical to communicating the proper understanding or placing unrelated information in the same matrix.
2. Decide on a matrix type. There are at least seven types of matrix diagrams. We will discuss the most frequently used two of these.

   The simplest matrix design is the L-shaped matrix, which is used to compare two variables. Figure 7.8 depicts an L-shaped responsibility matrix. By listing tasks along one axis, and functions, departments, regions, or individuals along the other, responsibility can be quickly demonstrated.

   In figure 7.8, the matrix communicates responsibility for the phases of TV design for a major electronics manufacturer. Any symbols can be used to denote the strength of relationships. (The symbols used here come from Japanese horse racing; at Japanese race tracks these symbols are posted next to the names of the horses that win, place, and show in each race.) Figure 7.7 quickly communicates several facts:

TV Design Matrix	A	B	C	D	Total	RF
Audio Module	◎		△	△	15	.18
Video Module		◎	△	△	15	.18
Electronics	△	△	◎	△	18	.21
Controls	△	△	◎	△	18	.21
Cabinet	△	△	△	◎	18	.21
Total	18	18	27	21	84	1.00

◎	Primary Responsibilty	9
○	Secondary Responsibilty	6
△	Keep Informed	3

Figure 7.8. *L-shaped matrix.*

- Teams A, B, and C must keep team D informed of their designs so that the cabinet is designed to accommodate the other phases.
- Team C has more involvement in the design than any other team. Therefore, if all design phases are equal, team C should have the most human resources. This is a real strength of this tool. Based on the relative weight of each phase, this matrix will help with the assignment of resources.
- The resource factor column indicates the relative amount of resources that will be required to coordinate the project. For instance, around 21 percent of the total coordination resources will be needed to plan, design, implement, and control electronic development; 18 percent for audio design; and so on. This doesn't indicate the quantity of resources that will be needed, but how the available resources should be used.
- The T-shaped matrix compares any one variable against two others. In the TV design example, this matrix would allow the relative investment cost of each phase to be added to the evaluation. For example, initial capital investment, staffing and training costs, and expected project time could be stated for each phase (Figure 7.9). Symbols for high, medium, and low could be used instead of actual numbers dur-

Cap.	Staff	Trig.	Time	TV Design Matrix	A	B	C	D	Total	RF
				Audio Module	◎		△	△	15	.18
				Video Module		◎	△	△	15	.18
				Electronics	△	△	◎	△	18	.21
				Controls	△	△	◎	△	18	.21
				Cabinet	△	△	△	◎	18	.21
				Total	18	18	27	21	84	1.00

◎	High	9
○	Medium	6
△	Low	3

◎	Primary Responsibilty	9
○	Secondary Responsibilty	6
△	Keep Informed	3

Figure 7.9. *T-shaped matrix.*

ing the early planning stages, which is another strength of matrix analysis. Even when complete quantitative data is unavailable, decisions can be made based on sound business judgment and practices.

3. Question the experts. Like Flowcharting, much of the essence of Matrix Design and Analysis is in separating important issues and elements from trivial ones. To gain this level of understanding, time should be spent with process experts before any observation ever takes place (an expert is one who has, employs, or displays special skill or knowledge derived from study, training or experience). In practice, the experts are the people who are most closely involved with the process on a consistent basis.

4. Identify the variables. As a result of the understanding gained in step 3, work with the experts to identify the variables to be evaluated. Make every effort to minimize the number of variables being evaluated—use only those that are essential to satisfying the statement developed in step 1.

5. Decide on the symbols. As stated in step 2, any symbols may be used to show relationship strength. Make sure that everyone understands the symbols to be used beforehand. Symbol use should be consistent

across the organization. This will eliminate wasting time repeatedly explaining the symbols.

6. Assemble an evaluation team. In some cases, the team of experts consulted in steps 3 and 4 may not be the right team for conducting the analysis. The proper team will be one that has expert knowledge of the processes involved in the analysis and also has a high enough level of knowledge of the organization to be able to draw the conclusions that may be called for. In general, this is more true of responsibility matrixes and matrixes dealing with capital expenditures. The more empowered a workforce becomes, the more likely that the same team will be able to participate in steps 3, 4, and 6.

7. Fill in the matrix. The most important considerations to keep in mind while completing the matrix is that each axis should be kept pure. For instance, in a responsibility matrix, make sure that the people, departments, units, regions and so on are all on the same axis (horizontal or vertical). Another important point is to decide whether quantitative data is desired. If it is not, don't bother with the math, which tends to make people draw conclusions that may not be desirable. Use the math to make the "correct" conclusions easier to draw.

This brings up a very critical point. Don't start with a conclusion and then construct a matrix around it. If the facts are broadly known and understood already, matrix analysis is probably a waste of time. Remember, this is a communication tool. Don't use it to manipulate results and actions!

Additional Information

Brassard, Michael. *The Memory Jogger+*, Methner, MA: Goal/QPC, 1989.

Storyboarding

What Is It?

Storyboarding is a creative tool used for planning, organizing, and communicating ideas through a simplified visual format. The storyboard is a quick sketch that highlights key issues and decision points reached during a group meeting. There are four types of Storyboards:

- Planning. In the Planning Storyboard, items are action-oriented and indicate what must be done and how the job will get done.
- Idea Generation. The Idea Storyboard is used for detailing specific ideas and generating new and unique solutions to problems.
- Communication. The Communication Storyboard answers the questions what? who? when? and how? regarding information that needs to be communicated.
- Organization. The Organization Storyboard is used to identify specific task areas in a project and the appropriate people responsible for each task.

How to Do It

The Storyboarding process has two distinct iterative sessions:

1. The creative session. The creative session should be used to generate ideas concerning a particular subject (for example, a solution to a problem). Participants write their ideas on cards. At the same time the idea is written, the participant announces it aloud so all participants can hear it. Vocalizing the idea reduces the number of duplicate ideas and stimulates other ideas. As the idea is submitted to the group, the card should be pinned to the board.

   The following are the Storyboarding rules for creative thinking:
   - Absolutely no criticism. Respect all participants' ideas.
   - Hitchhike on other participants' ideas. Feel free to modify or combine ideas of other participants.
   - Generate many ideas. Quantity, not quality, of ideas is the key in this phase.
   - Generate wild ideas. The wilder the idea, the better. There are no "wrong" ideas.

2. The criticism session. During the criticism session, ideas become "group property" for debate. Any participant can object to an idea on the board, while others should counter-object until consensus is reached. Ideas are either kept or discarded.

The following are the Storyboarding rules for critical thinking:
- Review and methodically critique each idea.
- Make ideas clear and precise. Often rewriting a card for clarity can produce consensus.
- Assign meaning to an idea. Individuals no longer "own" the ideas. Therefore, group consensus determines what the idea means.
- Keep only valid ideas. If the group feels an idea is invalid, it should be discarded.
- Don't use "killer phrases." Use constructive instead of destructive criticism. Consensus cannot be accomplished if participants are put on the defensive or are demoralized.

Steps in Storyboarding. These steps are basic Storyboarding guidelines that you may augment or delete according to your specific task and audience.

1. Storyboarding set-up.

The following equipment and facilities are recommended for a Storyboarding session:
- A room with ample wall space for drawing.
- Pens, push pins, tape, skein of yarn.
- 5″ × 7″ cards ("topic cards").
- 4″ × 6″ cards ("header cards").
- 3″ × 5″ cards ("subtopic cards").
- 2″ × 2″ cards (modifiers and qualifiers).
- Paper or board spanning entire length of wall.

A neutral facilitator should direct and organize the Storyboarding process. In the creative session, the goal is to generate ideas. In the criticism session, the facilitator's goal is to achieve consensus. In addition to these two basic objectives, the facilitator should follow these rules:
- Motivate, don't dictate.
- Pace the group.
- Direct participants to talk to the entire group, rather than to specific individuals.
- Be a diplomat.
- Praise the group's efforts.
- Don't mistake activity for accomplishment.

• Establish good rapport with participants; have fun!

Participants should be encouraged to combine their knowledge with that of other experts and should follow these rules:

• Use creative-thinking skills.
• Use critical-thinking skills.
• Share ideas with the group; don't talk to individuals during the process.
• Be specific when submitting ideas.
• Don't try to be a star.
• Pay attention to other participants and respect their ideas.

2. Determine a clear, concise, measurable goal for the discussion topic.

The goal should be clearly and concisely stated. If it cannot be written on a normal business card, it is too long. No more than one hour should be taken to determine the goal.

3. Construct the Storyboard framework.

A. Write the Storyboard topic on a 5″ × 7″ card. Pin the "topic card" on the top center of the Storyboard.

B. Write the word *purpose* on a 4″ × 6″ card. Pin it below and to the extreme left of the topic card.

C. Write the word *Miscellaneous* on a 4″ × 6″ card and pin it to the right of and below the topic card.

4. Finalize the purpose.

The facilitator should choose a participant to be the "pinner," the person who will pin idea cards to the Storyboard. The result of the initial creative session is the development of the purpose in greater detail than when the goal was initially determined. The final purpose should then be pinned under the purpose card on the Storyboard.

5. Finalize the headers.

This session begins the iterative process of Storyboarding. A creative session should be used to develop headers (4″ × 6″ cards) on the main topics of the Storyboard. The same rules used in the initial creative session apply. When all "headers" or topics are agreed on, these cards should be pinned in a horizontal row at the same level as the "purpose" and "miscellaneous" cards.

6. Finalize the subtopics.

The creative and critical process continues through the development of subtopics. Each header is selected at random and directed into subtopics. The subtopics are written on 3″ × 5″ cards and pinned under their respective headers. If any subtopics need modifiers or qualifiers, 2″ × 2″ cards can be pinned next to their related subtopic. (Repeat steps 5 and 6 until all "header" cards are completed.)

7. Refine the Storyboard.

The yarn can now be used to provide emphasis and to "tie" ideas together at various locations on the board, thus creating a picture of the topic and its interrelated ideas.

8. Save the Storyboard.

There may be times when a Storyboard cannot be left in its original displayed form. To "save" the Storyboard so that it can be reconstructed, use one of the following:

a. Number the cards.
  • Put the purpose cards together and number them consecutively.
  • Put the miscellaneous cards together and number them consecutively.
  • Number the header cards as columns, then number the subheaders with row and column.
  • Number modifiers appropriately

b. Use a computer spreadsheet program (such as, Lotus or Excel) to store the Storyboard.

c. Take a photograph or videotape of the Storyboard.

d. Copy the entire Storyboard, including relative position of the cards, by hand onto paper.

Types of Storyboards

The Planning Storyboard

• In the Planning Storyboard (Figure 7.10), all items are action-oriented and time-based. Participants determine a "topic" (the measurable goal) and the "purpose" ("create an action plan for implementing quality improvement strategy throughout the organization") for the session.

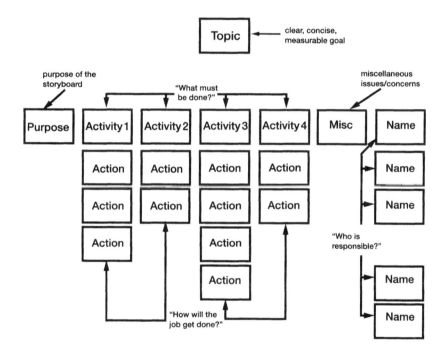

Figure 7.10. *The planning storyboard.*

• Heads identify activities, and subhead are the list of actions. Along the side of the Storyboard is the list of individuals who are responsible for each activity.

The Idea Storyboard

• The Idea Storyboard (Figure 7.11) is used to detail ideas concerning a specific issue and to generate new and unique solutions to problems.

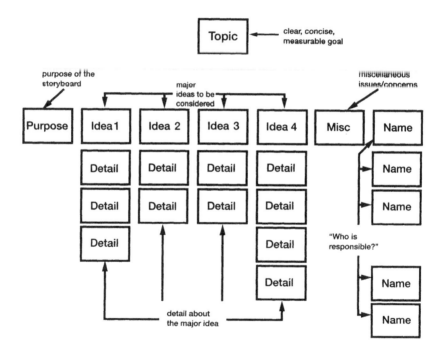

Figure 7.11. *The idea storyboard.*

• Head identify ideas and subheads are the details of each idea. Along the side of the Storyboard is the list of individual who are responsible for each idea.

The Communication Storyboard

· The Communication Storyboard (Figure 7.12) is used to answer the questions what? who? when? and how? about information that needs to be communicated either internally or external to the organization.

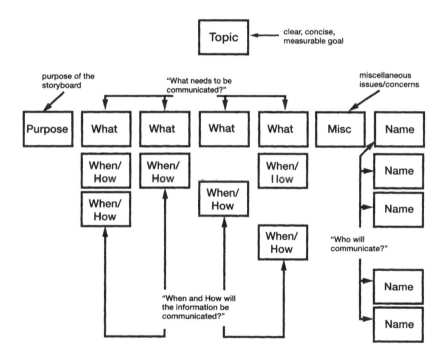

Figure 7.12. *The communication storyboard.*

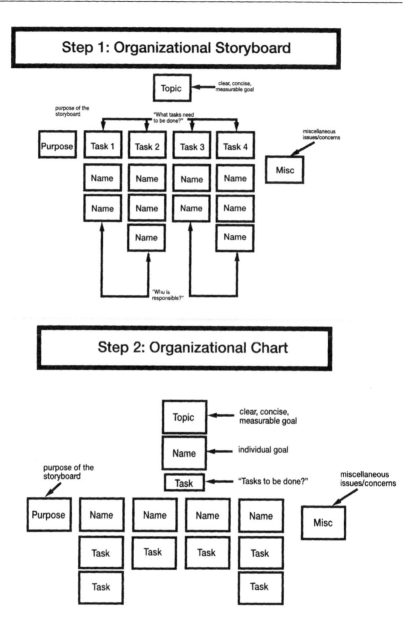

Figure 7.13. *Organizational storyboard.*

• Heads identify what needs to be communicated, and subheads indicate when and how the information will be communicated. Along the side of the Storyboard is the list of individuals who are responsible for communicating the information.

The Organizational Storyboard

The Organizational Storyboard (Figure 7.13) is used to identify both specific task areas in a project and the individuals who are responsible for each task. There are two steps to creating the Organizational Storyboard. First, tasks and individuals need to be identified. Second, the Storyboard should be rearranged into a suitable organizational chart. It is important to pay attention to the particular tasks, leaders, and doers when creating a successful organization chart.

Additional Information

Bunch, John. "The Storyboard Strategy." *Training and Development,* Vol. 45, No. 7, July 1991.

Hanke, Ed. An Exercise in Creativity. *Credit Union Management,* Vol. 16, No. 11, Nov. 1993.

Symons, Paula. "Shedding Some Light on Creativity." *Credit Union Management,* Vol. 15, No. 12, Dec. 1992.

Talbot, Mary. "Storyboard Your Meetings." *Success,* Vol. 40, No. 5, Aug. 1993.

Flowcharting

What Is It?

"A picture is worth a thousand words." Flowcharting, sometimes called *Flow Process Analysis* or *Process Flow Analysis,* is the act of drawing a "picture" of a process. It produces diagrams using connecting lines and symbols to show a step-by-step progression through a system or process. A Flowchart is the lowest-level tool available for showing cause-and-effect relationships. There are several types of Flowcharts. Some of these have very specialized uses. This discussion will be limited to Simple, Top-Down, and Multi-Process Flowcharts, and Process Mapping. These differ from one another in scope, objective, and use of symbols.

As you move from Simple to Top-Down to Multi-Process Flowcharts, you move along a continuum that progresses from very broad (limited detail) to very specific (extreme detail). Therefore, the choice of which of these to use should be based on the level of detail that is needed and the complexity of the process being analyzed and documented.

The Process Map adds two dimensions to the analysis that are not easily depicted with basic Flowcharts: time and space. The major advantage of the "map," as it is commonly called, is that it communicates ownership and duration. Typically, the Flowchart has no spatial component and defines time only in terms of chronology. The Multi-Process Flowchart comes closest to providing spatial representations.

Why Do It?

Flowcharts should be used to fully understand, document, and communicate systems and processes. Let's briefly define process terminology before we proceed further. The levels of composition are system, process, and task.

Systems. Systems work together to achieve some common, normally global objective. For instance, human physiology involves the working of several systems: nervous, circulatory, respiratory, digestive, reproductive, and so on. Systems, in turn, require the coordination of several processes.

Processes. Processes are broken down into tasks. The circulatory system, for instance, involves cardiac and vascular processes, one to pump blood, the other to transport it.

Tasks. Tasks occupy a level of detail that involves what must be done. For example, the tasks in the circulatory system would describe what each ventricle of the heart needs to do at each instant; what the arteries, veins, and capillaries need to do; and so on.

Because Flowcharts can produce and communicate understanding to such a detailed level, they should be prerequisite to approval of capital funds targeted for improvement, innovation, or modernization. In fact, before any improvement activity is implemented, Flowcharts should support decision making. No machinery, stores, not even a desk should be moved without the sanction of Flowcharting. They should also be demanded before any changes to organizational structure or responsibilities take place. Their objective would be to demonstrate that capabilities would be at least maintained and, ideally, enhanced. Flowcharts should be an integral part of every training process.

How to Do It

1. Define the scope of the analysis. Construct a complete, well-thought-out purpose statement. This statement will prevent analyses that are too narrow in scope to fully define the process or too broad to offer clear direction.
2. Approve the symbols. Many symbols are used in Flowcharting. In general, however, very few symbols are absolutely needed. The oval, rectangle, circle, diamond, triangle, square, and arrow will suffice for most efforts (Figure 7.14). Use the fewest symbols possible, and make sure everyone who is or will be involved understands the meaning of each symbol. This will make the interpretation of the charts much easier.
   - *Operation.* The circle denotes an operation. An operation is a process step that involves a "state change." This means that some, normally irreversible, change takes place in the product or service that is the final objective of the process. This sounds ominous, but really it is simple. In a manufacturing example, for instance, only process steps that involved "changing" the actual product (assembling, painting, and so on) would be considered operations. In an administrative example, steps involved with, for example, adding

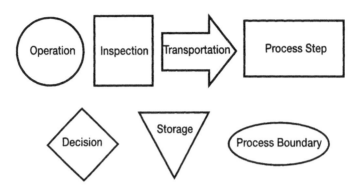

Figure 7.14. *Common flowchart symbols.*

information to a document would be considered an operation, whereas simply reviewing that information would not. Some support the position that an operation is anything that "adds value" to the end product or service. We certainly agree that, by definition, an operation is a value-adding process element. But, once an element's classification as an operation depends on its position in the value equation, unnecessary subjectivity is introduced. There is nothing subjective, however, about "state change," so using our definition will make improvement to processes easier to attain. This is because improvement begins by targeting non-value-adding elements of process for elimination.

- *Inspection.* The square denotes inspections. Any step that involves checking, verifying, counting, or grading or classifying would be called inspections. Based on the discussion on operations, inspections would, by definition, be non-value adding (NVA).
- *Transportation.* The arrow denotes transportation. Anytime something is moved in physical space or time, depict it in a chart with the transportation symbol. Since electronic data is "moved" in virtual space and time, it is handled specially (see Data-Flow Analysis later in this chapter).
- *Decision.* The diamond denotes decision points. When a process reaches a branching point where the path taken depends on a decision or condition, use a diamond. The decision or condition that causes the least disruption to the flow should always proceed from the bottom point of the diamond. The other(s) can proceed from either side, but right is normally preferred.

- *Storage.* The triangle (with a point down) denotes storage. Storage is used to represent steps in a process where the product being charted is placed in some physical location for some period of time. Sometimes, you may run across a D-shaped symbol. This is used to denote a delay and, while product may be idle during this period, be careful not to confuse this with storage. In storage, there is an intent to store the product or material, and many times the storage time is predetermined.
- *Process boundary.* The oval (with the long axis horizontal) denotes process boundaries. Use these to denote where the beginning and ending points of the chart are. These points may be different from the actual process boundaries from a functional standpoint. The main function of these is to establish points of connection and overlap to other process documentation.
- *Process step.* The rectangle (with the long axis horizontal) denotes process steps.
3. Question the experts. Much of the essence of Flowcharting is in separating important issues and elements from trivial ones. To gain this level of understanding, time should be spent with process "experts" before any observation ever takes place. By definition, an expert is one who has, employs, or displays special skill or knowledge derived from study, training, or experience. In practice, the experts are the people who are most closely involved with the process on *a consistent basis.*
4. Chart the process. As this questioning takes place, chart the process using the symbols approved in step 2. Make notes that indicate the reasons why process steps exist. Also note any procedural requirements that may by indicated be various successor and predecessor steps. This is done for two reasons. First, without a full knowledge of what *should* be done, it may be easy to omit critical steps that are not actually being observed; second, this forces every step to be justified.
5. Observe the process. The observer should do more than simply watch and record the process. During this time the observer must also begin to identify the nature of the improvement needed in the process. In order to develop the best possible improvements, you will have to understand causes of process deficiencies. The three general categories of causes are as follows:
   - Communication or "didn't know." Some people are consistently observed following a specific procedure while others are not. The key for this type of cause is inconsistency from one individual, department, and so on, to another.

- Non-adherence, or "knew, but didn't do." In some instances the experts will describe steps that will not be observed in practice consistently, if at all, even within the same individual, department, and so on. If experts have indicated that these steps are critical, especially if they are important predecessors to other steps, the non-adherence must be addressed.

    Steps that will not be adhered to can normally be predicted during questioning of the experts. These steps will be the ones that are described as "a pain," hard or unpleasant to do, or time consuming.

- Non-ability, or "didn't work." When procedures are followed as prescribed, the deficiencies must be caused by faulty process design or lack of or insufficient training.

6. Question the process. Compare the chart developed before the observation with the one resulting from observation. There will be elements that were observed but not described. These are "intra-improvement opportunities": they have been inspired by tinkering and will many times involve alternatives to the non-adherence to critical elements that are difficult, unpleasant, or inconvenient. All differences between the charts must be documented.

7. Question the experts again. Meet again with your experts so they can help you to reconcile the differences. Challenge each step, even those that are consistently followed. Force every step to be justified.

8. Improve the process. Use the following method to improve the process (remember, the experts are still the vital link):

- Eliminate as many NVA or nonessential steps as possible—a nonessential element is one that is not customer-driven. Keep only those that cannot be eliminated because of relationships to other steps.

- Combine the NVA or nonessential steps that remain with other steps, even other NVA or nonessential ones. After this, combine as many other steps as possible. Do not make any combinations that will compromise the effectiveness of the process. The goal of the combination should be to make steps easier, faster, more convenient, or less costly in some other way.

- Rearrange the order of remaining NVA and nonessential steps to minimize their impact on the process. After this, rearrange as many other steps as possible. The goals of rearrangement are the same as those of combination.

- Finally, *simplify* as many *value-adding* and *essential* steps as possible. Do not commit resources to simplifying NVA or nonessential elements. If they are important enough to simplify, they are probably more essential than believed. Simplification has the same goals as combination and rearrangement, only to a much greater degree.

9. Sell the improvement. Since so much care has been taken to involve the experts, the process of selling the improvements from step 8 should progress naturally. During this stage, take care of particulars such as ownership, timing, and measurement and follow-up.

10. Train the improvement. In our experience, this is probably the step most often neglected in most organizations. Many times, after substantial effort has been expended studying and improving processes, the improved procedures are never communicated. As a result, later effort is required to make the same or similar improvements all over again. This can be avoided if you use the chart itself as a training aide and use check-offs to ensure that everyone understands the procedure. Use the experts' reasoning to explain why the procedure is an improvement.

11. Install the improvement. The primary objective of installing the improvement is standardization. Until the process is standardized, the results of the improved procedure won't be realized. This is especially critical if capital expenditure decisions were based on the benefit to be derived from the new process. The keys to installing the improvement are:
    • Updating process documentation.
    • Incorporating the chart into the job summaries of everyone involved.
    • Posting the chart where it can be easily accessed and referred to.
    • Ensuring that all documentation showing the old procedure is removed.

Case Example

Simple Flowchart. The Simple Flowchart is used to show the essential steps of a process; very little detail is included. This type of chart is used to communicate overviews or overall conceptualizations. Figure 7.15 is an example of a simple flowchart for building a house. Obviously, no one unfamiliar with home building would use this chart as a guide for the actual construction. That same person could, however, get a good idea of what types of activities would be involved with the project. In general, use only rectangles in Simple Flowcharts. Not enough detail is shown to be concerned with decisions, and so on. A time-line could easily be added along

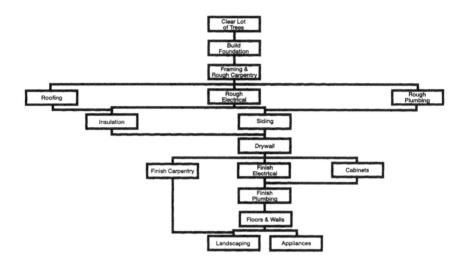

Figure 7.15. *Simple flowchart for building a house.*

the left or right edge of the chart. This would be useful for resource planning and coordination.

Top-Down Flowchart. The next level of charting detail is the Top-Down Flowchart. It communicates the major steps required to proceed from a specific input to a specific output. Steps to proceed to the next level of detail are listed below each of these major steps. Figure 7.16 expands on the chart from the home-building scenario. Though this is not very detailed, it is a clear enough "picture" to help resource decision making. Any prospective builder could look at this listing and almost immediately know what tasks will have to be out-sourced. The detail level on this chart should be confined to five or six items for each major step. If more items than this exist, each should be challenged and kept only if essential. As with the Simple Flowchart, only rectangles should be used. This is still a rather high-level, strategic tool, so more symbols would be meaningless.

The major disadvantages of the Top-Down Flowchart are that there is no reference to time, interrelationships are not indicated, and the process tends to look more linear than it really is.

Multi-Process Flow Chart. On the other end of the flowcharting continuum is the Multi-Process Flowchart. This chart is like a collection of Simple

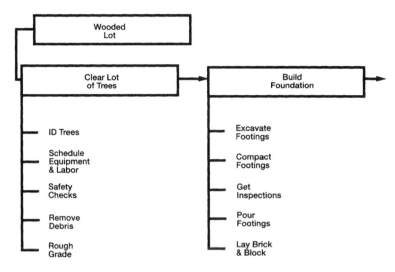

Figure 7.16. *Top-down flowchart for building a house.*

Flowcharts that have been expanded in detail and joined together (Figure 7.17). Use Multi-process Flowcharts to document and communicate process details to the task level and to show interrelationships between processes.

Process Mapping. Like the Flowchart, the Process Map is a "picture" of a process or system. Though both are visual representations of a process or system, Process Mapping offers a dimension that Flowcharting does not. This dimension is the advantage of diagramming all the functional areas, internal and external, that are involved in a process.

The flowchart is normally produced and displayed vertically, like in a grain silo. Because of this, flowcharting does not indicate cross-functional, interdepartmental, intercorporate, or international relationships and dependencies conveniently. The Process Map, on the other hand, is horizontal, like in a pipeline. Therefore, it indicates the interactions, interdependencies, and interrelationships that Flowcharting cannot. This is the spatial dimension referenced earlier. Another dissimilarity between Process Mapping and Flowcharting is that mapping uses only three symbols: the oval, denoting the endpoints of the process; the rectangle, denoting internal process steps; and the diamond, denoting decisions. When analyzing processes that span multiple departments, sites, or companies,

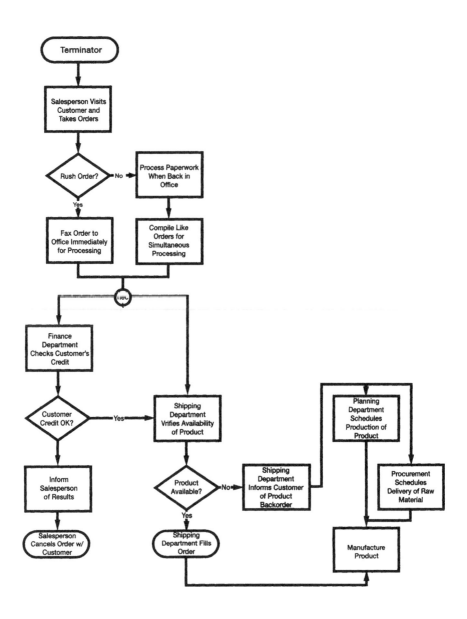

Figure 7.17. *Multi-process flowchart, Delta Company customer order process.*

mapping is in order. The higher the risk and penalty of suboptimization, the more appropriate mapping is.

The steps to using Process Mapping are as follows (these steps are the same as in Flowcharting with noted exceptions):

1. Define the scope of the analysis.
2. Define the scope of interactivity. Determine how wide the span of the analysis will be from a functional perspective. Which organizational functions will be involved and mapped? What externals will be included? What function (internal or external) triggers the beginning and ending of the process?

   The functional areas involved should be listed vertically down the left side of the map. The functions should be separated from one another using horizontal lines. Figure 7.18 demonstrates this with the blank map used for the process of writing this book.

   Mapping is used to develop a picture of *processes* not *functions*. Therefore, when the endpoints of a process are determined, make sure that these endpoints are process-oriented, not function-oriented. It is helpful to name processes in a manner that does not confuse

AUTHOR 1

AUTHOR 2

AUTHOR 3

AUTHOR 4

REVIEWERS

PUBLISHER

Figure 7.18. *Blank process map.*

them with their respective functions. For instance, rather than discussing the "human resource" process, it would be better to talk about the "recruitment" process, or, better still, the "employment slot open, employment slot full" process.

3. Add a timeline along the bottom of the chart. The units will be dependent on the process being mapped. The important thing is to make the units consistent, meaningful, and small enough to capture the *essential* detail of the map. This is the time dimension referred to earlier.

4. Question the experts.

5. Develop issues and problems list. This is perhaps the most important difference between "mapping" and "charting." The issues list is a record of concerns that come up that may be peripheral or unrelated to the central issue but are still important to the organization. The list serves as a "parking lot" for these items, thus allowing them to be retained in memory but preventing discussion of them from derailing the primary effort.

6. Chart the process. This is done identically to Flowcharting with one major and three minor exceptions:

  • The major exception is that there can be no "loop-backs" in the flow on a process map. This is because the map is time based, and a loop-back would indicate reverse time, which is impossible.

  • The minors exceptions are:

  1. *Always* proceed along the path of least resistance at decision points.

  2. Vertical alignment is important! Show elements vertically aligned only when they occur in the same reference of time.

  3. Clearly denote steps that are shown in detail on another chart (in Figure 7.19, these are shown with drop shadow).

   Figure 7.19 is the first page of a simplified map of the spring baseball camp of a Major League team. Time and cost have been left out to show the relationship mechanics more clearly.

7. Observe the process.

8. Quantify the process. Each rectangle on the map should be quantified in terms of time and cost. The maximum (M), minimum (m), and typical (T) times should be provided. Cost should be stated, at least, in terms of material cost and labor cost (Figure 7.20).

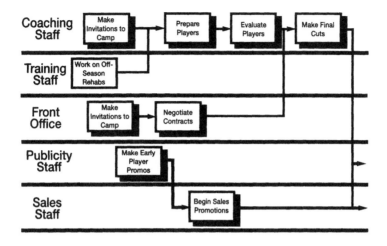

Figure 7.19. *Basic process map.*

Process Steps

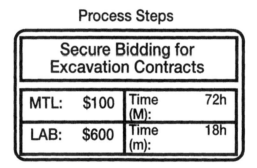

Figure 7.20. *Cost and time data for process steps.*

9. Question the process.
10. Question the experts again.
11. Improve the process.
12. Sell the improvement.
13. Train the improvement.
14. Install the improvement.

Additional Information

Burr, John T. "The Tools of Quality, Part I: Going with the Flow(Chart)." *Quality Progress,* June 1990, pp. 64–67.

Grove, A. S. "How to Run a Breakfast Factory." *Across the Board,* October 1983, pp. 34–45.

"Improving Performance with Process Analysis." *Risk Management,* November, 1992, pp. 47–51.

"Starting Over." *EuroBusiness,* December–January, 1993, pp. 50–52.

Henricks, Mark. "Process Flow Maps Locate Hidden Treasure by Analyzing Their Production Processes from Product Development to Distribution, OshKosh B'Gosh, Haggar, and Other Apparel Makers Are Boosting Results and Cutting Costs." *Apparel Industry Magazine,* February 1993, pp. 56–59.

Myers, Ken, and Ashkenas, Ron. "Results Driven Quality . . . Now!" *Management Review,* March, 1993, pp. 40–44.

Sherman, Stratford. "Are You as Good as the Best in the World?" *Fortune,* December 13, 1993, pp. 95–96.

Problem Stream Analysis

What Is It?

One of the most important steps toward empowering a team is developing decision-making ability. Decision making should be viewed as any other process. In other words, there are value-adding (VA) decisions and there are non-value-adding (NVA) decisions. VA decisions are those that involve strategy and support the business. These decisions require participation and expertise from all levels of an organization. The "better" an organization gets, the more time it will and must spend in VA decision making. NVA decisions are those that are involved with day-to-day process and operational management. To a large degree, NVA decisions involve fire fighting. Problem Stream Analysis formalizes, standardizes, and documents problem solving. It uses a hybrid of a Structured Tree Diagram. The diagram from Problem Stream Analysis is sometimes referred to as a Problem Chain because it takes a given result or process condition and traces its symptoms down to root causes.

Why Do It?

There are two overriding driving forces for Problem Stream Analysis. First, in order to spend the time needed on VA decision making, involvement in NVA decision making must be minimized. Second, since most operational decisions should ideally be made by an empowered team, the quality of the decisions being made must be high. Problem Stream Analysis accomplishes these objectives well. By tracing problems to their root causes, the time that would normally be spent "reinventing the wheel" for each incident is eliminated. And since there are a given number of possible causes already documented for each incident, a high likelihood exists that proper decisions will be made.

Problem Stream Analysis work best on discrete events. A discrete event is one in which something definable and identifiable *happens*. Problem chains don't work well on general, systemic process deficiencies. This is especially true of symptoms that are hard to tie to specific causes or where specific solutions are not clear. If a process is not well-defined enough to offer clean-cut cause-effect relationships, VA decision-making techniques like Process Decision Program Charting and Functional Decomposition should be used.

Functional Decomposition is a hierachial breakdown of a system into its elements for analysis. Once cause-effect relationships have been established, Problem Chaining will be effective. Problem Stream Analysis is one of the most reliable methods available for standardizing processes and ensuring adherence. Problem Stream Analysis can also be used to prepare for simulation and knowledge-based (expert systems) programming. In many cases Problem Chains can be compiled directly into program code—software programs are available to do this.

How to Do It

1. Write the problem statement.

The key to effective Problem Chaining is often in the quality, clarity, and accuracy of the problem statement. It should specifically and clearly define a problem that is easily detectable. If the problem statement addresses a condition that is hard to recognize, the chain will not be used when it should.

The problem statement must do more than simply describe the problem. Descriptions don't in themselves spur on or point to solutions. Examples of poor statements are:

• Machine 2000 in Process Alpha is not functioning properly.
• Today's shipment of Widget B did not arrive.
• The car won't start.

Better statements would be:

• What parameters ensure the proper functioning of Machine 2000 in Process Alpha?
• What factors and activities ensure the on-time arrival of Widget B.
• What factors ensure the proper cranking of a car?

By stating the problem this way, the focus will remain on the process itself. The key to effective Problem Chaining is defining and understanding the process.

2. Identify the check points.

The first level of the Problem Chain should communicate what things should be checked when problems arise. This will allow the problem to be closed-in on quickly. See the car problem example in Figure 7.21. Even the person with no automotive skills could use this chart to quickly narrow the possible causes of the problem by checking for the type of engine sounds. If the chart were complete, this would be even more evident because there would then be many more possibilities that could, otherwise, confuse the issue.

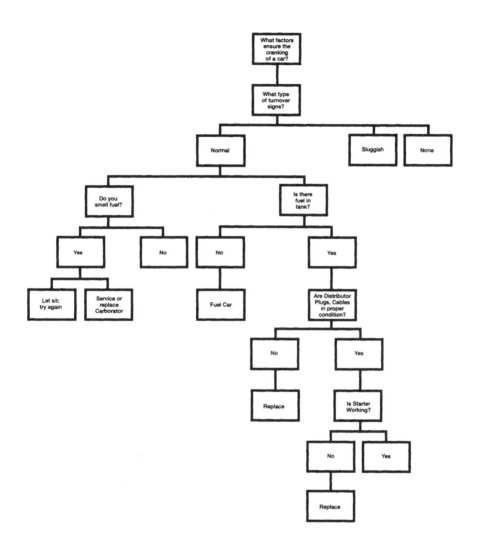

Figure 7.21. *Typical problem chain.*

A second advantage to constructing the chart this way is that team members begin to accept responsibility and feel more empowered because this type of knowledge increases confidence. It is also an effective training tool because it clearly demonstrates the process parameters that must be controlled if problems are to be avoided. When read from bottom to top, the chart says, "If these factors, parameters, or activities are controlled and maintained, then the overriding problem will be avoided." So, once this analysis is complete, it can move from a resolution tool to a preventive one.

3. Establish control points for the check points. Each check point should terminate at a control point. The control point dictates what action should be taken. In some cases, a check point will terminate without action. This may be because none is needed or because proper action is unknown. It is important to identify those points to which there is no known action. This knowledge allows the empowered team member to move up the chart until the first point at which the check is completely contained and to take corrective action there. This will correct some things that do not need correction, but the decision to do so is based on sound process knowledge. This again will increase the confidence of the team member.

4. Change the problem statement. Rephrase the problem statement to make it more descriptive and less probing of the problem itself. In this example, "Action required when car won't start" is a good statement to use. Do not restate any other statements in the chart.

5. Include the chart in the training process. The completed chart should be immediately incorporated into the training process. All team members should be taught how to interpret the chart. Each should be encouraged to refer to the chart as often as necessary. This is the step that makes Problem Stream Analysis critical to the team process. A necessary precursor to empowerment of teams is "enablement" of teams, and enablement is the process of transferring decision-making capabilities. Obviously, the earlier that this is done, the better, so preparing teams for the situations they are likely to encounter in a training process is a very powerful way to address team development needs.

6. Post the chart in the workplace. The chart should be posted or filed in the workplace. Ideally, it should become a part of work instructions or other types of manuals that are fully accessible to all teams involved with the process.

7. Change the chart as often as necessary. Open (non-action-terminated) control points should be closed whenever possible. In addition, some-

times process improvements will be made that make certain check and control points unnecessary. When this happens the chart should be updated immediately and then steps 5 and 6 followed.

8. Review the chart at least annually. Even if no changes have been made to the process, each chart should be reviewed and verified at least annually. Many times steps will come to light that need attention or improved focus. Taking a relatively benign look periodically can surface concerns that have been previously taken for granted.

Data Flow Analysis

What Is It?

Data Flow Analysis is a specialized Flowcharting tool. It demonstrates what information flows into a system and in what form, what happens to it, and where it goes when it leaves; who needs it; and uses it. It produces a picture of the information flow through a process or system. Almost all other Flowcharting techniques deal with the movement of something tangible and physical such as material, equipment, or people. Data Flow Diagrams are challenging because what they analyze is not always tangible. Many symbols are accepted for charting the flow of information; only three, however, are necessary for Data Flow Diagrams (Figure 7.22).

Figure 7.22. *Basic data flow analysis symbols.*

Why Do It?

No process can be fully understood until the flow of information through it is visible. In fact, data flow is such an integral part of process control that, without adequate information systems, many processes are in danger of failure. In addition, many process improvements will fail or not reach full potential because information systems are not extensive or healthy enough to support them. DFA must be done in parallel with other process analysis techniques in all but the very simplest of systems. Without this, there will be no guarantee that improvement will be successful and sustainable.

How to Do It

1. Clearly define the process to be analyzed.

   Since Data Flow Analysis is so boundary (input-output) oriented, the process should initially be defined based on its boundaries. This will help to ensure that the whole process and not some functional part of it will be captured. Sometimes it even helps to name the process based on these boundaries. Examples would be the order-to-delivery process, the idea-prototype process, and the position open, position filled (personnel recruitment) process.

2. Question the Experts. Like other Flowcharting efforts, spending time with the people who actually run the process is essential to the success of Data Flow Analysis. During this period the five Ws and one H (what, when, where, why, who, how) should be used extensively. Data systems typically have more hidden waste in them than other processes. Challenging old habits and procedures is the best way to identify this waste.

3. Follow the paper trail. Identify every form, report, and memorandum that is a *regular and required* part of the process. Even in the most advanced systems, if the paper trail is followed, most of the information required to sustain the system will be identified.

   For each document, collect and record the following information:

   • The purpose for the document. Be tough! Ask, "What does the information on this piece of paper do?; Why do you need the information?"

   • The information in the document that is actually used, who uses it, where it is used, and when it is used.

   • The distribution of the document—every copy must be accounted for!

   • The final disposition of the document. Is it filed? For how long? Is it destroyed? After what period of time?

   Remember, this should only be done for *regular and required* documentation. Nonstandard documentation will stick out later during charting.

4. Create a purpose statement for each regular and required document. Using the data from step 3, write a statement that justifies the existence of each document. The statement should include, in addition to the information in step 3, reporting frequency and identification of originators of all data contained in the document.

5. Chart the process. With the additions noted, steps 5 through 11 are identical to the steps described in Flowcharting. A simple chart is shown in Figure 7.23.

6. Observe the process.

7. Question the process.

8. Question the experts again.

9. Improve the process. Emphasis should be placed on eliminating nonessential steps of the process, repetitive data elements, and excess paperwork. Special attention should be paid to document

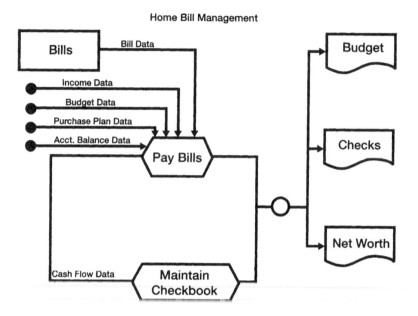

Figure 7.23. *Simple data flow chart.*

distribution; use the purpose statements for each document as a hard-and-fast guide to how many copies to circulate and to whom.

10. Train the improvement.
11. Install the improvement.
12. Identify technology that eliminates paper. Don't accept "improvements" that simply delay paper production or allow people to produce paper copies "as needed." If data is not used electronically as it was originally input or intended to be used, then waste may be hidden in the process. Information Technology can save time and eliminate wasted effort, but only if it is used properly.
13. Sell the improvement.
14. Train the improvement.
15. Install the improvement.

Komatsu Diagram

What Is It?

The Komatsu Diagram is a variation of the Tree Diagram. However, instead of text appearing at each branch of the tree, charts and graphs appear. These charts and graphs explain the state of the central issue, which is also a chart or graph.

Why Do It?

The Komatsu Diagram demonstrates cause-and-effect relationships or identifies components of a condition of process. It also indicates the process variables that are the most important to control, and clarifies what the objective of the control of these variables is. For instance, if a branch chart (one under the central chart or issue) has an inverse relationship to the central chart (when the branch variable increases, the trunk variable decreases), then it is immediately apparent whether to try to maximize or minimize that variable. Of course, care must be taken to ensure that relationships are direct before these kinds of assumptions can be made.

How to Do It

1. Choose a broad process measurement parameter.
2. Identify the major components or control causes for this parameter using Pareto Analysis or Force Field Analysis.
3. Construct the diagram (Figure 7.24)
   a. Place measurement parameter from step 1 at the trunk (top) of the diagram just as you would the central issue in a Tree Diagram.
   b. Place the components or causes as roots from the trunk. Note: For clarity, show only one level of detail on the chart.
4. Design process-control procedures around the diagram. In Figure 7.24, the diagram would obviously dictate the control of caloric intake, fat intake, and exercise.
5. Implement the procedures.

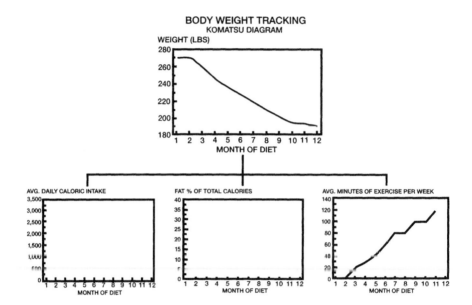

Figure 7.24. *Komatsu diagram body weight tracking.*

Spider or Target Diagram

What Is It?

The Spider or Target Diagram is a tool that visually represents performance of 8 to 12 parameters on a single chart. It is named by its resemblance to a spider web or, when used properly, to a target.

Why Do It?

This diagram quickly and clearly points out, by area, whether performance is acceptable or not. This makes resource management and improvement efforts much easier to plan and predict. It can also be used as a basis for recognition and reward systems—when used this way, the diagram can eliminate subjectivity and assure fairness between individuals, teams, departments, divisions, and so on.

How to Do It

1. Determine parameters to be tracked. Though any number of parameters may be used, the diagram works best with 8 to 12. It is important to involve as many of the people who will be rated or affected by the tracking as possible.
2. Put all parameters on the same scale for performance. For example, each could be evaluated on a five-point scale, ten-point scale, and so on.
3. Develop the guidelines for point performance for each parameter.
4. Publish all guidelines.
5. Draw the chart.
   a. Draw a "target" containing the number of rings as the maximum point value on your scale. Put numbers on the circles to represent the scaled rating. Begin from the outer circle and put the highest rating on the inner circle. This will allow the diagram to be used as a "target" (Figure 7.25).
   b. Draw straight lines out from the center of the circles. The number of lines should equal the number of parameters that you will track. Distribute the lines around the circles as evenly as possible.
   c. Place labels on these lines to represent the parameters (Figure 7.26).
   d. Use Executive Diagnosis to rate or weight the parameters.

Figure 7.25. *Target diagram with point levels.*

Figure 7.26. *Blank spider diagram.*

Figure 7.27. *Completed spider diagram.*

    e. Add a single marker to each line to represent its parameter's rating
       or weight.
    f. Draw a line to connect the markers (Figure 7.27).
  6. Interpret the diagram. Those parameters that deserve the most atten-
     tion will be the ones closest to the outer circle.
  7. Make plans to improve the performances of these parameters.

Brainstorming

What Is It?

Some have defined insanity as "doing the same things you've always done, but expecting different results than you've always gotten." In order to "stop the insanity," the molds of habit and tradition must be broken. Brainstorming was developed in the 1960s by advertising executive Alex Osborn as a group idea-generation technique to help do this. Brainstorming is designed to generate ideas in volume. These ideas lead to problem solving and breakthrough thinking. Because Brainstorming requires participation from everyone in the group, many times the ideas come from members who would otherwise not be consulted or included in the process. This advantage alone, aside from improvements gained from solutions and breakthroughs, is critical to organizational performance. The expansion of involvement throughout the organization leads to improvements in morale, job satisfaction, and, consequently, commitment. The more dedicated an organization becomes to "teamwork philosophies," the more critical this commitment will become.

Why Do It?

Brainstorming is a useful idea-generation tool during periods of

- strategic planning
- problem solving
- breakthrough thinking
- innovation

How to Do It

1. Develop the purpose statement. Clearly state the purpose of the Brainstorming session before any meeting planning or communication takes place. The statement should indicate whether the group will engage in strategy, problem solving, or innovation. The overriding role of the purpose statement is to focus the group. The most effective statements for Brainstorming are often presented in question form and should be complete phrases containing at least a noun and a verb. Of the "five Ws and one H" (who, what, why, when, where,

how), "what" and "how" are more effective for use in purpose statements than the others because they don't easily allow answers that affix blame. Use the purpose statement to keep the Brainstorming effort focused on improvements to the process and away from finger pointing. Examples of good purpose statements are:
- What are the factors involved with the increase in customer complaints at the North Road branch office?
- What are the critical areas needing improvement if we are to become the benchmark of the industry in safety?
- What changes can we make to the design of the Model Z Widget in order to create a marketing advantage of at least three years?

2. Choose the facilitator. Before being allowed to lead sessions, make sure that potential facilitators have had as much training in group dynamics, communication (especially listening and negotiating), and leadership as feasibly possible. They should also fully understand the rules of facilitation:
- Do not promote or allow personal attacks.
- Do not offer opinions, even if asked by the group.
- Do not participate in voting.
- Do not manipulate or influence discussion or voting. This includes exerting influence by calling for votes while discussion is swayed toward a given point of view.
- Speak only to keep discussion active.
- Do not allow individuals or subgroups to dominate the discussion.
- Do not allow the group to discard outcomes that are uncomfortable or differ from expectations.

   Because of these rules, the facilitator sometimes has more success when he or she is not a stakeholder in the outcome of the Brainstorm. When this is impossible, drafting the most influential member of the group can be effective because it allows others more opportunity for involvement.

3. Communicate the rules. The success of Brainstorming depends to a large degree on how effective the facilitator is at helping the group obey the rules of Brainstorming:
- Every member of the group has an equal voice.
- Only one member is allowed to give an idea at a time and then only according to the sequence that has been agreed upon.
- No explanation of ideas is asked or given, but clarification is allowed.
- No evaluation or criticism of ideas is allowed.

- "Far out" ideas are welcomed.

- Expanding on the ideas of other members is encouraged.

- No ideas can be combined or eliminated without the permission of the member(s) giving them.

- Voting cannot take place until all ideas have been exhausted.

   No matter how often the group members have been through Brainstorming, these rules should be reviewed before each session. If the group neglects any rules during the session, the rules should be reviewed as many times as necessary. It may help to post the rules conspicuously whenever sessions are active.

4. Generate the ideas. Several methods are used for generating and collecting ideas:

- The most common method is *Round Robin*. For this method the group should be seated in a U-shape with the facilitator at the open end. The steps for this method are:

a. Any member volunteers to give *one* idea.

b. The facilitator paraphrases the idea after hearing it and asks the "giver" for approval of the wording.

c. Once the "giver" approves the wording, the facilitator records the idea on a flipchart or overhead velux. The idea should be coded to identify the member who gave it, either by color or initials. It should also be given a sequence letter (beginning with "A") for later reference. The 27th idea should be given the sequence "AA", the 28th, "AB", and so on.

d. The facilitator then calls for an idea from the member to either side of the last "giver" (once this direction has been established it should be maintained throughout the session).

e. That member can either give an idea or "pass" to the next member.

f. Steps b and c are repeated each time an idea is given.

g. Control goes to the next member and steps e and f are repeated.

h. Once a full round of "passes" is achieved, the facilitator begins the next phase.

   - *Brainwriting* was developed at the Battelle Institute in Germany. For it, the group should be seated at a round table. The steps for this method are:

a. Each member is given a sheet of legal paper and a pencil or pen of a unique color. Each is instructed to turn the paper sideways and fold it into a number of columns equal to half the size of the group, but no less than three or more than five. The rest of the process is done in complete silence.

b. Each member lists two to four ideas on his or her paper. Unrelated ideas should be placed in different columns.

c. All papers are placed in the center of the table and shuffled.

d. Each member takes a sheet from the center. If any member gets a sheet that he or she has already had, the entire group should exchange sheets in one direction.

e. Each member adds as many ideas as possible in three minutes to the list that he or she picked. Members should use the ideas already on the list for stimulation and should be encouraged to modify or make them more complete. Totally unrelated ideas are also allowed, but should be entered in a new column. Columns on the back of the paper can be used if necessary.

f. Repeat steps c through e the number of times as there are group members or until 30 minutes have elapsed, whichever occurs first.

g. The facilitator transfers all ideas onto a flipchart or overhead velux and proceeds to the next phase. The ideas should be sequenced as in Round Robin.

- *Mind Mapping* is designed to achieve breakthrough thinking. The human mind stores and processes information in associative rather then compartmental "chunks." Mind Mapping tries to parallel this process and, thereby, makes idea generation more effective and creative. The steps are:

a. The facilitator writes the purpose (or central) statement in a box in the center of a flip chart. (It may be useful to tape three flipcharts together on a wall (use markers that will not bleed through).

b. Use consensus to determine the major issues related to the central statement.

c. The facilitator writes these issues as branches from the central statement. The rest of the process is done in complete silence.

d. Each member should be given a unique color marker.

e. All members gather around the flip chart and add limbs to branches on the chart when they have an idea that is related to what is already on the chart. When a member generates an idea unrelated to any of the branches, another branch is added by that member.

f. Once a member has no more ideas, he or she sits down but can return to the chart if new ideas come up as long as the session is active.

g. When all members are seated, the facilitator transfers the ideas to a flipchart and sequences them, as in Round Robin, and then moves to the next phase.

5. Clarify ideas. This is not a period for detailed explanation or defense of ideas. If a member questions an idea, then the member who gave the idea should clarify it as briefly as possible. The facilitator may help by rephrasing the idea for more clarity if necessary. This step and the next one are the reasons that maintaining the identity of the member giving each idea is so important—without this, even the member who gave an idea will sometimes not remember giving it.

6. Combine redundant ideas. No matter which method is used for generating ideas, redundantcy will occur. These ideas should be combined to aid voting. Before any ideas are combined, all members who were involved with giving them must agree to have them combined. No pressure should be exerted to combine ideas. Ideas that are only simi lar (as opposed to identical) should not be combined unless there is agreement and the essence of each idea is retained in the combination.

7. Rank the ideas. Several methods are useful for ranking:
   • *Multi-Voting* is useful for a large number of ideas, 50 or more. It allows the group to quickly and equitably reduce the number of ideas on the list. The steps to Multi-Voting are:
   a. Assign each member a number of votes equal to roughly 20 percent of the total number of ideas remaining.
   b. Have each member write numbers from one to the number of votes assigned on a sheet of paper.
   c. Have each member secretly assign letter sequences for the ideas they feel merit further investigation to the numbers on their paper. Only one sequence can be assigned to each number.
   d. After all voting is complete, the facilitator should go to the flipchart and ask for the number of votes for each idea by a show of hands. The facilitator should then record the total votes given to each idea next to the idea on the chart.
   e. Ideas with less than two votes should be lined through on the chart lightly enough to still be legible.
   f. If more than 50 ideas remain, the process should be repeated. This time the facilitator should use a differently colored marker to record the voting.

• *Nominal Group Technique* is similar to Multi-Voting in that it too can quickly reduce the number of ideas on a list. It should be used when there are 25 to 50 ideas. The steps to Nominal Group Technique are:

a. Assign each member a number of votes equal to twice the number of team members.

b. Have each member write the sequence letters of the ideas that remain on a sheet of paper.

c. Have each member distribute votes to ideas as desired. For instance, if a member has ten votes, those ten votes could be spread to as many as ten ideas or as few as one.

d. After all voting is complete, the facilitator should go to the flipchart and ask for the number of votes for each idea. The facilitator should then tabulate and record the total votes given to each idea next to the idea on the chart.

e. Ideas with less than two votes should be lined through on the chart lightly enough to still be legible.

f. Only one round should be necessary.

• Force Ranking is probably the most widely used ranking technique for Brainstorming. It should be used when the number of ideas remaining is less than 25. To Force Rank:

a. Choose a number equal to about one-half the number of members, but never less than four.

b. Have each member write the sequence letters of the ideas that remain on a sheet of paper.

c. Have each member secretly assign the ranking "1" to the idea they feel has the most merit. Have them continue to assign ranks up to the number from step a. All other ideas should get the next highest ranking. For example, if there are eight members in the group, the top four ideas would be ranked. After each member has chosen the four ideas that each feels is best, all other ideas should receive the ranking of "5."

d. After all voting is complete, the facilitator should go to the flipchart and ask for the ranking of each idea from each member. The facilitator should then record the rankings next to each idea on the chart.

e. The rankings for each idea should then be totaled.

f. The ideas with the lowest totals are the ones that should be chosen. The number of ideas depends on the number from step a). If there are eight members, then the four ideas with the lowest totals are chosen.

8. Move on to planning. After the most critical ideas have been identified, the group must identify what actions need to be taken. Force Field Analysis is a useful technique for determining the next steps.

9. Save the charts. The charts from Brainstorming should always be saved. Later, after improvement is made, they can be revisited to see if any of the ideas that were not given high priority have become easy to implement. They can also spur new learning and idea generation after better understanding of processes has been gained by other efforts.

Case Examples

During a major expansion, a grim discovery is made: the budgeted estimate for a significant portion of the project is $1 million short of providing the funds that will actually be needed. Approving additional funds will not be easy and can only be considered as a last resort. The implementation team uses Brainstorming to figure out how to complete the project within the budget and with no compromise to effectiveness.

A major service corporation has used Continuous Improvement philosophies to reduce customer complaints to the lowest level in its 50-year history. It has been at this level for five years even though expenditures on training and incentives have continued to rise each year. The organization uses Brainstorming to help it "revolutionize" its customer service.

Force Field Analysis

What Is It?

"All systems naturally move from a state of order to one of disorder." Almost every general physics course introduces this as a basic premise early in the curriculum. Kurt Lewin developed Force Field Analysis as a tool for identifying the forces that impact and shape management systems. His premise was that a situation can only be held static by opposing factors, some driving change and others resisting it. Think of Force Field Analysis as a sort of "balance sheet" of system performance.

Why Do It?

Use Force Field Analysis when there is a need to identify the factors, issues, and concerns (the forces) that are preventing progress and those that, if enhanced, can drive an organization toward improvement. Force Field Analysis is effective during problem identification as well as problem-solving efforts. When engaged in another tool, such as idea generation, Force Field Analysis can be invaluable.

How to Do It

1. Draw a large T on a board, flipchart, or paper.
2. Write the current situation above the T.
3. Write a goal statement or desired state to the far right of the top of the T.
4. Use Brainstorming or some other idea-generation technique to identify the forces involved in the situation. Record those that are or could be driving you toward the desired state on the left side of the T. Record the forces that are restraining movement on the right side.

Case Examples

An organization is trying to implement Total Quality Management. The implementation team must identify all of the factors that will influence this effort throughout the organization (Figure 7.28).

A major newspaper is faced with declining circulation and, therefore, declining advertising profits. It must quickly determine the factors that control its circulation so that it can begin to prime itself for survival (Figure 7.29).

Force Field Analysis Case Example 1

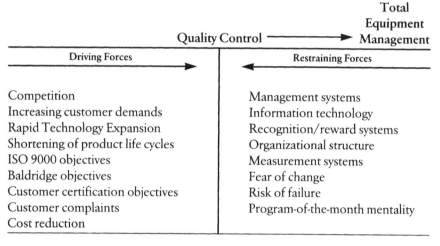

Quality Control	⟶	Total Equipment Management

Driving Forces ⟶	Restraining Forces ⟵
Competition	Management systems
Increasing customer demands	Information technology
Rapid Technology Expansion	Recognition/reward systems
Shortening of product life cycles	Organizational structure
ISO 9000 objectives	Measurement systems
Baldridge objectives	Fear of change
Customer certification objectives	Risk of failure
Customer complaints	Program-of-the-month mentality
Cost reduction	

Figure 7.28.

Force Field Analysis Case Example 2

Low Circulation	⟶	Flexibility

Driving Forces ⟶	Restraining Forces ⟵
Declining circulation	Unequal community coverage
Changing societal roles of women	Organizational structure
Changing societal roles of minorities	Budgetary policies
Increasing influence of cable, pay TV, sports	Inadequate gender diversity
Declining advertising profits	Inadequate culture diversity
Coupon package mailings	Advertising rates
Third party advertising	Advertising sales policy

Figure 7.29.

Additional Information

Lynch, Robert F., Werner, Thomas J., and Lynch, Livia, C. *Continuous Improvement: Teams and Tools.* Atlanta, GA, Qual Team, Inc. 1992.

Cost-Benefit Analysis

What Is It

Cost-Benefit Analysis is an analytical tool that can be used to:

• Compare the costs and benefits of alternative solutions or projects and thereby select the best ones.
• Evaluate and reassess ongoing projects.
• Compare with a new system the cost of operating and maintaining an old system.

How to Do It

Five steps should be completed to conduct a Cost-Benefit Analysis.

1. Determine the parameters of the assessment. Specifically this relates to:
   a. The time period to be used in calculations.
   b. The reliability and exactness of data.

   Most Cost-Benefit Analyses use a three-to-five-year time span. Anything less than three years will favor solutions or projects that are "quick hit" and not factor in projects that begin to return considerable benefits in later years. If a solution or project will accrue benefits for significantly longer than five years, it may be necessary to lengthen the time span accordingly.

   A direct relationship exists between the cost of doing a Cost-Benefit Analysis and the degree of reliability and exactness of data that are used in the calculation. The greater the detail and reliability, the larger the cost. We recommend you seek out the controller of your organization when determining the appropriate reliability and exactness of data for each application. If ballpark estimates will suffice, don't consume resources that can be better allocated to other efforts.

2. Quantify the financial and nonfinancial benefits. A benefit is anything that has a positive affect on an organization's performance. This can include, but is not limited to, reducing cycle times, improving productivity and quality, cost avoidance, and enhanced efficiency. If your organization has a sophisticated accounting system, most benefits can be easily quantified. Some benefits are nonfinancial because no clear and direct link exists between a solution and its bottom-line impact. Examples of nonfinancial benefits include improvements in employee

morale, job satisfaction, and organizational image. Even though these benefits are difficult to quantify we suggest you contact your customers to, at the very least, ask for their assistance in weighting or prioritizing each benefit.

It is also important to note the assumptions underlying each benefit and to identify any risks, the probability and potential impact of each risk occurring, and how each risk will be managed.

3. Quantify the direct and indirect costs. When quantifying costs we suggest you focus on significant costs relevant to equipment, facilities, material, and people. These costs can be categorized as direct or indirect. A direct cost is directly attributable to a project or solution. Examples include salaries and benefits, outside services (such as consultants), training, travel, utility charges, and lease and rental fees. Indirect costs are all other costs (such as, lost business and customer complaints). Costs can be identified using either past performance or history, interviewing key decision makers, or through Functional Decomposition. Functional Decomposition allocates costs by breaking down a process into its major tasks and steps, key cost drivers can then be determined. Remember to take inflation into consideration when determining costs. As with benefits, it is important to note underlying assumptions, risks, and so on, for each cost.

4. Determine cost-benefit ratio. In order to calculate the cost-benefit ratio, the net present value (NPV) must be identified. The NPV discounts future net benefits to their present value. In order for this calculation to be reliable, it is imperative to select the right rate of discounting. Again we suggest you seek out your organization's controller to assist you in selecting the most appropriate discount rate. High discount rates penalize projects with benefits occuring farther in the future. Listed below is the formula for computing the NPV.

$$NPV = CI = \frac{CR}{(1 + \text{interest})}$$

CI   = Initial cash investment
CR   = Expected cash return
Periods = Number of interest periods at the interest rate

The resulting calculation will be either a positive number, a negative number, or zero. A positive number means the project generates more benefits than costs. Zero means there is no gain or loss, and a negative number means the project lost money. From a purely NPV perspective, the option with the highest NPV is usually the solution most often selected.

5. Select the solution or project. Before final selection of a solution or project, we highly recommend performing a double check to ensure the numbers used are realistic. We encourage you to identify the variables that will have the highest impact on the NPV formula. Reevaluate assumptions underlying all cost and benefit estimates, identify risks, the probability of each risk happening, and contingency plans for addressing each risk. For some projects it may be necessary to identify low and high estimates for each variable to see how they affect the attractiveness of each alternative. The final decision should be based on the following variables:

- The option or solution with the best financial return.
- Strategic importance of the solution or project.
- Regulatory requirements, that will affect the solution or project.
- The organization's capability to take on additional debt.
- Stakeholder perceptions (shareholders, suppliers, customers, and so on) about the solution or project.

Case Example

You are a member of a cross-functional team that has been charged with making a recommendation to senior management of either 1) designing and implementing a new information system internally, or 2) continuing to use the existing system that does not provide employees with timely and accurate information to make business decisions. A breakdown of the costs of each option are outlined in Table 7.4.

Additional Information

Anwar Tahmasp Khan. *Cost-Benefit Analysis*. National Institute of Public Administration, 1965.

Dasgupta, A., and Pearce, D. *Cost-Benefit Analysis*. New York: Barnes and Noble, 1972.

Lesourne, Jacques. *Cost-Benefit Analysis and Economic Theory* City: North Holland Publishing Company, 1975.

Pearce, David. *Cost-Benefit Analysis,* New York: St. Martins Press 2nd ed., 1983.

Sassone, Peter, and Schaffer, William. *Cost-Benefit Analysis: A Handbook* New York: Academic Press, 1978.

Table 7.4
Cost-Benefit Analysis Example
Design System

Costs	Year 1	Year 2	Year 3
Labor for design + inflation adjustment = (1.03)	$100,000	$103,000	$106,000
Labor support + inflation adjustment = (1.03)	50,000	51,500	53,045
Utility + inflation adjustment = (1.03)	45,000	46,360	47,741
Total cash outflows	195,000	200,860	206,786
Benefits			
Efficiency	147,000	180,000	195,000
Expense reductions	130,000	150,000	160,000
Total benefits	277,000	330,000	355,000

Current System

Costs	Year 1	Year 2	Year 3
Labor + inflation adjustment = (1.03)	$100,000	$103,000	$106,000
Computer center operations + inflation adjustment = (1.03)	400,000	412,000	424,360
Total cash outflows	500,000	515,000	530,360
Benefits			
Expense reductions	175,000	190,000	195,000

Advanced Tools: Morphs

What Is It?

"Morphs" combine one or more basic tools; the combinations that result greatly increase the usefulness and effectiveness of the basic tools alone. Many other combinations than the ones presented here are possible. We have chosen two that, in our experience, have been the most useful. Morphs are named by the tools they contain.

Why Do It?

In most organizations today, communicating ideas involves "selling". The window of time that the audience is "sellable" is small in most instances; employees simply have too many other concerns and considerations, for a lot of time to be spent listening to long pitches. Morphs are designed to add punch to the sell by connecting different representations of data. They associate, for example, implementation-level tasks with ownership so that relationships that might otherwise be strained can be easily communicated. Using morphs adds credibility to conclusions and recommendations. At the same time, they increase the "comfort level" of decision makers because there is less ambiguity associated with approvals.

Examples of Morphs

Tree Morphs. The Tree Morphs (Figure 7.30) allow for analysis to be conducted and displayed at the implementation level of a Structured Tree Diagram.
   Use the right-hand side of the morph for:

- A Matrix showing responsibilities, ownership, interrelationship to other projects and processes, project cost, past performances, and so on. By definition, this would be named a Tree-Matrix Morph.
- A Gantt chart showing the critical path of a project. This is a Tree-Gantt Morph.
- A bar or line chart, if the right-hand side of this morph is envisioned as a graphical grid. This produces the Tree-Measure Morph. This is very useful for showing trend, impact, and basis data to support the implementation conclusions of the Tree Diagram.

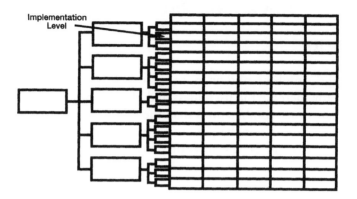

Figure 7.30. *Tree morph structure.*

Matrix Morphs. The Matrix Morphs take matrix elements, normally implementation tasks, and explode them out using:

- A Gantt chart, the Matrix-Gantt Morph.
- A bar or line chart, the Matrix-Measure Morph.

Perhaps the most widely known and used morph is the "House of Quality" used in Quality Function Deployment. It is also, by far, the most complex.

Comment Analysis

What is it?

Comment analysis is used to categorize, sort, and analyze written or transcribed comments. There are many instances where it is feasible and informative to capture and analyze comments. For example, many questionnaires have open-ended questions. Also, comments can be gathered and analyzed from telephone interviews, and focus groups provide an abundance of comments. Until the advent of recent versions of word processing software and spreadsheets, it was difficult to organize and analyze these comments. Fortunately, most current Windows™ or Macintosh™-based word processing and spreadsheet software allow the user to sort comments into useful categories. Most spreadsheets provide greater control over the sorting routines than do word processors, but, over the last 15 years, I have found that most word processors are more than adequate.

Why Do It?

Comments contain a great deal of information about the context, nature, characteristics, and innuendo of the information being gathered that just cannot be captured from quantitative data. Analyzing comments allows you to develop themes and trends that would not emerge from quantitative data. And, using word processing software and spreadsheets to help you sort the comments into a predefined structure greatly increases the speed with which you can identify trends in the data.

How Do You Do It?

Well-designed questionnaires allow the respondent to submit written comments at the end of each section of a questionnaire. For example, a questionnaire on leadership can include a section in which respondents write additional comments. The written comments are then transcribed into either a word processor or spreadsheet table with appropriate heading. For example, the written comments below were transcribed from an organizational assessment questionnaire into a simple four-column table. The columns are labeled and the comments sorted by organizational codes:

Org Code   The organization code number that identifies the location of the department

Supr Code   The supervisor or non-supervisor code

Sec Code   The section code (e.g., B = leadership). The section code could also be a *theme* code, such as training. But any agreed-upon code would be sufficient.

Sorted by Questionnaire Organization Code

Org Code	Supr Code	Sec Code	Comments
	Non	B	Favoritism is a big offender and morale crushing throughout the department.
00510	Sup	A	It is difficult to do a good job at communicating when you are working so hard and things are changing so fast.
00668	Sup	A	I think this organization does a good job with communication. We have worked very hard to improve this one the last 18 months. Good job Laura Estes!!
00668	Non	B	Teamwork training is always helpful.
00668	Sup	C	This survey is confusing, regarding unit and department. As a supervisor, I wasn't sure how to complete many of the questions, e.g., "my unit" as the unit I supervise? Or "my unit" as peers??

The following examples, taken from the same organizational assessment questionnaire, are sorted by supervision code and section code.

Sorted by Questionnaire Supervision Code

Org Code	Supr Code	Sec Code	Comments
00669		A	There is no communication within the Marketing Department.
00669	Non	A	My supervisor and I usually only communicate through profs. I guess that I should be fortunate that we communicate at all! My supervisor claims that he does not have time to communicate! So profs it is!
00669	Non	A	New employees are constantly hired without anyone in the SBU (other than the directly affected unit) knowing about it.
00669	Non	A	See "teamwork" comment. Applies here to interdepartment communication, too.
	Non	B	Favoritism is a big offender in morale crushing throughout the department.
00668	Non	B	Teamwork training is always helpful.

Sorted by Questionnaire Organization Code

Org Code	Supr Code	Sec Code	Comments
00510	Sup	A	It is difficult to do a good job at communicating when you are working so hard and things are changing so fast.
00668	Sup	A	I think this organization does a good job with communication. We have worked very hard to improve this one the last 18 months. Good job Laura Estes!!
00669	Non	A	My supervisor and I usually only communicate through profs. I guess that I should be fortunate that we communicate at all! My supervisor claims that he does not have time to communicate! So profs it is!
00669	Sup	A	Downward communication at Laura's staff's level is not good. Information has to be actively obtained. The attitude is "careful management of information, only to the extent of the organization's perceived ability to handle it." It is better at Laura's level, but still not adequate.
00669	Non	A	New employees are constantly hired without anyone in the SBU (other than the directly effected unit) knowing about it.
00669		A	There is no communication within the Marketing Department.

Other Uses

Written comments come in all shapes and formats. We designed an interview protocol to be used to provide a structured interview format about organizational architecture with a group of senior executives of a Fortune 100 company. The following is a portion of the interview protocol we used to collect the data.

We collected the data, transcribed it into a table, sorted the data, and developed trends in about one-fourth the time it would take sorting the written data by hand.

VMS = Very much so, FTM = For the most part, SW = Somewhat,
OS = Only slightly, NAA = Not at all, DNA = Does not apply

1 Setting Strategy:	VMS	FTM	SW	OS	NAA	DNA	Comments:

2 Managing Customers	VMS	FTM	SW	OS	NAA	DNA	Comments:

3 Managing Culture	VMS	FTM	SW	OS	NAA	DNA	Comments:

Sorted by Questionnaire Section

Org Code	Level Code	Sec Code	Comments
00510	AVP	1	In my particular unit, every employee has worked for ZCCG and the SBU for a considerable amount of time. I think the people are bored, yet not self-motivated enough to take on additional responsibility or move on to other areas. Each individual knows their own job. I think the team gets along well, but work hasn't anything to do with it.
00510	AVP	1	Very poor teamwork within unit. More attention needs to be placed on impact of decisions that may affect others.
00520	VP	1	I think, on a whole, the entire workforce has changed and all people in all fields are expected to do more for the same pay. It's a vicious world out there. I think the unit has problems, but I think the people are very lax in their responsibilities.
00520	VP	2	SBU management appears to be very separate from the rest of the SBU regarding open communications. This leaves them unaware of the underlying atmosphere out in the trenches. It appears that little accurate information about the real world gets passed to ??? by her direct reports. No one is willing to rock the boat!
00530	VP	2	SBU management gives "lip service" to teamwork, but actions speak louder than words.

Some Additional Tips

Again, spreadsheet software provides more sorting options than found with word processing software. For example, a spreadsheet can designate the order of the columns to be sorted. With a word processor, sorting can only be done one column at a time. Unfortunately, it takes more time to set up a written comments table in a spreadsheet than it does in a word processor. And finally, more people have access to word processors than they do to spreadsheets.

We have used up to seven columns for codes to sort written data, and have had as many as 100 pages of written comments. This tends to be the outer limits of sorting written comments unless you have more than 12 megs of RAM or a lot of time. Both MicroSoft Word and Word Perfect have excellent help lines that can help you sort through any sorting problems you may have.

CHAPTER 8

Team Assessment Instruments

Overview of Team Assessment Instruments

Name of Instrument	Purpose
1. Team Leader Feedback Questionnaires	A 360° feedback/assessment instrument designed to evaluate the overall performance of the team leader by team members.
2. 360° Team Member Feedback	A 360° feedback/assessment instrument designed to judge the overall performance of a team member by other team members.
3. 360° Feedback Form	A feedback form designed to evaluate the performance of a consultant or facilitator.
4. Post-Project Team Evaluation	A 360° feedback/assessment instrument designed to provide each team member with an opportunity to judge the overall success of the team from a project perspective.

(table continued on next page)

Name of Instrument	Purpose
5. Meeting Evaluation Questionnaire	A survey that evaluates the effectiveness of meetings according to a number of attributes.
6. Performance Management Questionnaire	A performance management evaluation form designed to identify gaps in the performance management structure of a team.
7. Feedback to the Consultant	A generic competency review form that can be used by many different stakeholders.
8. Team Readiness Questionnaire	A comprehensive team readiness questionnaire based on Catalyst Consulting Group Organizational Architecture.

360° Feedback and Assessment

What is 360° Feedback/Assessment?*

360° feedback/assessment* requires many different stakeholders (customers, managers, peers, support personnel) to judge the performance of an organization, a team, or an individual. This chapter discusses types of 360° feedback/assessment, the benefits of its use, and identifies some implementation issues that must be addressed before a 360° feedback/ assessment program is started. Figure 8.11 illustrates the sources of performance data in a 360° feedback/assessment program.

Benefits of 360° Feedback/Assessment

Research and our experience have shown that the following benefits derive from implementing a successful 360° feedback/assessment program.

- Increased alignment. Alignment occurs when senior management, middle management, and employees are all rowing in the same direction to the same destination. If everyone in a company knows and acts as expected, alignment with business goals and objectives increases. A

---

*Assessment occurs when performance information is used to make personnel decisions such as wage increases, transfers, pormotions, bonuses, and so on. Feedback occurs when performance information is used to identify individual strengths and weaknesses as part of a personal development process. The process leads to an action plan that puts the strengths to best use and eliminates or mitigates the weakness.

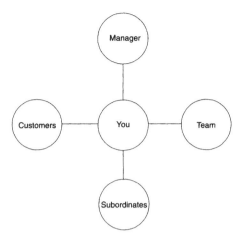

Figure 8.1. *360° Feedback/assessment sources of performance data.*

360° feedback/assessment program defines, communicates, and measures the behaviors that are expected of executives, managers, or employees. This alignment helps to eliminate or mitigate major course corrections during a business performance year, increasing the velocity and accuracy of hitting the company customer satisfaction, human resource management, productivity, and cash-flow targets for the current and future performance years.

• Increased information. Communication is increased because more people participate in providing assessment and feedback to more managers and employees. Many participants in 360° feedback/assessment programs have stated that the increased feedback helped them to better understand how they contributed to the organization, and how they could better capitalize on their strengths and mitigate their weaknesses. This increased scope of information provides a more realistic and candid perception of performance. In individual cases, 360° feedback/assessment often reduces rater bias found in typical single-rater performance-appraisal systems, as long as the rater is assured anonymity when rating the person being assessed.

• Increased candor. One of the frequently cited reasons for developing a 360° feedback/assessment program is the lack of candor found when one person assesses performance. As already indicated, anonymity in a 360° feedback/assessment program allows people to be candid without fear of disclosure. To be sure, the implementation of 360° feedback/assessment programs indicates that there are both candor and trust problems in an organization. A successful 360° feedback/ assessment programs is, *logically*, self-terminating.

- A Reduction in single-rater bias. Anyone who rates the performance of another person brings with them a unique rating bias. For example, many managers will admit to being tough raters, which means they are less likely to give the highest rating for any reason. Others only use the middle of the rating range. Still others assume that once an employee has accomplished one assignment successfully, that employee will accomplish all other assignments successfully. Rating bias is most damaging when only one rater, usually the immediate manager, is allowed to rate the performance of an employee. But having a large number of people evaluate one person's performance mitigates the biases and provides a more realistic and accurate view of that person's performance.

- Multiple uses. When group data are obtained and aggregated, managers often find that 360° feedback/assessment programs provide them with additional information about individual, team, and departmental performance that can be used for selection, deployment, compensation, training needs analysis, customer satisfaction, and process improvement.

Information-Gathering Methods for 360° Feedback/Assessment

Methods for gathering information for 360° feedback/assessment include interviews, open-ended questions, focus groups, checklists, scaled and rated questionnaires, surveys, and performance-appraisal forms designed for use by peers, subordinates, superiors, and customers: These methods fall into two broad categories (See Table 8.1).

- Qualitative methods. Qualitative methods of assessment and feedback include face-to-face interviews, focus groups, Nominal Group Technique, and structured interviews. These methods, especially when they are structured (that is, ask the same questions with every interviewee), provide rich and deep feedback. The only major drawback with interview-based 360° assessment/feedback is that the results are difficult to aggregate when management wants to look across more than one department or organization.

- Quantitative methods. Questionnaires are the most prevalent quantitative methods used in 360°. Questionnaires ensure that the same questions are asked about everyone, they are quick to complete, and the data can be statistically analyzed, making cross-department and organi-

Table 8.1
Comparison of Qualitative and Quantative Methods of 360°
Feedback/Assessment

	Pros	Cons
Qualitative Methods	- Rich, deep information - Pin-point specific performance information	- Time consuming
Quantitative Methods	- Quick and easy to complete - Cross-organizational analysis	- Superficial information that may require further follow-up

zational comparisons possible. Further, developers and users alike appear to be more comfortable with attaching numbers to assessment/feedback, but there is little or no evidence that the quantitative techniques are any more efficacious than qualitative techniques.

If you choose to use quantitative techniques, make sure that you provide space for written comments at the end of each section and at the end of the questionnaire. You will quickly learn that written comments are the single best source of performance information available to you and the employee.

Content

The content of any 360° assessment/feedback instrument should accurately detail the behaviors the company wants its managers and employees to demonstrate. In short, you will get what you measure! This often means that the content for managers will be different from that of employees.

- Competencies. Competencies are broadly defined categories of performance such as leadership, team building, and communication broken down into specific examples. Many companies use a standard set of competencies for all managers and employees. Other companies use a standard set of competencies but define them differently for managers and employees.
- Job-level content. Performance information is often gathered at a specific job level, providing a comprehensive view of individual performance. Increasingly, evidence suggests that the more job-specific the content, the more meaningful it will be to users, and the more likely the users will incorporate the findings into an action plan.

Table 8.2

Comparison of Level of Analysis in 360° Feedback/Assessment

	Pros	Cons
Competencies	- Communicates a standard set of behavior - Reduces overall cost of data gathering techniques - Cross-organizational analysis	- Less likely they will be accepted as meaningful at all levels of company
Job-Level Specific	- Greater buy-in - Greater acceptance of results - Greater likelihood results will be incorporated into an action plan	- More cost in the development of data-gathering techniques - More analysis costs

Implementation Issues

If the 360° feedback/assessment is to prove beneficial to the individual and the organization, a number of issues need to be considered and resolved prior to and during implementation. If handled improperly, these issues could have legal repercussions for the company and could have a negative impact on motivation and performance. Some of the key issues to consider:

- Why do you want to introduce 360° feedback? Before introducing a feedback tool of this kind, it is important to figure out why you want to use it. Here are some typical questions to think about. Is the organization going through change? What type of change? Can a 360° instrument be used in the change and, if so, how and who can it help? How much time will be needed to develop the instrument and tailor it to the needs of the organization? With which group of people will the instrument be used (executives, managers, teams) and why?
- How will the information be used? Information is generally used for personal development in the current job or to prepare for advancement or new assignments or other developmental assessment to make personnel decisions such as salary increases, bonuses, or promotions. In development, the results should be given to the individual. To help analyze and interpret the results, we recommend that a person experienced in feedback should work with the individual. If you are planning

to use the information for assessment,* there are some additional concerns. The first administration of the assessment instrument should be used for developmental purposes only because the individual must be given an opportunity to practice new performance expectations. Also, because of the legal issues surrounding 360° assessment/feedback, the program should be subjected to reliability and validity studies to determine its correlation with success.

Case law regarding 360° assessment and feedback is still in its infancy and very unsettled. However, courts and jurists have made it reasonably clear that as long as 360° is used for personal development, improving personal skills such as interpersonal communication and coaching, they usually side with the company. When 360° is used for assessment, that is, hiring, firing, transferring, or promoting, then 360° is held to the same standards used in testing: reliability and validity must be established.

• Who will be included in the feedback? The first consideration is to determine at which level performance information is most needed. Leadership and managerial feedback participants are chosen based on their specific needs and the needs of the unit. Individual performance feedback typically includes everyone in a department or on a team.

• Who will conduct the feedback? It is very important to have a person trained in providing feedback.

• How will the data be processed? Plans must be developed to gather data, collate it, calculate ratings, and generate reports. These tasks can be automated to some extent, but any 360° feedback/assessment program can be labor intensive.

• At what level will the process begin? When organizations are promoting cultural change, the process typically begins with the senior management team.

• Post-evaluation help. Organizations must have funds to pay for training, facilitators, and individual counseling for individuals who have been identified as needing help. Corrective action is absolutely essential for individuals that receive assessment. While the number of individuals who have this experience is small, the consequences can be very painful for the individual and the organization. Giving an individual a negative assessment without giving them the resources to address

---

*Most vendors adamantly refuse to allow their programs or instruments to be used as an assessment technique.

the problems will almost always guarantee resentment on their part. This resentment may be used to discredit the program. Further, if the assessment is used to terminate the individual without remedial help, that person may decide to take legal action.

- The validity of commercial instruments. If vendor instruments are used to make personnel decisions, it is advisable to conduct a validity study. Many vendors have conducted validity studies, but three problems are associated with these. First, the sample size is typically too small and, therefore, extrapolating results to the general population is questionable. Second, most vendor validity studies only report those items or blocks of items that have predicted success on the job (promotions, compensation, performance ratings). Third, in many vendor validity studies the items that are good predictors of success are items usually associated with a traditional model of managerial behavior; therefore, if you are trying to move your company away from traditional management behaviors, using an instrument based on traditional management behavior will not get you where you want to go.

  Our advice would be to design an instrument in-house, with the help of a consultant or vendor, that measures the kinds of behavior your organization wants as part of their business strategy.

- Costs. 360° feedback/assessment programs are expensive to implement. The least expensive parts of the program are designing the instrument and analyzing the results.

Some War Stories

The Good. Many consulting firms use what they call multi-rater performance-appraisal systems, another name for 360° feedback/assessment. The results are used for both development and assessment purposes. In such cases employees ask their clients, managers, subordinates, and peers to provide feedback on standardized forms about their performance. The forms contain both rating scales and areas for comments. The data are gathered and tabulated. Almost always, more evaluations are obtained from clients and fewer from co-workers, and the ratings are weighted accordingly. This makes sense, given the fact that most consulting firms earn fees from clients, and client service is of prime importance. This very broad and deep evaluation system gives management, and the individual, a very accurate picture of the individual's performance.

The Bad. Often, when a new tool comes into existence, everyone rushes to use it. In one such case, a well-meaning manager thought that using a

360° feedback/assessment was just what his department needed. As an experiment, he decided that two of his four teams should evaluate their respective individual members. The results would be used to make personnel decisions. Sounds good so far, but this decision was made in late November with personnel decisions due in December. This case was primed for litigation! Why?

First, the manager did not communicate performance criteria to be used in the assessment. Second, team members did not have a chance to practice the desired behaviors. Third, he did not conduct the program with all teams, which could have left him open to charges of unequal treatment, especially if teams in the 360° feedback/assessment program received more positive rewards as a result of the evaluation. Fourth, he did not set up a post-assessment program to help those that needed help. Fifth, the manager had no way of knowing whether or not the content used to make the assessment sufficiently covered the work being done by the employees.

360° Feedback/Assessment and Case Law

The case law for 360° feedback/assessment is not yet firmly established. The courts have *generally* said that any reasonable construct (such as, leadership, teamwork, communication) will do as long as it is only used for personal development. If 360° feedback/assessment is used for assessment, it must be task or behavior based.

Summary

In summary, 360° feedback/assessment can be a powerful tool in the search for improved performance, but it does have costs, risks, and consequences. 360° feedback/assessment only begins with the development or purchasing of the questionnaire. The real challenge, both economic and psychological, is how the results of the program are handled after the data have been collected.

Team Leader Feedback Questionnaire

The purpose of this questionnaire is to provide the team leader with feedback about his or her performance. Each section of the questionnaire captures some specific information about linkage and alignment, individual performance goals, team performance goals, commitment, and feedback and coaching.

Directions: Please circle the appropriate answer, using the following scale:

VMS = Very much so, FTM = For the most part, SW = Somewhat, OS = Only slightly, NAA = Not at all, DNA = Does not apply, No opinion

Linkage and Alignment:

1. The team leader ensured that the goals of the work unit are aligned with the strategic goals of the firm.
   VMS   **FTM**   **SW**   **OS**   **NAA**   **DNA**
2. The team leader communicated the company goals for a given operating period.
   VMS   **FTM**   **SW**   **OS**   **NAA**   **DNA**
3. The team leader communicated and reinforced company mission.
   VMS   **FTM**   **SW**   **OS**   **NAA**   **DNA**
4. The team leader set specific work-unit standards linked with strategic goals.
   VMS   **FTM**   **SW**   **OS**   **NAA**   **DNA**
5. The team leader provided an understanding of how work is linked with strategic goals.
   VMS   **FTM**   **SW**   **OS**   **NAA**   **DNA**

Comments:

Individual Performance Goals:

6. The team leader developed performance goals with employees.
   VMS   **FTM**   **SW**   **OS**   **NAA**   **DNA**
7. The team leader determined the priority of performance measures with employees.
   VMS   **FTM**   **SW**   **OS**   **NAA**   **DNA**
8. The team leader made assignments based on individual skills.
   VMS   **FTM**   **SW**   **OS**   **NAA**   **DNA**

9. The team leader explained facts affecting the individual's appraisal.
   VMS   **FTM**   **SW**   **OS**   **NAA**   **DNA**

10. The team leader set clear-cut performance measures for each project.
    VMS   **FTM**   **SW**   **OS**   **NAA**   **DNA**

Comments:

Work-Group Performance Measures:

11. The team leader developed performance measures to evaluate work-group projects.
    VMS   **FTM**   **SW**   **OS**   **NAA**   **DNA**

12. The team leader communicated performance measures to the work group.
    VMS   **FTM**   **SW**   **OS**   **NAA**   **DNA**

13. The team leader encouraged frank and open exchanges of ideas.
    VMS   **FTM**   **SW**   **OS**   **NAA**   **DNA**

14. The team leader determined if the work group had clear understanding of responsibilities.
    VMS   **FTM**   **SW**   **OS**   **NAA**   **DNA**

15. The team leader made clear-cut, expedient decisions when necessary.
    VMS   **FTM**   **SW**   **OS**   **NAA**   **DNA**

Comments:

Gaining Commitment:

16. The team leader communicated high personal standards to all personnel.
    VMS   **FTM**   **SW**   **OS**   **NAA**   **DNA**

17. The team leader demonstrated strong commitment to achieving unit objectives.
    VMS   **FTM**   **SW**   **OS**   **NAA**   **DNA**

18. The team leader allowed team members to participate in setting deadlines for projects.
    VMS   **FTM**   **SW**   **OS**   **NAA**   **DNA**

19. The team leader developed good relationships with subordinates.
    VMS   **FTM**   **SW**   **OS**   **NAA**   **DNA**

20. The team leader encouraged candor without fear of repercussions.
    VMS   **FTM**   **SW**   **OS**   **NAA**   **DNA**

21. The team leader showed concern for work-group morale.
    VMS   **FTM**   **SW**   **OS**   **NAA**   **DNA**

22. The team leader emphasized team work as opposed to individual competi-
tiveness.
VMS   **FTM**   **SW**   **OS**   **NAA**   **DNA**
23. The team leader made efforts to resolve conflicts with the individual
involved.
VMS   **FTM**   **SW**   **OS**   **NAA**   **DNA**

Comments:

Feedback and Coaching:

24. The team leader conscientiously provided timely feedback to individuals.
VMS   **FTM**   **SW**   **OS**   **NAA**   **DNA**
25. The team leader developed specific plans to improve individual performance.
VMS   **FTM**   **SW**   **OS**   **NAA**   **DNA**
26. The team leader helped team members determine realistic career objectives.
VM3   **FTM**   **3W**   **O3**   **NAA**   **DNA**
27. The team leader recognized and praised good performance.
VMS   **FTM**   **SW**   **OS**   **NAA**   **DNA**
28. The team leader went to bat for individuals with superiors/clients.
VMS   **FTM**   **SW**   **OS**   **NAA**   **DNA**
29. The team leader encouraged the team when they made extra effort.
VMS   **FTM**   **SW**   **OS**   **NAA**   **DNA**
30. The team leader used positive reinforcement more than negative reinforcement.
VMS   **FTM**   **SW**   **OS**   **NAA**   **DNA**
31. The team leader ensured that formal appraisals were consistent with feedback.
VMS   **FTM**   **SW**   **OS**   **NAA**   **DNA**
32. The team leader provided economic or other incentives whenever possible.
VMS   **FTM**   **SW**   **OS**   **NAA**   **DNA**

Comments:

Additional Comments for the Team Leader:

Please Return to: _____

360° Team Member Feedback Questionnaire

Requested by: _____ Department: _____

The purpose of this survey is to provide the person identified above with candid feedback concerning how frequently they perform the behaviors listed below. Please take the time to complete the comments section. It is very important that you provide written comments because these explain the reasons for your assessment. To ensure anonymity, all written comments should be typed.

Please check (√) the category that best fits your relationship with the person requesting that you complete this survey.

Manager ____ Peer ____ Subordinate ____ Team member ____ Customer ____ Other ____

Directions: Please circle the appropriate answer, using the following scale:

VMS = Very much so, FTM = For the most part, SW = Somewhat, OS = Only slightly, NAA = Not at all, DNA = Does not apply, No opinion

Planning:

    1. Helps determine customer wants and needs.
       VMS   **FTM**   **SW**   **OS**   **NAA**   **DNA**
    2. Understands link between customer wants and business plan objectives.
       VMS   **FTM**   **SW**   **OS**   **NAA**   **DNA**
    3. Negotiates customer- and productivity-focused performance measures.
       VMS   **FTM**   **SW**   **OS**   **NAA**   **DNA**
    4. Negotiates which performance data sources will be used for performance measures.
       VMS   **FTM**   **SW**   **OS**   **NAA**   **DNA**

Comments:

Productivity:

5. Actively participates in process analysis for productivity improvment.
VMS   FTM   SW   OS   NAA   DNA

6. Provides suggestions to eliminate, simplify, or automate processes.
VMS   FTM   SW   OS   NAA   DNA

7. Seeks out new resources regarding equipment or methods of production.
VMS   FTM   SW   OS   NAA   DNA

8. Balances customer wants and productivity improvement with business objectives.
VMS   FTM   SW   OS   NAA   DNA

9. Meets minimum production standards.
VMS   FTM   SW   OS   NAA   DNA

Comments:

Feedback:

10. Provides informal feedback of performance to team members.
VMS   FTM   SW   OS   NAA   DNA

11. Provides nonjudgmental, behavioral descriptions of others' performance.
VMS   FTM   SW   OS   NAA   DNA

12. Suggests ways to realign individual/team performance with business plan.
VMS   FTM   SW   OS   NAA   DNA

13. Encourages candor within the team.
VMS   FTM   SW   OS   NAA   DNA

14. Recognizes and praises good performance.
VMS   FTM   SW   OS   NAA   DNA

Comments:

Assessment:

15. Collects assessment information from a variety of sources, including customers, team members, and managers.
VMS   FTM   SW   OS   NAA   DNA

16. Ensures that formal assessment is consistent with informal assessment.
VMS   FTM   SW   OS   NAA   DNA

17. Fairly assesses achievement of business plan objectives against performance measures.
VMS   FTM   SW   OS   NAA   DNA

18. Encourages frank and open exchanges of different views of performance.
VMS   FTM   SW   OS   NAA   DNA

19. Ensures there is a clear understanding of roles and responsibilities.
    VMS   **FTM**   **SW**   **OS**   **NAA**   **DNA**
20. Negotiates new performance measures if needed.
    VMS   **FTM**   **SW**   **OS**   **NAA**   **DNA**

Comments:

Development:

21. Develops specific plans to improve performance.
    VMS   **FTM**   **SW**   **OS**   **NAA**   **DNA**
22. Determines realistic career objectives.
    VMS   **FTM**   **SW**   **OS**   **NAA**   **DNA**
23. Provides/seeks increasingly more difficult assignments and exposure.
    VMS   **FTM**   **SW**   **OS**   **NAA**   **DNA**
24. Balances education and training needs with business needs.
    VMS   **FTM**   **SW**   **OS**   **NAA**   **DNA**

Comments:

Intra-Team Activities:

25. Seeks to learn all tasks the team is responsible for performing.
    VMS   **FTM**   **SW**   **OS**   **NAA**   **DNA**
26. Contributes to team meetings.
    VMS   **FTM**   **SW**   **OS**   **NAA**   **DNA**
27. Cooperates readily with all team members.
    VMS   **FTM**   **SW**   **OS**   **NAA**   **DNA**
28. Actively implements other team members' ideas once accepted by team.
    VMS   **FTM**   **SW**   **OS**   **NAA**   **DNA**

Comments:

What is the single most important thing this team member needs to do to improve his or her individual performance?

Please Return to: _____

360° Feedback Form

I have provided you with consulting services during the recent performance year. Trying to practice what I preach, below you will find a 360° feedback form. Please complete and return the form to me. If you choose to remain anonymous, send the completed form to your human resource consultant. Lucia will collect the data and type any comments before presenting the information to me. Please complete only those sections that apply to your business.

Directions: Please circle the appropriate answer, using the following scale:

VMS = Very much so, FTM = For the most part, SW = Somewhat, OS = Only slightly, NAA = Not at all, DNA = Does not apply, No opinion

1. Business analysis:
   Discussed, analyzed, and understood business issues facing the SBU/ department.

   | VMS | FTM | SW | OS | NAA | DNA |

Comments:

2. Solutions:
   Alternative solutions were offered, discussed, and evaluated.

   | VMS | FTM | SW | OS | NAA | DNA |

Comments:

3. Cost of implementation:
   Costs were discussed and estimated? Were the estimates accurate?

   | VMS | FTM | SW | OS | NAA | DNA |

Comments:

4. Written documentation:
Written documentation was clear, concise, and increased your understanding.
VMS　　　**FTM**　　　**SW**　　　**OS**　　　**NAA**　　　**DNA**

Comments:

5. Oral communication:
Oral communication was clear, concise, and increased your understanding.
VMS　　　**FTM**　　　**SW**　　　**OS**　　　**NAA**　　　**DNA**

Comments:

6. Project specifications:
Specifications for products and services were determined prior to their production/provision.
VMS　　　**FTM**　　　**SW**　　　**OS**　　　**NAA**　　　**DNA**

Comments:

7. Timeliness:
Milestones were delivered on due dates.
VMS　　　**FTM**　　　**SW**　　　**OS**　　　**NAA**　　　**DNA**

Comments:

8. Quality of the deliverables:
Deliverables met product (or service) specifications.
VMS　　　**FTM**　　　**SW**　　　**OS**　　　**NAA**　　　**DNA**

Comments:

9. Project status:
You were kept informed about project status throughout the project.
VMS   **FTM**   **SW**   **OS**   **NAA**   **DNA**

Comments:

10. Business and technical knowledge:
Knowledge and understanding about your business was exhibited.
VMS   **FTM**   **SW**   **OS**   **NAA**   **DNA**

Comments:

11. Use Again:
Would you use my services again?
VMS   **FTM**   **SW**   **OS**   **NAA**   **DNA**

Comments:

Additional Comments:

Please Return to: _____

Post-Project Team Evaluation

The purpose of this survey is to provide the team with an aggregated analysis of how well the team performed based on a set of variables identified from past research. Please take the time to fill out the ratings and complete the comments section. It is very important that you provide written comments because these comments explain the reasons for your rating. Please check (√) the category that best fits your relationship with the person requesting that you complete this survey.

Team Leader _____ Team coordinator _____ Content expert _____ Team support _____

Directions: Please circle the appropriate answer, using the following scale:

VMS = Very much so, FTM = For the most part, SW = Somewhat, OS = Only slightly, NAA = Not at all, DNA = Does not apply, No opinion

Sponsor Support:

1. How would you rate the amount of time the sponsor spent with the team?
   VMS   **FTM**   **SW**   **OS**   **NAA**   **DNA**
2. Did the sponsor actively listen to team members' suggestions and ideas?
   VMS   **FTM**   **SW**   **OS**   **NAA**   **DNA**
3. Did the sponsor provide resources when they were needed?
   VMS   **FTM**   **SW**   **OS**   **NAA**   **DNA**
4. This team sponsor provided more support than other team sponsors in the past.
   VMS   **FTM**   **SW**   **OS**   **NAA**   **DNA**

Comments about sponsor support:

Team Management:

1. a. Did the team manager spend adequate time with the team?
   VMS   **FTM**   **SW**   **OS**   **NAA**   **DNA**
   b. Was the the degree of management the team manager supplied during the project adequate?
   VMS   **FTM**   **SW**   **OS**   **NAA**   **DNA**
2. Did the team manager actively listen to team member suggestions and ideas?
   VMS   **FTM**   **SW**   **OS**   **NAA**   **DNA**
3. a. Did the manager get you the resources you needed when you needed them?
   VMS   **FTM**   **SW**   **OS**   **NAA**   **DNA**

b. Did the team manager keep focused and aligned with the project plan?

VMS   **FTM**   **SW**   **OS**   **NAA**   **DNA**

c. Did the team manager control boundary crossings?

VMS   **FTM**   **SW**   **OS**   **NAA**   **DNA**

4. This team sponsor provided more support than other team sponsors in the past.

VMS   **FTM**   **SW**   **OS**   **NAA**   **DNA**

Comments about team management:

Conceptual Design Team:

1. a. Did the conceptual design team present their vision, mission, and ideas about product specification prior to the start of the team?

VMS   **FTM**   **SW**   **OS**   **NAA**   **DNA**

b. How close did the final product come to matching conceptual design team model?

VMS   **FTM**   **SW**   **OS**   **NAA**   **DNA**

Comments about the conceptual design team:

Team Building:

1. a. How would you rate the team-building activities conducted prior to the start of the team?

VMS   **FTM**   **SW**   **OS**   **NAA**   **DNA**

b. How would you rate the trust among team members?

VMS   **FTM**   **SW**   **OS**   **NAA**   **DNA**

What sort of team building activities do you think would be appropriate or would create better bonds between team members?

_____

_____

Project Plan:

1. Was on-line documentation used during the project?
   VMS   **FTM**   **SW**   **OS**   **NAA**   **DNA**
2. Were customer requirements used to guide the development of the products or services?
   VMS   **FTM**   **SW**   **OS**   **NAA**   **DNA**
3. Was the mission used to guide the development of the products or services?
   VMS   **FTM**   **SW**   **OS**   **NAA**   **DNA**
4. Were product or service specifications used to guide the development of the products and services?
   VMS   **FTM**   **SW**   **OS**   **NAA**   **DNA**
5. Were milestones and due dates met as outlined in the project plan?
   VMS   **FTM**   **SW**   **OS**   **NAA**   **DNA**
6. Were JIT reviews conducted for each subcomponent?
   VMS   **FTM**   **SW**   **OS**   **NAA**   **DNA**
7. a. Were team members scheduled and dedicated to this project?
   VMS   **FTM**   **SW**   **OS**   **NAA**   **DNA**
   b. Were scheduled and dedicated team members available as scheduled?
   VMS   **FTM**   **SW**   **OS**   **NAA**   **DNA**
8. a. Were roles and responsibilities defined before the beginning of the project?
   VMS   **FTM**   **SW**   **OS**   **NAA**   **DNA**
   b. Were roles and responsibilities revised during the project as needed?
   VMS   **FTM**   **SW**   **OS**   **NAA**   **DNA**
9. Were planned and estimated hours compared against actual hours for each team member?
   VMS   **FTM**   **SW**   **OS**   **NAA**   **DNA**
10. Were planned subcomponent costs and actual costs compared at the end of the project?
    VMS   **FTM**   **SW**   **OS**   **NAA**   **DNA**
11. Was the team's span of control defined and reinforced during the project?
    VMS   **FTM**   **SW**   **OS**   **NAA**   **DNA**
12. Were performance measures developed as part of the project plan?
    VMS   **FTM**   **SW**   **OS**   **NAA**   **DNA**
13. Has customer feedback been collected and compared to product specifications?
    VMS   **FTM**   **SW**   **OS**   **NAA**   **DNA**
14. Was a process map developed for how work would flow through the team?
    VMS   **FTM**   **SW**   **OS**   **NAA**   **DNA**

Comments about project planning:

Physical Work Evironment:

1. Team members were in close, physical proximity of each other.
   VMS   **FTM**   **SW**   **OS**   **NAA**   **DNA**
2. The team had all the resources required to perform their tasks.
   VMS   **FTM**   **SW**   **OS**   **NAA**   **DNA**
3. A conference room was provided so that team meetings would not be interrupted.
   VMS   **FTM**   **SW**   **OS**   **NAA**   **DNA**
4. Boundary crossings were kept to a minimum.
   VMS   **FTM**   **SW**   **OS**   **NAA**   **DNA**
5. The sponsor provided written and vocal support for the team.
   VMS   **FTM**   **SW**   **OS**   **NAA**   **DNA**
6. Team members were provided team training (how to work as a team) before the project began.
   VMS   **FTM**   **SW**   **OS**   **NAA**   **DNA**
7. Both individual and team rewards and recognition were provided for excellent performance.
   VMS   **FTM**   **SW**   **OS**   **NAA**   **DNA**
8. The team and its sponsor were debriefed at the end of the project.
   VMS   **FTM**   **SW**   **OS**   **NAA**   **DNA**

Comments about the physical work environment:

Please Return to: _____

Meeting Evaluation Questionnaire

Directions: Please circle the appropriate answer, using the following scale:

VMS = Very much so, FTM = For the most part, SW = Somewhat, OS = Only slightly, NAA = Not at all, DNA = Does not apply, No opinion

1. Agenda: Were the objectives, roles/responsibilities of participants, and outcomes of the meeting clearly communicated?
   VMS   **FTM**   **SW**   **OS**   **NAA**   **DNA**
2. Preparedness of the leader: Did leader utilize effective meeting management and team process tools/techniques?
   VMS   **FTM**   **SW**   **OS**   **NAA**   **DNA**
3. Preparedness of the participants: Did participants complete all pre-work, did they actively participate in the discussion?
   VMS   **FTM**   **SW**   **OS**   **NAA**   **DNA**
4. Punctuality: Did the meeting start and end on time?
   VMS   **FTM**   **SW**   **OS**   **NAA**   **DNA**
5. Focus: Did people adhere to the agenda topics?
   VMS   **FTM**   **SW**   **OS**   **NAA**   **DNA**
6. Management: Did the leader keep the meeting on track?
   VMS   **FTM**   **SW**   **OS**   **NAA**   **DNA**
7. Usefulness: Was the meeting useful in accomplishing something of value?
   VMS   **FTM**   **SW**   **OS**   **NAA**   **DNA**
8. Logistics: Was the meeting room large enough, quiet, and comfortably ventilated? Were the seating arrangements appropriate?
   VMS   **FTM**   **SW**   **OS**   **NAA**   **DNA**
9. Appropriateness: Was a meeting the most appropriate format for accomplishing the objective?
   VMS   **FTM**   **SW**   **OS**   **NAA**   **DNA**
10. Adequacy of resources: Were the appropriate resources (flipchart, overhead projector, personal computer, and so on) available to complete the task at hand?
   VMS   **FTM**   **SW**   **OS**   **NAA**   **DNA**
11. Action planning: Were commitments formalized and/or action plan developed to ensure all commitments would be completed on a quality and timely basis?
   VMS   **FTM**   **SW**   **OS**   **NAA**   **DNA**

Suggestions for improvement:

Please Return to: _____

Performance Management Questionnaire

Periodically we will be monitoring our progress. The purpose of this survey is to find out how we're doing as a department and determine how we can continue to improve. Answers are anonymous and confidential; summary results will be shared.

Directions: Please circle the appropriate answer, using the following scale:

VMS = Very much so, FTM = For the most part, SW = Somewhat, OS = Only slightly, NAA = Not at all, DNA = Does not apply, No opinion

Department Mission:

1. I know and understand our department's mission.
   VMS   **FTM**   **SW**   **OS**   **NAA**   **DNA**
2. I am clear on what my responsibilities are and how they contribute to meeting the department's mission.
   VMS   **FTM**   **SW**   **OS**   **NAA**   **DNA**
3. In my team, the department's mission is the focus by which goals and objectives are established and decisions are made.
   VMS   **FTM**   **SW**   **OS**   **NAA**   **DNA**

Comments:

Team Objectives:

4. The team's objectives are clearly defined and understood.
   VMS   **FTM**   **SW**   **OS**   **NAA**   **DNA**
5. The team has a clear understanding of how it will be measured and evaluated in achieving its objectives.
   VMS   **FTM**   **SW**   **OS**   **NAA**   **DNA**
6. Team objectives are reviewed regularly to ensure they are still appropriate.
   VMS   **FTM**   **SW**   **OS**   **NAA**   **DNA**
7. My team members cooperate to accomplish the team objectives.
   VMS   **FTM**   **SW**   **OS**   **NAA**   **DNA**

Comments:

Individual Objectives:

8. My individual objectives are clearly defined and I understand them.
   VMS   **FTM**   **SW**   **OS**   **NAA**   **DNA**

9. I have a clear understanding of how I will be measured and evaluated in achieving my individual objectives.
VMS   FTM   SW   OS   NAA   DNA

10. My individual objectives are reviewed regularly to ensure they are still appropriate.
VMS   FTM   SW   OS   NAA   DNA

11. I believe what I am doing adds value.
VMS   FTM   SW   OS   NAA   DNA

12. I understand the individual competencies that are required for my successful performance.
VMS   FTM   SW   OS   NAA   DNA

13. I take actions to ensure I meet customer requirements.
VMS   FTM   SW   OS   NAA   DNA

Comments:

Roles and Responsibilities:

14. Each team member's role and responsibilities are clearly defined and understood by all members.
VMS   FTM   SW   OS   NAA   DNA

15. Team members change their roles when it is required for the team to achieve its objectives.
VMS   FTM   SW   OS   NAA   DNA

16. Team members exhibit interdependency and collaboration rather than competition.
VMS   FTM   SW   OS   NAA   DNA

17. Team members have a clear understanding of each others' skills and expertise.
VMS   FTM   SW   OS   NAA   DNA

18. Team members are encouraged to seek out others' skills and expertise to answer questions, solve problems, train, and so on.
VMS   FTM   SW   OS   NAA   DNA

19. Team members seek information and support from other functional areas (such as, underwriting and research and product development) when needed to meet the team's objectives.
VMS   FTM   SW   OS   NAA   DNA

20. Team members are encouraged to initiate change when they see a better way to do things.
VMS   FTM   SW   OS   NAA   DNA

21. Team members feel that they have input on the changes occurring in the department.
VMS   FTM   SW   OS   NAA   DNA

22. My job responsibilities are what I thought they would be.

Comments:

Commitment of Members:

23. Team members have a strong sense of belonging to the team.
    VMS   **FTM**   **SW**   **OS**   **NAA**   **DNA**
24. Team members give and receive pertinent information from other team members needed to accomplish their work.
    VMS   **FTM**   **SW**   **OS**   **NAA**   **DNA**
25. Team members exhibit a healthy level of trust and openness.
    VMS   **FTM**   **SW**   **OS**   **NAA**   **DNA**
26. Team members have developed effective ways of working together and know how to use one another as resources.
    VMS   **FTM**   **SW**   **OS**   **NAA**   **DNA**
27. Team members reward/recognize personal achievements.
    VMS   **FTM**   **SW**   **OS**   **NAA**   **DNA**
28. Team members feel free to try new approaches without having their motives questioned.
    VMS   **FTM**   **SW**   **OS**   **NAA**   **DNA**
29. Team members work toward resolving work-related conflict.
    VMS   **FTM**   **SW**   **OS**   **NAA**   **DNA**
30. Team members function smoothly because we have rules of behavior that guide us in how we are to treat one another.
    VMS   **FTM**   **SW**   **OS**   **NAA**   **DNA**

Comments:

Leadership:

31. My team leader keeps us focused on our mission and objectives.
    VMS   **FTM**   **SW**   **OS**   **NAA**   **DNA**
32. My team leader discusses issues and gets facts and opinions before decisions are made or problems are solved.
    VMS   **FTM**   **SW**   **OS**   **NAA**   **DNA**
33. My team leader encourages initiative and welcomes leadership efforts by team members.
    VMS   **FTM**   **SW**   **OS**   **NAA**   **DNA**
34. My team leader is flexible and shifts style to address the needs of the situation and the people involved.
    VMS   **FTM**   **SW**   **OS**   **NAA**   **DNA**
35. My team leader provides ongoing, informal, and clear feedback on performance.
    VMS   **FTM**   **SW**   **OS**   **NAA**   **DNA**
36. My team leader encourages candor without fear of repercussions.
    VMS   **FTM**   **SW**   **OS**   **NAA**   **DNA**
37. My team leader recognizes and praises good performance.
    VMS   **FTM**   **SW**   **OS**   **NAA**   **DNA**

38. My team leader provides guidance in our efforts to solve business problems rather than solving the problems for us.
VMS   **FTM**   **SW**   **OS**   **NAA**   **DNA**
39. My team leader shares all pertinent information needed to perform our job.
VMS   **FTM**   **SW**   **OS**   **NAA**   **DNA**
40. My team leader gives us responsibility for implementing resolutions to business problems.
VMS   **FTM**   **SW**   **OS**   **NAA**   **DNA**
41. My team leader ensures that we come to agreement about how objectives are going to be accomplished and measured.
VMS   **FTM**   **SW**   **OS**   **NAA**   **DNA**
42. My team leader links bonuses and other awards to our performance.
VMS   **FTM**   **SW**   **OS**   **NAA**   **DNA**
43. My team leader is open to feedback on his or her own performance.
VMS   **FTM**   **SW**   **OS**   **NAA**   **DNA**
44. My team leader encourages us to challenge the status quo.
VMS   **FTM**   **SW**   **OS**   **NAA**   **DNA**
45. My team leader is open to new ideas and ways of doing things.
VMS   **FTM**   **SW**   **OS**   **NAA**   **DNA**

Comments:

Group Processing:

46. All team members consider planning essential activity.
VMS   **FTM**   **SW**   **OS**   **NAA**   **DNA**
47. All team members participate in the planning process.
VMS   **FTM**   **SW**   **OS**   **NAA**   **DNA**
48. The time spent in meetings is used *effectively* in addressing business issues, solving problems, and building commitment.
VMS   **FTM**   **SW**   **OS**   **NAA**   **DNA**
49. All members' ideas and opinions are solicited, listened to, and valued.
VMS   **FTM**   **SW**   **OS**   **NAA**   **DNA**
50. When suggestions for changes are made or new ideas presented, team members are supportive.
VMS   **FTM**   **SW**   **OS**   **NAA**   **DNA**
51. Team members exhibit clear understanding of how we approach problem solving as a group.
VMS   **FTM**   **SW**   **OS**   **NAA**   **DNA**
52. Team members spend time planning before they act; they know what will be done, who will do it, and by when.
VMS   **FTM**   **SW**   **OS**   **NAA**   **DNA**
53. Team members are skilled at diagnosing and working on business problems.
VMS   **FTM**   **SW**   **OS**   **NAA**   **DNA**

Comments:

Overall perception:

54. Employees work across teams and cooperate to accomplish overall objectives.
    VMS   FTM   SW   OS   NAA   DNA
55. Employees produce quality products and services.
    VMS   FTM   SW   OS   NAA   DNA
56. Employees' products and services meet customer requirements.
    VMS   FTM   SW   OS   NAA   DNA
49. All members' ideas and opinions are solicited, listened to, and valued.
    VMS   FTM   SW   OS   NAA   DNA
57. Employees add value to this company.
    VMS   FTM   SW   OS   NAA   DNA
58. Team members respect the current management team (dept. head, team leaders, team heads).
    VMS   FTM   SW   OS   NAA   DNA
59. Team members communicate effectively within this unit.
    VMS   FTM   SW   OS   NAA   DNA
60. Cooperation and teamwork are encouraged in this unit.
    VMS   FTM   SW   OS   NAA   DNA

Provide your overall perception (strengths and weaknesses) of this department/team.

_____

_____

Please Return to: _____

Feedback to the Consultant

Purpose. The purpose of this questionnaire is to provide me feedback about my performance. This information will by used be me to improve the consulting skills I bring to you.

Directions: Please circle the appropriate answer, using the following scale:

VMS = Very much so, FTM = For the most part, SW = Somewhat, OS = Only slightly, NAA = Not at all, DNA = Does not apply, No opinion

1. Did this consultant meet your expectations in setting strategy?
   VMS   **FTM**   **SW**   **OS**   **NAA**   **DNA**

Comments:

2. Did this consultant meet your expectations in managing customers?
   VMS   **FTM**   **SW**   **OS**   **NAA**   **DNA**

Comments:

3. Did this consultant meet your expectations in managing culture?
   VMS   **FTM**   **SW**   **OS**   **NAA**   **DNA**

Comments:

4. Did this consultant meet your expectations in designing organizational structures?
   VMS   **FTM**   **SW**   **OS**   **NAA**   **DNA**

Comments:

5. Did this consultant meet your expectations in managing business systems?
   VMS   **FTM**   **SW**   **OS**   **NAA**   **DNA**

Comments:

6. Did this consultant meet your expectations in designing management information systems?
   VMS   **FTM**   **SW**   **OS**   **NAA**   **DNA**

Comments:

7. Did this consultant meet your expectations in designing and managing the infrastructure?
   VMS   **FTM**   **SW**   **OS**   **NAA**   **DNA**

Comments:

8. Did this consultant meet your expectations in creating and managing organizational capacity?
   VMS   **FTM**   **SW**   **OS**   **NAA**   **DNA**

Comments:

9. Did this consultant meet your expectations in building teamwork and instilling cooperation?

VMS   **FTM**   **SW**   **OS**   **NAA**   **DNA**

Comments:

10. Did this consultant meet your expectations in developing individual capacity?

VMS   **FTM**   **SW**   **OS**   **NAA**   **DNA**

Comments:

Please Return to: _____

Team Readiness Questionnaire

The following questionnaire is used to determine whether or not an organization is ready to implement teams. Please respond **Yes, No,** or **Don't Know** to each of the following questions. Also, please take the time to offer written comments—they will help us interpret your ratings.

Strategy

Teams should be part of a business strategy and part of a business plan. Below are questions that examine the link between teams and the business strategy.

1. Are the following performance-measurement categories addressed and implemented in the business strategy?
   _____Customer acquisition and satisfaction
   _____Productivity improvement
   _____Cash-flow improvement
   _____Human resource management
   _____Head count reduction
   _____Removal of layers of management
   _____All of the above
2. Are the following questions addressed and used in the business plan?
   _____Who is the customer?
   _____What are their requirements?
   _____What are the performance measures that are linked to customer requirements?
   _____What are the performance measures that are linked to customer encounters?
3. Will the designing and implementation of teams have an impact on the support of other ongoing operations and initiatives such as:
   _____Re-engineering
   _____Reorganization
   _____Compensation
4. Will the following issues have driven this organization to discuss the implementation of teams? Check all that apply.
   _____Re-engineering
   _____Reorganization
   _____Compensation
   _____A need for increased productivity
   _____A need for customer satisfaction and retention

_____A need to reduce the number of layers between the CEO and the floor

_____A substantial increase in cash flow

_____The overwhelming success other companies have had with teams

Comment on specific strategic issues that could have an impact on the successful implementation of teams?

Culture

One of the biggest barriers to the successful implementation of teams is the existing organizational culture. The following questions, answered honestly, will bring greater understanding about the potential effect organizational culture will have on teams.

5. Given 100% to divide the following styles of communication, what percentage would you assign to each?
   The total must add up to 100%
   _____% Upward communication
   _____% Downward communication
   _____% Horizontal communication
   100%
6. How would you characterize communication style within the organization?
   _____Is Communication frank and candid?
   _____Is Communication frequent?
   _____Is Communication honest?
   _____Is Communication filtered and devoid of hidden agendas?
   _____Can management be challenged from below?
7. How would you characterize status differences between managers and employees?
   _____Status differences are easily discernible.
   _____Status differences are part of the compensation package.
   _____Status differences are minimized.
8. Does management encourage
   _____Risk taking.
   _____Employee empowerment.
   _____Cross-functional operations.
   _____Innovation.

9. Pick the *one* statement that best describes how managers typically make decisions in your company.

_____Managers solve the problems themselves.

_____Managers obtain information from subordinates, and then make the decision.

_____Managers share the problem with subordinates, but solve the problem themselves.

_____Managers share the problem with the group, get the group's ideas, but make the decision themselves.

_____Managers share the problem with the group, and together the manager and group solve the problem.

10. How would you characterize cross-functional cooperation and reinforcement?

_____Does management encourage and reinforce cross-functional cooperation?

_____Do the unit heads encourage and reinforce cross-functional cooperation?

_____Do employees encourage and reinforce cross-functional cooperation?

What specific cultural issues could have an impact on the successful implementation of teams?

Business Systems

Business systems provide both direction and control of an organization.

11. How would you characterize the business planning process?

_____ Formal

_____ Informal

_____ Nonexistent

12. How would you characterize the links between the business plan and individual/team performance measures?

_____ Rolled down from the business plan.

_____ Rolled down from the department business plan.

_____ Indirect links to the business plan.

_____ No links to the business plan.

_____ There are no performance measures.

13. How would you characterize the systems for rewarding teamwork and cooperation for employees?
    _____ Compensation supports individual effort exclusively.
    _____ Compensation provides for team rewards.
    _____ Both.
14. How would you characterize the link between performance measures and pay-for-performance?
    _____ Linked to achieving the goals and objectives of the business plan.
    _____ Linked to achieving the goals and objectives of the department business plan.
    _____ Linked to achieving the goals and objectives of the team business plan.
15. Are there mechanisms to recognize employees for teamwork and cooperation?
    _____ Yes, and they are used.
    _____ Informally, some managers recognize teamwork and cooperation.
    _____ Scattered and inconsistent.
16. How would you characterize administration control policies?
    _____ Formal
    _____ Informal
    _____ Promote centralized decision making

What specific issues could have an impact on the successful implementation of teams?

Individual Capability

Individual capability addresses the ability of individual employees to work in a customer-focused team environment.

17. Are employees encouraged to make and maintain links with the following?
    _____ Customers (someone who purchases a product or service from outside the organization)
    _____ Sponsors (someone who provides the funds to support a project from within the organization)
    _____ Users (someone within the organization who uses the products or services)

18. How would you characterize employees' abilities in the following?
_____ Employees are capable of managing conflict.
_____ Employees are capable of managing interpersonal process.
_____ Employees are capable of managing team processes, such as developing norms and assigning tasks.
19. How would you characterize management's ability in the following?
_____ Managers are capable of managing conflict.
_____ Managers are capable of managing interpersonal process.
_____ Managers are capable of managing team processes, such as developing norms and assigning tasks.
20. How would you characterize employees' enthusiasm for increased involvement and participation?
_____ Employees are interested in new job challenges and the opportunity to learn different skills.
_____ Employees are interested in providing input in developing performance measures.
_____ Employees are interested in job rotation and cross-training.
21. How would you characterize management's relationship with employees?
_____ Management treats employees with respect.
_____ Management views employees as the organization's number one resource.
_____ Management actively supports the utilization of teams.

What specific individual capability issues could have an impact on the successful implementation of teams?

_____

_____

Organizational Capability

Organizational capability determines the degree to which an organization's management and training systems can support an initiative.

22. Characterize the organization's product and services. Choose one.
_____ Well-defined
_____ Loosely defined (such as in staff functions)
_____ Depends on which business unit
23. Team training (developing business plans, managing processes, process mapping, performance measures, and so on) has been provided. Choose all that apply.
_____ To upper management
_____ To middle management
_____ To supervisors
_____ Some combination of the above

_____ To all employees
24. Do teams support the core competencies of the organization? Choose one.
_____ Yes
_____ To a greater degree rather than a lesser degree
_____ To a lesser degree rather than a greater degree
25. Do you have the human resources, time, and capital to fund the following:
_____ Team training
_____ Redundant business systems
_____ New technology
_____ Redesign of infrastructure

What specific organizational capability issues could have an impact on the successful implementation of teams?

_____

_____

Information System

The information system involves the technology employees use and its impact on their ability to function.

26. Employees have access to the information they need.
_____ Yes
_____ Only what management thinks they need
_____ On a need-to-know basis
_____ None
27. Are the right platforms in place?
_____ Yes
_____ No
28. Are the right applications in place?
_____ Yes
_____ No
29. The existing information system
_____ Provides timely and accurate data.
_____ Is routinely updated.
_____ Crashes often.
30. The technology employees use allows them to have an impact on their performance.
_____ Yes
_____ To some extent, but the system drives the work.
_____ The technology dominates the work.

What specific information technology issues could have an impact on the successful implementation of teams?

_____

_____

Infrastructure

Infrastructure refers to the physical layout of buildings and offices, automation, transportation, and other forms of conveyance.

31. Evaluate the existing physical layout. Chose all that apply.
    ____ Space is readily adaptable.
    ____ Space is readily available.
    ____ Clear physical or technological boundaries can be established between work groups.
    ____ There is an adequate number of conference rooms for team meetings.
    ____ Technology and electrical systems are easily adapted to team needs.
32. How would you characterize the degree to which automation impacts work?
    ____ Little or no impact
    ____ Some impact
    ____ Machine-driven with parts being supplied
    ____ Fully automated

What specific infrastructure issues could have an impact on the successful implementation of teams?

_____

_____

Please describe, in your own words, why you think teams would increase the overall effectiveness of your company, what managerial and employee barriers need to be removed to ensure the success of teams, and your estimate of the likelihood that teams will be successful.

_____

_____

_____

_____

_____

_____

Your estimated likelihood that teams can be successfully implemented _____%:

CHAPTER 9

Team Effectiveness Interventions

Overview of Team Effectiveness Intervention

This matrix is a quick reference guide that can be used to select the most appropriate tool for a given purpose or application.

Tool	Purpose
1 Role Negotiation	To help team members and management identify unresolved issues and determine accountability.
2 Communication Maps	To identify patterns of communications within a team, locating possible communication bottlenecks.
3 Team Process Consultation	To resolve interpersonal conflict, improve communication, and develop problem-solving skills.
4 Team Building	To set goals, allocate work, examine team processes, and coordinate team activities.

(table continued on next page)

5 Coaching for Effective Performance	To provide informal feedback to team members and team management and to help all concerned maintain alignment with team goals.
6 Norms	To help the team decide, in advance, the way they will interact with one another on a day-in-day-out basis.
7 Guidelines for Meeting Management	To set up a meeting, determine its agenda, and develop action steps.

Role Negotiation

What Is It?

Role Negotiation is an exchange process that enables each team member to negotiate a change in the behavior of another team member. This technique involves a four-step process that leads to the creation of "negotiation contracts" that document changes agreed upon between both parties.

Why Use It?

Role Negotiation is primarily used to resolve conflicts pertaining to power, authority, and influence that often arise during the transition to a team environment. This type of intervention is appropriate when problems between team members can be attributed to an unwillingness to adjust behavior from a self-centered to a team-centered approach to business. Use Role Negotiation for the following:

• To reduce role ambiguity.
• To minimize conflict between team members.
• To enhance individual and team accountability.
• To improve group cohesiveness.
• To sustain mutually beneficial work relationships.

Steps

Role Negotiation is a first step in team transition and should not be used as the only method for team development. The following are general guidelines for the facilitator-aided intervention.

Step 1: Intervention Set-Up. During this step, the facilitator sets the climate and the ground rules for the intervention. These are the six key rules:

1. Participants must communicate openly and honestly.
2. Participants must be specific and concrete in expressing their expectations for others' behavior (that is, what they want others to do—more, less, or remain unchanged).
3. It is inappropriate to use the session to discuss personal feelings about teammates. The aim is to look at the mutual concerns about work behavior patterns.
4. The facilitator must ensure that team members are participating equally in the exchange process.
5. Expectations must be documented by both the receiver and the sender.
6. Role Negotiation is completed when agreements to change are clearly documented and acceptable to all parties.

Step 2: Issue Diagnosis. In this step, individual team members determine how their own effectiveness can be improved if others change their work behaviors. Each team member develops a list of things he or she would like each of the other team members to do:

- Do more of or do better (for example, increase frequency of candid feedback).
- Do less of or stop doing (for example, limit number of "progress checks" on subordinates to one per week).
- Continue doing (for example, continue providing monthly reports on status of projects).

Once this activity is completed, the lists are exchanged so that each team member has all of the lists that pertain to him or herself. From these lists, each team member creates a master list of requested behavior changes. Each master list is then divided into three categories for his or her own behavior modifications:

- Do more of or do better.
- Do less of or stop doing.
- Continue doing.

The facilitator writes each team members' name on the board and creates a chart listing the suggested behavior changes from each person's master list. (*Note: Questions at this stage are for clarification purposes only.*)

Step 3: Negotiation. The facilitator pairs off team members and instructs the individuals in each pair to discuss the most important behavior changes they want from each other and the changes they are willing to make in return. They both mark change requests on their own list and on their teammates' list so that the facilitator can help them identify the most negotiable issues. The pairs negotiate the list until each team member is satisfied that they will make changes in their own behavior and see behavior changes in the other team member. All agreements are formally documented, and penalties for nonfulfillment are discussed. The recorded agreements are known as "negotiation contracts." The facilitator must reinforce the importance of adhering to the negotiation contracts.

Step 4: Follow-Up Meeting. This meeting determines whether the negotiation contracts have been honored and assesses their effectiveness in solving the team's problem. If a lack of clarity still remains around roles, contracts can be renegotiated by repeating step 3 at this meeting.

Additional Information

Beckhard, Richard, "Optimizing Team-Building Efforts," *Journal of Contemporary Business,* Vol. 1, No. 3, Summer 1972.

Beckhard, Richard, and Reuben Harris. *Organizational Transitions: Managing Complex Change.* Reading, Mass.: Addison-Wesley, 1977.

French, Wedell, and Cecil, Bell. *Organizational Development.* Prentice-Hall, 1984.

Herman, Stanley, "A Gestalt Orientation to Organization Development" in *Contemporary Organization Development: Conceptual Orientations and Interventions.* Warner Burke (Ed.) Washington, D.C.: NTL Institute for Applied Behavioral Science, 1972.

Herman, Stanley, and Michael Korenich. *Authentic Management: A Gestalt Orientation to Organizations and their Development.* Reading, Mass.: Addison-Wesley, 1977.

Communication Maps

What Is It?

A Communication Map is a graphic representation of communication patterns within an organization. It provides insight into who communicates with whom, whether the communication is one-way or two-way, how important the communication is, and the frequency of the communication. A Communication Map can be developed for any size organization, but maps that show the communicaton at fewer than thirty people are the easiest to understand.

Why Use It?

The Communication Map will provide a simple and straightforward method of graphing the frequency and importance of communication within a defined group and can provide valuable insight into communication problems. A specific example would be as a follow-up to an employee survey. One of the most common findings in employee satisfaction surveys is that communication from management and across the organization is inconsistent or unreliable. Further, there is limited information about the frequency and importance of communication within an organization. The communication map can provide greater insight into this. Given the data from the map, adjustments can be made to improve the overall reliability and consistency of the information. A map can also pinpoint where communication bottlenecks occur and the degree to which each person has influence and control. For instance, there are times when excessive influence and control by the wrong person can have a negative impact on the organization and lead to decreased productivity. There can also be cases where there is a weak leader and the informal network of power that results within the organization may actually contribute to productivity.

How to Do It

1. **Develop a simple questionnaire** that asks each participant two questions. One is about the average frequency of the communication and the other is about its importance (that is, discussion, talking, advising, instructing). Be sure you define the rating scale for the group under review.

Directions: Please indicate, by circling the appropriate answer, the average frequency and level of importance of communication you have with each of the following individuals. Do not complete the row for yourself.

Dept.	First	Last	Frequency	Importance
0	Kathy	Miller	High Medium Low	High Medium Low
1	Joan	Reese	High Medium Low	High Medium Low
1	Bill	LaFond	High Medium Low	High Medium Low
1	Jill	Berggman	High Medium Low	High Medium Low
2	Bess	Eaton	High Medium Low	High Medium Low
2	Kathy	Molloy	High Medium Low	High Medium Low
3	Dan	Fuller	High Medium Low	High Medium Low
4	Bill	Jones	High Medium Low	High Medium Low
4	David	Wade	High Medium Low	High Medium Low
4	Roger	Smith	High Medium Low	High Medium Low

2. **Calculate average rating frequency and importance for each participant** (where high = 3, medium = 2, low = 1). In the example given, the average frequency of contact with Joan Reese, for those who completed the survey, is 1.9, while the importance is 2.4.

Dept	First	Last	Frequency	Importance	Total
0	Kathy	Miller	3.0	3.0	6.0
1	Joan	Reese	1.9	2.4	4.3
1	Bill	LaFond	1.6	2.7	4.3
1	Jill	Berggman	3.0	2.4	5.4
2	Bess	Eaton	1.7	2.6	4.3
2	Kathy	Molloy	2.9	2.8	5.7
3	Dan	Fuller	1.7	2.1	3.8
4	Bill	Jones	2.9	2.9	5.8
4	David	Wade	1.5	2.1	3.6
4	Roger	Smith	1.6	2.5	4.1

3. **Place the manager in the middle** of the "importance and frequency" grid. Add other participants based on their average importance and frequency ratings finding their location by using the importance and frequency axes of the grid (see Figure 9.1).

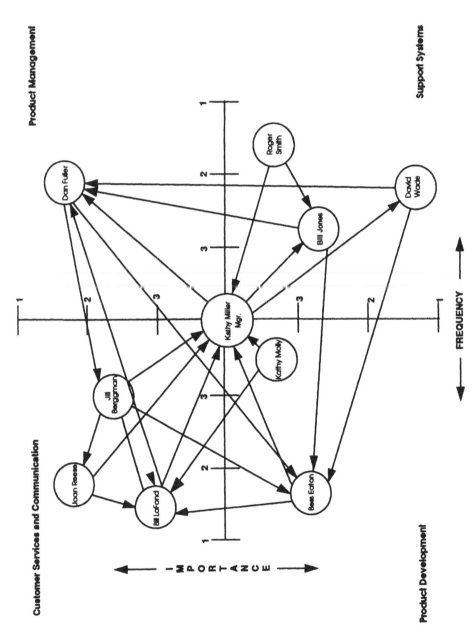

Figure 9.1. *Marketing department communication map.*

4. **Identify the top two most-frequent contacts** for each participant.

5. **Add direction arrows** for the top two most-frequent contacts for each participant.

6. **Analyze and interpret results.** The average ratings indicate that every one in this department has the most important and frequent contact with Kathy Miller (the manager). Bill Jones has the second highest ratings, but his most frequent contacts are with workers with relatively lower ratings. This could be an indication that Jones is taking up slack for the supervisor, acting as a bottleneck for some function, or acting as a mentor to these positions. Clarification is needed. Dan Fuller has the second highest contact rating in the department but one of the lowest importance ratings. The reasons for this need to be investigated as well.

7. Develop action plan.

Team Process Consultation

What Is It?

Process Consultation is an intervention to help diagnose problems and assist the team to resolve them. It typically aims to reduce interpersonal conflict, improve communication skills, develop problem-solving skills, and improve team effectiveness in the organization. This intervention requires significant team member involvement in the diagnosis and correction of group problems. These can relate to tasks the team is performing, the process by which it accomplishes the tasks, or interpersonal conflict between members. Typically, data are collected on the human interactions that occur within the team and are then communicated to group members, allowing time to discuss, diagnose, and solve team problems.

How to Do It

Four major steps precede feedback of information to the group. These steps are outlined below.

Step 1. Exploratory Meeting.

1. **Schedule a meeting with the team leader to:**
   a. Identify characteristics of the team (age, skill mix, sex, and so on).
   b. Identify problem areas and concerns (see Figure 9.2 for questions).
   c. Identify problem indicators.
   d. Assess the team leader's level of commitment. Determine the degree of openness, willingness, and authenticity of communication. If the team leader is not committed, reassess the appropriateness of this intervention.
   e. Identify a suitable approach for data collection.
2. **Meet with individual team members**
   Arrange to meet with each team member individually to establish trust and rapport. Identify the following:
   a. Attitudes regarding the current level of group functioning.
   b. How well their needs are being met by the current group interactions.
   c. Problem areas and indicators.

Figure 9.2.

Key Analysis Questions

1. Participation
   a. Who are the high and low participators?
   b. Is there any shift in participation among team members?
   c. Who talks to whom?
2. Influence
   a. Who are most and least influential?
   b. How do team members influence (through coercion, formal authority, coalitions) each other?
3. Decision making
   a. Who assumes leadership in the team?
   b. Is the leader appointed?
   c. Is there conflict over who the leader is and his or her preferred role?
   d. How are decisions made?
      (1) By formal authority?
      (2) By majority rule or voting?
      (3) By consensus?
      (4) By unanimous consent?
   e. Does anyone make contributions that are ignored?
4. Task and maintenance functions
   a. Does anyone ask for or make suggestions regarding the task the team is working on?
   b. Is there any giving or asking for additional facts, thoughts, opinions, or alternatives?
   c. Who helps or hinders team discussions?
5. Group atmosphere
   a. Are communications open and unfiltered?
   b. Do team members listen to one another?
   c. Is there a high degree of trust?
   d. How is conflict resolved? Is it openly discussed or is conflict avoided?
   e. Is the group cohesive?
6. Membership
   a. Are there any cliques?
   b. Are all members equally committed to the team?
   c. Are all members treated equally regardless of their formal title or authority?
7. Norms
   a. Are the norms of the group clearly understood by each team member?
   b. What happens when someone breaks a norm?
   c. Have the norms been formalized via a charter, or are they implied?

Step 2. Approach Development.

1. **Evaluate data** obtained from interviewing the team leader and team members to further define problem areas and priorities. Confirm that Process Consultation is an appropriate intervention.

2. **Identify when observations should take place.** Choose a setting in which it is easy to observe interpersonal and group processes. It is important to have access to a situation where the group members are interacting with each other in their usual fashion.

3. **Identify the data collection method(s)** that you will use. For instance, you might consider observing a staff meeting or a regularly scheduled work task. (Choose a task that requires significant interdependence among the group members.)

Step 3. Data Collection. Data can be collected through observation, interviews, or group discussion (questionnaires or surveys should be avoided). Several data collection tools are reviewed below.

Process Consultation Instrument (PCI) (see Figure 9.3)

The purpose of the PCI is to identify, record, and classify verbal and nonverbal interactions that occur within a group. This includes facial expressions, gestures, body language, emotional signs, and comments that are either expressive or directed toward other people. These interactions are arranged in two broad categories known as task behaviors and maintenance behaviors. A group that is functioning effectively will have sufficient amounts of both task and maintenance behaviors.

Directions for Using PCI. The PCI is suitable for groups of three to seven members. The instrument should be used for short periods of observation (5 to 10 minutes) to provide a snapshot of a team's level of interactions. Write the name of each group member on the top of the instrument. When using the PCI, identify and categorize each unit of interaction observed for all group members. A unit is defined as a communication sufficiently complete to permit another person to interpret it (this can range from a nodding of the head, a smile or uttering a single word or simple sentence).

Process Consultation
Data Collection Instrument

Interaction Category	(Name of Team Member)	(Name of Team (Member)	(Name of Team (Member)	Group
1. Seems Friendly				
2. Dramatizes				
3. Agrees				
4. Gives Suggestions				
5. Gives Opinion				
6. Gives Information				
7. Asks for Information				
8. Asks for Opinions				
9. Asks for Suggestions				
10. Disagrees				
11. Shows Tension				
12. Seems Unfriendly				
Total				
Participant's Share				

Figure 9.3.

Before attempting to utilize the PCI, it is essential to understand the definitions for each of the 12 categories in the instrument and to practice using the instrument to obtain familiarity with the line where each category is located. Each of the categories is discussed below.

1. **Seems Friendly.** Any act of hospitality, expressions of sympathy or empathy, or demonstrations of affection. Examples include:
   a. Confiding in one another
   b. Acts of apology
   c. Urging unity or harmony
   d. Expressions of solidarity
   e. Praising, rewarding, encouraging others
   f. Smiling
2. **Dramatizes.** Any act that emphasizes hidden meaning or emotional implications or is self-revealing. Examples include:
   a. Jokes, comments, or stories with a double meaning.
   b. Symbolic actions; shrugs, bodily or facial expressions portraying great amazement, surprise, fear, or anger.

3. **Agrees.** Any act that shows accord or assent about facts, inferences, or hypothesis. Examples include:
   a. Nonverbal acts (such as nodding the head).
   b. Verbal comments such as "I think you are right," "Yes, that's true."
4. **Gives Suggestions.** Any act that directs the attention of the group to task problems. Examples include:
   a. Identifying a problem to be discussed.
   b. Pointing out the relevance of a remark.
   c. Calling a meeting to order.
   d. Opening a new phase of actions.
   e. Attempting to guide or counsel.
5. **Gives Opinions.** Any act that involves a moral obligation, offers a belief, or indicates adherence to a policy. Examples include:
   a. Any statement that is not based on fact. These statements frequently begin with "I think," "I believe," and so on.
   b. Statements that denote value judgments. (Note: "Gives Opinions" should be distinguished from category 6 "Gives Information" primarily because "Gives Opinions" uses inference or value judgments.)
6. **Gives Information.** Any act reporting factual or potentially verifiable observations or experiences. Examples include:
   a. Providing facts, figures, statistics, and so on.
   b. Describing a previous experience.
7. **Asks for Information.** Any act that requests a descriptive, objective type of answer. Examples include:
   a. Requests for information based on an individual's observation, experience, or empirical research.
   b. Requests for factual answers. (If an inference, evaluation, or expression of a feeling is requested, it should be tabulated as category 8, "Asks for Opinions.")
8. **Asks for Opinions.** Any act that seeks an interpretation, a value judgment, a statement involving beliefs or values, or feedback regarding one's level of understanding. Examples include:
   a. Request for a diagnosis of a situation.
   b. Reaction to an idea.
9. **Asks for Suggestions.** Any act that requests guidance in the problem-solving process, is neutral in emotional tone, and attempts to turn the initiative over to another. Examples include any open-ended, nonvalue-laden questions.
10. **Disagrees.** Any act that rejects another's statement of information, opinion, or suggestion. Examples include:
    a. Statements that reject another person's position.
    b. Turning the head in disagreement.

11. **Shows Tension.** Emotional signs of anxiousness that indicate a conflict between acting and withholding action. Examples include:
    a. Appearing disconcerted, alarmed, dismayed, or concerned.
    b. Nonverbal cues such as trembling, flushing, and licking of the lips.
    c. Nervous laughter.
12. **Seems Unfriendly.** Any act that is personally negative and not content-oriented. Examples include:
    a. Judging another's behavior.
    b. Interrupting, deprecating, or ridiculing another individual.

Tabulating the PCI. The PCI is a sophisticated instrument that requires a thorough knowledge of group dynamics. An overview of the potential levels of analysis follows.

Level I. Participants share total observed interactions. The first level of analysis identifies the spread of participation throughout the team. Individuals who attempt to gain status or influence others will generally have the highest levels of participation.

Level II. Percentage of total group interaction in each category. This level of analysis identifies the team participation in each of the 12 categories. The team levels are then compared to established norms to identify potential problem areas. For example, if the group's aggregate percentage for the category "Agrees" is 27 percent, the group may not be encouraging the participation of members who have dissenting opinions.

Level III. Percentage of total group participation that each member contributes in each category. This level of analysis identifies the type of contribution and frequency of each member's participation. It can be used to identify members who need to be encouraged to participate or those who provide strong task or maintenance behaviors.

Level IV. Percentage of an individual's total participation for each category. This facilitates the comparison of each team member's contribution with the estimated norms. This information is extremely useful in identifying the roles each member plays under a variety of conditions.

Role Nominations Exercise (see Figure 9.4)

This exercise can be used to clarify and define the roles that members in the team play and to identify team members who help or hinder team development and interaction.

Directions for Using the Instrument. The Role Nominations Exercise is a simple way to identify team members' perceptions of each other. Each

Role Nominations Form

	(Name of Team Member)	(Name of Team Member)	(Name of Team Member)
Task Roles			
Initiator Contributor			
Information Seeker			
Information Giver			
Coordinator			
Orienter			
Evaluator			
Growing and Vitalizing Roles			
Encourager			
Harmonizer			
Gatekeeper and Expediter			
Standard Setter or Ego Ideal			
Follower			
Anti-Team Roles			
Blocker			
Recognition Seeker			
Dominator			
Avoider			

Figure 9.4.

member fills out the Role Nominations Form (Figure 9.4) by placing check marks in the columns corresponding to the roles that each member has played most frequently in the group, including him or herself (Members can play more than one role). Each of the role characteristics is grouped under one of three categories: task roles, growing and vitalizing roles, or anti-team roles. Each of the characteristics is discussed below.

Task Roles
1. **Initiator Contributor.** A team member who takes control of tasks and gives valuable input to the team's task completion.
2. **Information Seeker.** A member who gathers information from the team.

3. **Information Giver.** The team member who is a valuable information resource to the team, providing input for task accomplishment.
4. **Coordinator.** The person who coordinates the team's activities (such as, allocating responsibilities or keeping people on schedule).
5. **Orienter.** The member who seems to determine the team's direction and focus.
6. **Evaluator.** The member who judges or evaluates the others.

Growing and Vitalizing Roles

7. **Encourager.** The person who is a moral support for the team, keeping energy and optimism alive.
8. **Harmonizer.** The person who restores harmony when there is team conflict.
9. **Gatekeeper and Expediter.** The person who controls information flow in and out of the team, helping to maintain cohesive team attitudes and opinions.
10. **Standard Setter or Ego Ideal.** The person who controls team standards, especially motivation and commitment; this person usually represents a model that other members strive to follow.
11. **Follower.** A supporter of the team whose input is important but is always within team norms.

Anti-Team Roles

12. **Blocker.** This team member may withhold information the team needs or slow down the team's productivity by creating conflict.
13. **Recognition Seeker.** This person is preoccupied with personal achievement even at the expense of team achievement.
14. **Dominator.** This person strives for team control without consideration for others
15. **Avoider.** This team member avoids important task issues or interaction with other team members.

Analyzing the Role Nominations Exercise. After each member completes the Role Nominations form individually, the team should combine the forms and discuss any findings.

What Happened in the Group During the Role Nominations Exercise (see Figure 9.5)

Figure 9.4 can be used as a checklist by an observer to sum up his or her observations of the team's interactions. The form can also be filled out by

What Happened in the Group During the Role Nominations Exercise?

1. What was the general atmosphere in the group?
   Formal _____ Informal _____
   Competitive _____ Cooperative _____
   Hostile _____ Supportive _____
   Inhibited _____ Permissive _____
   Comments: _____
   _____
   _____
   _____

2. Quantity and quality of work accomplished
   Accomplishment: High _____ Low _____
   Quality of production: High _____ Low_____
   Goals: Clear _____ Vague _____
   Methods: Clear _____ Vague _____
                          Flexible _____ Inflexible _____
   Comments: _____
   _____
   _____
   _____

3. Leader behavior
   Attentive to group needs _____
   Supported others _____
   Concerned only with topic _____ Took sides _____
   Dominated group _____ Helped group _____
   Comments: _____
   _____
   _____
   _____

4. Participation
   Most people talked _____ Only few talked _____
   Members involved _____ Members apathetic _____
   Group united _____ Group divided _____
   Comments: _____
   _____
   _____
   _____

Figure 9.5.

all members to start an evaluation discussion. The form is completed by placing checks next to descriptions that best describe the characteristics of the group's level of functioning. Additional comments may be added where clarification or a more detailed description is needed. The exercise identifies the general atmosphere in the team, the quantity and quality of work accomplishment, leader behavior, and participation level.

Step 4. Integration. There are three techniques that may be used in combination to develop the process skills of the group:

1. **Agenda-setting exercises** are used to raise the team's awareness of their own internal process.
   a. Suggest to the team that they spend a few minutes at the end of their meeting to review the meeting. Ask:
   (1) How clear were communications?
   (2) How involved did team members feel?
   (3) Were member resources fully utilized?
   b. Suggest follow-up team analysis and problem-solving sessions to:
   (1) Work on team process issues.
   (2) Discuss the manner in which the team's working agenda is processed.
   (3) Address interpersonal process issues.

   (These sessions should not be suggested until the team is "emotionally" ready to explore relationships and interpersonal issues.)

2. **Coaching or counseling of individuals or teams.**

   These sessions help members to observe and diagnose processes, assimilate feedback, and become active in solving their own problems. Guidelines to consider are as follows:
   a. Be sure that the team or individual has understood the feedback and related it to observable behavior.
   b. Be sure that members have begun an active process of trying to solve the problem for themselves.
   c. If you are not sure about where the team stands on points a and b, probe and encourage with further questions.

3. **Structural suggestions.**

   Team structure relates to work processes, role and decision-making clarity, and the way the team interacts with the formal hierarchy.

Risks and Issues of Concern Involving Team Process Consultation

Process Consultation requires a unique set of skills. Expertise in group dynamics, group problem solving, and assessing nonverbal communications is required. The success of the intervention is dependent on the following:

1. Collecting data on the various group processes.
2. Training or helping members to understand group processes.
3. Providing assistance in the diagnosis and correction of problem areas.

Remember that all of the data-collection methods only reveal a snapshot of the team. They do not necessarily represent the team's typical interaction. Still, they are useful aids for beginning to analyze the team. Data-collection methods should be used to:

1. Promote a discussion within the team to determine if the observed data is representative of normal interactions.
2. Identify member reactions.
3. Identify problem areas and their causes.
4. Develop action plans to improve team effectiveness.

Additional Information

Bales, R. F. *Interaction Process Analysis*. Reading, Mass.: Addison-Wesley, 1950.

Bales, R. F., and Hare, A. P. "Diagnostic Use of the Interaction Profile." *Journal of Social Psychology*, 1965, pp. 239–258.

Chapple, E. D. "Measuring Human Relations: An Introduction to the Study of Interaction of Individuals." *General Psychology Monograph*, 1940, 22, pp. 3–147.

Luft, J. "The Johari Window." *Human Relations Training News*, 1961, pp. 5–7.

Walton, Richard. *Interpersonal Peacemaking Confrontations and Third-Party Consultation*. Reading, Mass.: Addison-Wesley, 1969.

Patton, Bobby R., and Griffin, Kim. *Decision-Making Group Interaction*. New York: Harper & Row, 1978.

Shein, E. H. *Process Consultation: Its Role in Organization Development*. Reading, Mass.: Addison-Wesley, 1969.

Guidelines for Analyzing Performance Problems

Directions: Read each of the following questions until you find an alternative that 1) you have the authority to implement and, 2) provides the greatest return on investment. If you cannot secure the appropriate commitment from resources, break the problem down and focus on solving a portion of the problem.

1. Is There a Problem?
    a. What is the difference between the individual's actual and desired performance?
    b. Describe the performance problem. When does it occur? Where does it occur? How often does it occur?
    c. How long has there been a problem?
    d. How will you know when the problem is solved?
2. Is It Important?
    a. What impact does the incorrect performance have on:
        (1) Achieving the business strategy or performance objectives?
        (2) Cash flow?
        (3) Productivity?
        (4) Quality?
    b. Is the cost of doing something worth the outcome?
        (1) If the cost of correcting the problem exceeds the outcome, ignore the performance problem.
3. Is It a Communication Problem?
    a. Does the individual:
        (1) Know he or she is supposed to take the desired action?
        (2) Know what the desired action is?
        (3) Know when to take the desired action?
        (4) Lack the necessary authority?
        (5) Have clear objectives that reflect the organization's mission and strategy?

The desired performance has to be realistic, measurable, and attainable. Clarify performance expectations, delegate authority; and, commensurate with the tasks, clarify departmental and individual's priorities and provide the performer with timely and accurate data to perform better.

4. Is It a Skill Problem?
   a. Has the individual correctly performed the task or skill before? If not, arrange formal training or coaching (explain the task, demonstrate it, allow individual to perform it, provide feedback).
   b. How often?
      (1) If the task is done intermittently, poor performance may be due to a lack of practice. (Provide closer supervision and increased feedback.)
   c. Is there regular feedback on performance? (If not, increase feedback on the strengths and weaknesses of performance.)
   d. Are the individual's present skills sufficient for desired performance? If not, does the individual have the physical and mental potential to perform as desired (if not, simplify the job, transfer, or terminate).
5. Is It a Problem with the Reward System?
   a. Does the performer know the desired standard? (If there are no standards, mutually create them. If a standard exists, communicate it.)
   b. Is there a favorable outcome for performing? (If not, recognize and reward desired performance.)
   c. Does the individual receive negative consequences for nonperformance? (If not, develop progressive means of punishment.)
   d. Does the individual receive any feedback on performance? (If not, coach the performer, and, if possible, redesign the job to provide timely feedback.)
6. Is It a Problem of Adequate Resources?
   a. Does the performer:
      (1) Have access to sufficient materials (books, reference guides, personal computer, and so on) to achieve the desired performance? (Provide appropriate materials.)
      (2) Have sufficient administrative and technical support? (Provide adequate support.)
      (3) Have sufficient time to perform? (Reprioritize the performer's duties and responsibilities.)
      (4) Encounter any other obstacles (noise in environment, administrative policies, interruptions, and so forth) that inhibit performance.
   b. If the individual lacks the necessary resources:
      (1) Provide additional resources, if available.
      (2) Clarify priorities.
      (3) Reduce performance standards if additional resources are unavailable.

Team Building

What Is It and When Should It Be Used?

Team Building is an intervention for improving both the efficiency and quality of the team (output) and the way team members work together (input). Team Building interventions are typically directed toward five major areas:

1. Setting goals or priorities.
2. Analyzing or allocating the way work is done.
3. Examining the way a team is working and its processes.
4. Examining relationships among members.
5. Coordinating team activities with other work units and teams.

How to Do It

Listed below are the steps for successful Team Building:

1. **Preparing for Team Building.** Involve team members in developing a list of suggested interview questions relating to goal clarity, work processes, role clarity, decision-making processes used by the group, problem solving, communications, and conflict management. Once this list is finalized, obtain consensus from the team on the Team-Building process to be used and agree on process outcomes.
2. **Data Collection.** Interview team members to become familiar with the team's functions and objectives and to identify team issues and concerns. Use open-ended questions, leaving the majority of the explanation to the team members.
3. **Data Analysis.** Categorize the issues into general themes and sub-themes. After the data have been collected, an executive summary should be written and disseminated to all team members.
4. **Team Strategy Session.** Distribute the executive summary of interviews to all team members prior to scheduling a team strategy session. Team members should clearly define each issue and problem in detail and rank them in terms of their importance. At this stage, it is important to separate symptoms of problems from their root causes. Individual team members may be selected to collect any additional data. When consensus has been reached regarding the root causes of the most important problems and issues, the meeting should focus on identifying a list of potential solutions to the problems.

5. **Action Planning.** When the list of possible solutions has been pared down, the team should begin to develop action plans to bring about the desired changes. A well-written action plan should identify the key tasks or steps to be completed, who is responsible for each step, resource requirements, and start and completion dates. This document should be distributed to each team member and serve as a map to focus effort and hold individuals accountable.

   Conclude the process by conducting a "sanity check" to assess how well the Team Building process met each individual's expectations. Key questions that may be asked are:
   a. Did we focus on the critical issues?
   b. Was the Team Building process effective?
   c. How can we improve the process in the future?
   d. Are the action plans realistic and achievable?
   e. How would you rate the overall session?

6. **Follow-up.** A review session is usually held at about three to nine months after the initial experience to assess team progress. At this time, the baseline measurements are compared to objectives to determine 1) how well the team has implemented the action plan, 2) which objectives have been accomplished to date and reasons for poor performance, 3) what additional resources are required to ensure success, 4) what new issues have developed since the last session, and 5) what should be done about these new issues and problems.

Risks and Issues of Concern Involved with Team Building

Successful Team Building depends on getting the right people together with a large block of uninterrupted time to identify high-priority problems. It also depends on developing realistic solutions and action plans, implementing solutions with enthusiasm, and conducting a follow-up session to check the process.

Initial Team Building efforts are generally more effective if they focus on task issues rather than relationship issues. Task issues are a safer, less-resisted area to start with. Nevertheless, interpersonal issues that get in the way of team effectiveness issues should not be ignored if they get in the way of developing task solutions.

Additional Information

Beckhard, Richard. "Optimizing Team-Building Efforts." *Journal of Contemporary Business,* Vol. 1, No. 3, Summer 1972, pp. 23–32.

Brauchle, Paul, and Wright, David., "Fourteen Team-Building Tips." *Training and Development,* Vol. 46, Issue 1, Jan. 1992.

Dyer, William G. *Team Building: Issues and Alternatives.* Reading, Mass.: Addison-Wesley, 1977.

Fordyce, J. K., and Weil, R. *Managing with People: A Manager's Handbook of Organization Development Methods.* Reading, Mass.: Addison-Wesley, 1971.

Hughes, Keith. "A Manager's Guide to the Art of Team Building." *Security Management,* Vol. 37, Nov. 1993.

Likert, R. *New Patterns of Management.* New York: McGraw-Hill, 1951.

Litton, P. W., and Bottger, P. C. "Individual versus Group Problem Solving: An Empirical Test of Best Member Strategy." *Organizational Behavior and Human Performance,* 1982.

Patten, T. *Organizational Development Through Team Building.* New York: John Wiley & Sons, 1981.

Quick, Thomas. *Successful Team Building.* New York: AMACOM, 1992.

Stoner, Charles, and Hartman, Richard. "Team Building: Answering Tough Questions." *Business Horizons,* Vol. 36, Sept.–Oct. 1993, pp. 70–78.

Woodman, R., and Sherwood, J. "The Role of Team Development in Organizational Effectiveness: A Critical Review." *Psychological Bulletin,* Vol. 88, July–Nov. 1980.

Coaching for Effective Performance

What Is It?

Coaching is an open discussion in which timely and candid feedback is given on a team member's performance. Its main focus is to provide guidance to help improve performance. It can be formal or informal and can come from a variety of sources, including the manager, customers, or other team members. Coaching can also take place when a team member models good performance for another team member who needs to improve his or her performance.

Why Do It?

Coaching is an effective tool for increasing levels of performance, eliminating performance problems, and maintaining high performance standards of individual team members. It is most often used to:

- Build trust and respect among team members.
- Increase motivation and productivity.
- Break down communication barriers.
- Accomplish team objectives.
- Keep on track with the business plan.
- Transfer knowledge (both intellectual and experiential).

Steps

The following steps are recommended as a general framework for ongoing and continually evolving coaching activities. Keep in mind, though, that coaching may not be a linear process.

Step 1: Establish an Open Environment. To be effective, coaching should identify what the team member is doing right, as well as identify areas in need of improvement. To provide useful feedback, the "coach" must:

- Encourage full participation—coaching is two-way communication.
- Be open to what is said—listen and think before responding.
- Encourage honest and candid discussions.
- Use behavioral examples to illustrate performance standards you hope to achieve.

- Consider all discussions opportunities for improvement.
- Ask questions.

Step 2: Prepare for the Discussion. Before conducting a coaching session, decide ahead of time what you intend to accomplish and how you will proceed. Ask yourself the following questions:

- Is there a performance problem I hope to eliminate?
- Has the team member requested advice on working more effectively with other team members?
- Does the team member need reinforcement to maintain already effective performance?

The answers to these questions will help you determine the purpose of your coaching discussion: to eliminate a performance problem, improve already good performance, or sustain high performance levels.

Step 3: Determine a Plan of Action. An action plan will help you focus the coaching discussion on achieving the specific goal determined in step 2. No matter what the particular purpose of the coaching discussion, you should follow this plan of action rigorously. The action plan should include the following:

1. When and where the coaching discussion will take place (generally this should be done in privacy and away from office distractions).
2. What will be discussed. Focus on specific actions and behaviors.
   - Avoid generalizations (discuss what you observe rather than what you perceive as an individual's "attitude").
   - Avoid making judgments or discussing personalities
   - Discuss any obstacles getting in the way of success
3. Identification of problems (use constructive criticism by acknowledging what isn't working rather than destructively criticizing what you think is wrong).
4. Discuss and reach agreement on ways to improve.
5. Make a commitment to follow-through on any agreements reached during the coaching discussion.

Step 5: Follow the Action Plan. During the coaching discussion, follow the specific plan of action you've created. Compare your actions and outcomes to what you planned. Ask for feedback from the team member you are coaching to determine what you can do to make the session more effective.

Step 6: Review and Adjust Your Coaching Methods. After completing the coaching discussion, determine what worked, what didn't work, and what you need to do differently. The answers to the following questions will help you focus on the plan of action for future coaching discussions:

- Did you change your plan of action in the middle of the discussion?
- Did the discussion make you uncomfortable or uneasy at certain points?
- Did you find it difficult being completely candid with the team member?
- Did you leave the discussion feeling as if nothing was accomplished?

Additional Information

Deegan, Arthur. *Coaching: A Management Skill for Improving Performance.* Reading, Mass.: Addison-Wesley, 1979.

Frankel, Lois, and Otazo, Karen. "Employee Coaching: The Way to Gain Commitment, Not Just Compliance." *Employment Relations Today,* Vol. 19, No. 3, Autumn 1992.

Gaines, Harry. "Ten Tips for Effective Coaching." *Executive Excellence,* Vol. 10, No. 3, March, 1993.

Rosenberg, DeAnne. "Coaching Without Criticizing." *Executive Excellence,* Vol. 9, No. 8, August, 1992.

Wolff, Michael., "Become a Better Coach." *Research-Technology Management.* Vol. 36, No. 1, Jan./Feb. 1993.

Yager. Ed., "Coaching Models." *Executive Excellence,* Vol. 10, Mar. 1993.

Norms

What Is It?

Unfortunately, most teams do not establish in the beginning written rules for the way they will interact with one another. If teams do not establish these written rules purposely, after a month or so they develop unwritten rules, expectations, and undocumented policies and procedures for how they interact with one another. These are the unwritten norms. Norms exist around such things as who gets to read the first copy of drafts, which team members support one another, or how the team leader is approached when all team members are present.

Why Do It?

The most-effective teams formally define their norms very soon after they have started. Norms serve many purposes, the most important one being that everyone looks for some way to predict other team members' behavior. Norms accomplish the following:

- Reflect the core values of the team.
- Provide team members with some limited guarantees that if "X" does this, it means that.
- Provide consistency within the team.
- Help the team avoid potentially embarrassing situations.
- Reduce ambiguity.
- Reduce conflict.
- Promote team cohesion.

This list points to both the positive and negative influences norms can have on a team. An example of the negative influence of norms is the Space Shuttle *Challenger* disaster in 1986. Because of several delays, there was an enormous amount of pressure to launch the Space Shuttle—in spite of evidence that a potential problem existed with the boosters. The shuttle was launched and seven lives were lost. *Why?* Because one of the unwritten norms was that no one would challenge a decision made by the team leaders. Conformity was highly valued, even to the point of making a disastrous decision.

It is very important that a team establish formal norms as soon as possible. It is also important to frequently set aside some time to reexamine the norms to see if they still work. Below are some examples of norms.

Active Listening. Team members agree to carefully listen to other team members' ideas, suggestions, and perceptions without interrupting.

Paraphrasing. Once a team member has presented an idea, suggestion, or perception, it is incumbent upon other team members to check their understanding by paraphrasing what that member said.

Process checking. Any team member can call for a process check (that is, clarify a point, get a vote on clarity) any time during a meeting. Process checks are required before moving on to new business.

Open-mindedness. Team members will not reject another team member's suggestion without first hearing all the details.

Frankness. Team members are expected to voice their opinions without fear of retribution from other team members or the team leader.

Solidarity. All discussions held by the team will be kept within the team unless the team agrees to seek outside opinions.

Decision making. All team members will be asked to participate in all team decisions. A process check will be made for each decision.

Confrontation. Positive confrontation is expected from every team member. No team member will be penalized for a positive confrontation.

How to Do It

The following steps are designed to help teams establish their own norms. This works best when team members meet early on and develop consensus on their norms, but developing norms at a later stage can also greatly increase a team's effectiveness.

Equipment Needed. Two flips charts or one flip chart and a white board.

Steps

1. Prepare a flip chart formatted as follows. Use the other flip chart or white board for writing and rewriting norms.

Current Rules of Conduct	Desired Rules of Conduct

2. Identify and examine the team's current norms.

Current Norms	Desired Norms
Discussing team failures with department members not on the team	
Bad decision making	
Lack of candor	
No one listens to other team members' suggestions	
Other	

3. Come to consensus about the kind and number of norms (consensus about their exact meaning is unnecessary at this stage).
4. Have each team member make a list of behaviors they would like to see the team adopt.
5. Ask for a desired rule of conduct from each team member. *Remember that these behaviors should be in the context of a business objective, mindful of people's differences, something the team values as a group, and something that can be observed.*
6. Post each behavior on a flip chart. Post flip chart on the wall.
7. Continue process until each team member's list is exhausted.
8. Write each rule of conduct on a separate piece of paper before adding it to the desired list on the flip chart. You may have to rewrite it several times before the team comes to consensus on its wording.
9. Clarify each suggested rule one at a time. Discard redundancies. Do a process check after each rule.
10. Do several process checks along the way for each new rule of conduct. When everyone agrees with its meaning, post it to the flip chart.

Solidarity

All discussions held by the team will be kept within the team unless the team agrees to seek outside opinions.

11. Have new norms typed and sent to all team members.

Current Rules of Conduct	Desired Rules of Conduct
Discussing team failures with department members not on the team	Solidarity—All discussions held by the team will be kept within the team unless the team agrees to seek outside opinions.
Bad decision making	
Lack of candor	
No one listens to other team members' suggestions	

Tips for Establishing Norms

- Make sure everyone on the team has input.
- Be supportive of all team members' suggestions. Clarify suggestions if needed.
- Establish about seven norms.
- Avoid defensiveness.
- Don't include norms that cannot be practiced by the team.
- You may want to consider evaluating team members on how well they live up to the norms. See the section on 360° Feedback and Assessment in Chapter 8 for some tips.
- The Process Check. The process check is a simple procedure that anyone in a team can use to determine how team members think about a particular topic. Someone simply calls for a process check and team members signal their positions by using hand signals.

Affirmative	Undecided	Negative

If there are negative or undecided votes, clarify what needs to be done to bring the matter to a close.

Guidelines for Meeting Management

Planning for the Meeting

1. Identify the purpose, objectives, and desired products or outcomes for each meeting.
2. Decide who should attend the meeting.
3. Develop a meeting agenda and any other background or handout materials and distribute to each attendee before the meeting.
4. Advise participants what role they will play for different items on the agenda.
5. Identify the facilities (room) and resources needed (such as, flip charts, felt markers, grease board, overhead projector) to achieve the objectives for the meeting. Schedule the meeting room to ensure its availability.
6. If appropriate, select seating arrangements for participants. Seating location can have a dramatic effect on the interactions of a participant (for example, seating someone at the end of the table can isolate them or curtail their influence).

Leading the Meeting

1. Appoint a notetaker at each meeting (notes should include decisions made, who's responsible for what, unresolved issues, next steps, and so on).
2. Begin the meeting by restating the objectives, desired outcomes or products, and process procedures.
3. The leader should moderate the meeting (during conflict it is important to maintain an open, nondefensive style), keep discussions focused, encourage participation, assess group process, and obtain consensus on actions to be taken.
4. Before ending the meeting, summarize the main points of discussion, decisions made, agreed upon responsibilities and timelines, and next steps.
5. Debrief participants to assess their satisfaction with the meeting, issues that adversely affected meeting effectiveness, and suggestions to improve group process.
6. As a group, decide on the next meeting's agenda.

(text continued on page 284)

Meeting Record-Keeping Form

Date	Location
Agenda Items	Time Allotted
Attendees	Copies to
Activity	Responsibility
Room Set-up and Requirements	Contact Person

Meeting Planning Worksheet

Team	Date and Location
Attendees	
Absentees	
Discussion Points	Made By
Action Steps	Responsibility

(text continued from page 281)

Follow-up

    1. Distribute notes to all participants.
    2. Ensure action items do not fall through the cracks.
    3. Hold participants accountable for tasks assigned to them.
    4. Develop periodic progress reports.

BIBLIOGRAPHY

Albrecht, Karl and Zemke, Ron. *Service America: Doing Business in the New Economy.* Warner Books, 1985.

Beckhard, R., and R. Harris., *Organizational Transitions: Managing Complex Change.* Reading, MA: Addison-Wesley, 1987.

Belbin, R. Meredith. *Management Teams: Why They Succeed or Fail.* Butterworth-Heinemann, Ltd. Oxford, England: Linacre House Jordon Hill,1992.

Block, Peter. *The Empowered Manager: Positive Political Skills at Work.* San Francisco: Jossey-Bass, 1989.

Boyett, Joseph H. and Conn, Henry P. *Workplace 2000: The Revolution Reshaping American Business.* New York: Dutton, 1991.

Boyett, Joseph and Conn, Henry. *Pay For Knowledge: How to Improve Employee Flexibility, Productivity Brief.* Houston: American Productivity Center, 1990.

Carr, Clay. *Team Power: Lessons from America's Top Companies on Putting Teampower to Work.* Englewoods Cliffs: Prentice Hall, 1992.

Crosby, Philip B. *Quality is Free.* New York: Mentor, 1979.

Davidow, William H. and Uttal Bro. *Total Customer Service: The Ultimate Weapon.* New York: Harper Perennial,1989.

Davis, Stanley M. *Managing Corporate Culture.* Ballinger Publishing Company, 1984.

Denison, Daniel R. *Corporate Culture and Organizational Effectiveness.* New York: John Wiley and Sons, 1990.

Dyer, William. *Team Building Issues and Alternatives.* Reading, MA: Addison-Wesley, 1987.

Francis, David and Young, Don. *Improving Work Groups.* San Diego, CA: University Associates, 1979.

Galbraith, J. *Organization Design.* Reading, MA:. Addison-Wesley, 1977.

Gryna, Frank M. Jr. *Quality Circles: A Team Approach to Problem Solving.* New York: AMACOM 1981.

Hackman, Richard and Oldham Greg. *Work Redesign.* Reading, MA: Addison-Wesley, 1977.

Hicks,, Douglas. *Activity-Based Costing for Small and Medium-Sized Businesses.* New York: John Wiley & Sons, 1992.

Hanna, David. *Designing Organizations for High Performance.* Reading, MA: Addison Wesley Publishing Company 1987.

Hronic, Steven, *Vital Signs.* New York: Amacom, 1994.

Hunt, V. Daniel. *Quality in America: How to Implement a Competitive Quality Program.* Homewood, IL: Business One Irwin, 1992.

Jenkins, Douglas and Gupta, Nina. "The Payoffs of Paying for Knowledge," *National Productivity Review.* Spring, 1985, pp. 121–130.

Kanter Rosabeth Moss. *The Change Masters.* New York: Simon & Schuster, Inc. 1983.

Kotter, J. P. and Heskett, J. L. *Corporate Culture and Performance.* New York: Free Press: 1992.

Kohn, Alfie. *Punished by Rewards.* New York: Houghton-Mifflin, 1993.

Larson, Carl E. and LaFasto, Frank M. J. *TeamWork: What Must Go Right/What Can Go Wrong.* Troy, NY: Sage Publications, Inc., 1989.

Lawler, Edward E. III; Mohrman, Susan Albers; Ledford, Gerald E. *Employee Involvement and Total Quality Management: Practices and Results in Fortune 1000 Companies.* San Francisco: Jossey Bass, Inc. 1992.

Lawler, Edward and Ledford, Gerald. *Skill Based Pay.* San Diego: Center for Effective Organizations, 1984.

Lawler, Edward. *High Involvement Management.* San Francisco: Jossey-Bass Inc. Publishers, 1986.

Lewis, Betty, "Team-Directed Workforce from a Worker's View." *Target Journal,* Volume 6, Number 4, Winter 1990.

Lynch Robert and Werner, Thomas. *Continuous Improvement Teams & Tools.* Atlanta, GA: QualTeam, Inc., 1992.

Manning, George and Curtis, Kent. *Group Strength: Quality Circles at Work.* South-Western Publishing Co., 1988.

Orsburn, Jack, Moran, Linda, Musselwhite, Ed, and Zenger, John. *Self-Directed Work Teams.* Homewood, IL: Business One Irwin, 1990.

O'Toole, James. *Making America Work: Productivity and Responsibility.* The Continuum Publishing Company, 1981.

Parker, Glenn M. *Team Players and Teamwork: The New Competitive Business Strategy.* San Francisco: Jossey-Bass, 1991.

Pasmore, William A. *Designing Effective Organizations: The Sociotechnical Systems Perspective.* New York: John Wiley and Sons, 1988.

Patton, Bobby and Giffin, Kim. *Decision-Making Group Interaction.* New York: Harper & Row Publishers, 1990.

Peters, T. and Waterman, R., Jr. *In Search of Excellence: Lessons from America's Best Run Companies.* New York: Harper & Row, 1982.

Porras, Jerry. *Stream Analysis: Powerful Way to Diagnose And Manage Organizational Change,* Reading, MA: Addison Wesley Publishing Company, 1987.

Recardo, Ronald. *Appropriate Reward Systems for a JIT Environment.* Paper presented at APICS JIT conference in Washington, D.C., June 1989.

Recardo, Ronald. "JIT With Two R's: Recognition and Rewards." *Target Journal,* Summer 1990

Rummler, Geary and Brache, Alan. *Improving Performance.* San Francisco: Jossy-Bass, 1990, Revised 1995.

Sayles, Leonard R. "Doing Things Right: A New Imperative for Middle Managers,". *Organizational Dynamics,* May 1993, pp, 5–10.

Schein, Edgar. *Process Consultation.* Reading, MA: Addison Wesley Publishing Company, 1988.

Seashore, Stanley, Lawler, Edward, Mirvis, Philip, and Cammann, Cortlandt. *Assessing Organization Change.* New York: John Wiley & Sons, 1983

Semler, Ricardo, "Managing Without Managers," *Harvard Business Review,* Cambridge, MA, September–October 1989, pp. 76–84.

Stacey, Ralph. *Managing the Unknowable,* San Francisco: Jossey-Bass, 1992.

Stacey, Ralph. "How I Learned to Let My Workers Lead," *Harvard Business Review,* Cambridge, MA, November–December 1990, pp. 66–82.

The Catalyst Consulting Group. *High Performance Work Teams Training Manual.* South Glastonbury, CT, 1993.

Tichy, Noel. *Managing Strategic Change.* New York: John Wiley & Sons, 1983.

Tosi, Henry and Tosi, Lisa. "What Managers Need To Know About Skill Based Pay". *Organization Dynamics,* 1987, pp. 52–64

Tosi, Henry L. *Organizational Behavior and Management: A Contingency Approach.* Boston: PWS-Kent Publishing Company, 1990.

Tregoe, Benjamin B. and Zimmerman, John W. *Top Management Strategy: What it is and How to Make it Work.* New York: Simon and Schuster, 1980.

Tzu, Sun. *The Art of War.* New York: Delacorte Press, 1983.

Ulrich, Dave and Lake, Dale. *Organizational Capabiity: Competing from the Inside Out.* New York: John Wiley & Sons, 1990.

Van De Ven, Andrew and Ferry, Diane. *Measuring and Assessing Organizations.* New York: John Wiley & Sons, 1980.

Varney, Glenn. *Building Productive Teams.* San Francisco: Jossey-Bass Publishers, 1990.

Vicere, Albert A. "The Strategic Leadership Imperative for Executive Development," *HR Planning,* Volume 15, Number 1 1992, pp. 15–31.

Wade, David, "Inside 360° Assessment and Feedback," *Western New England Organization Development Newsletter,* Hartford, Connecticut, Spring 1993.

Wade, David and Bumpass, Susan, "Measuring Participant Performance: An Alternative," *Australian Journal of Educational Technology,* Volume 6, Number 2, Melbourne, Australia, Summer 1990.

Wade, David and Hughey, Anthony, "Steering Clear of the Doldrums: How Aetna's Payroll Department Improved Morale and Increased Productivity by Implementing Self-directed Teams," *PayTech Magazine,* March/April, 1995, pp. 24–27.

Wade, David, "Teams Revisited: Why Teams Fail, Why Teams Succeed," *New England Organization Development Newsletter,* Hartford, Connecticut, Spring 1994.

Walton, Richard. *Interpersonal Peacemaking.* Reading, MA: Addison-Weslely Publishing Company, Inc, 1969.

White, Alan F. "Organizational Transformation at BP. An Interview with Chairman and CEO Robert Horton," *HR Planning,* Volume 15, Number 1 1992. pp.3–14.

Wilson, David C. *A Strategy of Change: Concepts and Controversies in the Management of Change.* Routeledge, 1992.

Ziethaml, Valerie, et al. *Delivering Quality Service.* New York: Free Press, 1990.

Index

For Product Safety Concerns and Information please contact our EU representative GPSR@taylorandfrancis.com Taylor & Francis Verlag GmbH, Kaufingerstraße 24, 80331 München, Germany

T - #0021 - 230425 - C0 - 229/152/17 [19] - CB - 9780884158523 - Gloss Lamination